THE HISTORY *of the* Country Club *of* PADUCAH

BY VICKI HUNKLER

Acclaim Press™
Your Next Great Book

P.O. Box 238
Morley, MO 63767
(573) 472-9800
www.acclaimpress.com

Book and Cover design: M. Frene Melton

ISBN: 978-1-942613-62-6 | 1-942613-62-8
Library of Congress Control Number: 2017900443

First Printing: 2017
Printed in the United States of America
10 9 8 7 6 5 4 3 2 1

Contents

Introduction

Illustrated with more than 300 photographs, this account of the Country Club of Paducah's rich and colorful history is a journalistic approach written by Vicki Hunkler.

The facts she discovered through numerous conversations with members, and through the study of the board minutes and the archives at the McCracken County Public Library and *Paducah Sun* newspaper are interesting and enlightening.

She weaves this story through a framework of milestone events that took place between the incorporation of the Country Club of Paducah in 1913 and the beginning of 2017. The men and women whose ideas, decisions, and accomplishments are highlighted in this history are the reason the club exists today.

No other history has been written about the Country Club of Paducah, which makes it not only engaging, but also a necessity as we build on the past and move forward.

Let us salute the past and celebrate the future of the club and its members!

Acknowledgments

I want to express my sincere appreciation to every person who contributed a piece of information, a clipping, or a photograph for *The History of the Country Club of Paducah*. Although I cannot begin to list them all, I do want to acknowledge a few individuals who shared their memories through photographs, clippings, numerous interviews, and whose own personal histories at the club are woven into the book.

Special thanks to Bill Bone, Sue Fendley, Tom Garrett, Edward Hely, Vic Speck, George Sullivan, and Tommy Thomas for their contributions to the history of golf; and to Hal Sullivan, Rose Ann Fiorita, and Judy Green for their information on the history of tennis; and to Pat Brockenborough, Sally Shelton Crowe, Mark Curtis, Pat Kerr, Claire Key, Diane Lengsfeld, Gloria Livingston, Barbara and Mike Livingston, Barbaranelle McClennahan, Jerry Page, Mary Jane Harris Park, Lucy and Bill Paxton, Dr. Rob Robertson, Kristie Wilson, and Virgie Wilson, whose family keepsakes, files, and photographs are a vital part of the story.

Bill Usher, Ed Hough, and Phyllis Curtis contributed to this history through numerous interviews and photographs before they passed away. Without their input, my job would have been far more difficult and the history certainly less colorful and thorough.

I appreciate the assistance of the club's management and staff, Tim Straley, Angie Skees, Hollie Treas, Larry Hantle, and Chris Dallas. I must also thank my husband, Chris, for two years of support and patience.

And, of course, thank you to the generous sponsors of this book whose early support and confidence in the finished product are greatly appreciated.

This book offers a journalistic approach to history. I hope you enjoy *The History of the Country Club of Paducah* as much as I have loved researching, writing, and photographing it.

—Vicki Hunkler, March of 2017

The Sponsors

We thank these club members for their generous support. Without them, this publication would not have been possible.

Platinum

Mike and Barbara Livingston

Gold

Jim and Brenda Brown
Adam Chustz
Bill and Peggy Conyer
Mark and Debby Curtis in memory of Jim and Sue Curtis, Lafon Craft and in honor of Doc Craft
Rose Ann, Angela and Teddy Fiorita in memory of Ted Michael Fiorita
Tom and Sandra Garrett in memory of Tom and Helen Garrett
Tom and Toni Greene
Ken and Beth Hunt in memory of Mary Lou Hunt
Aubrey and Betty Lippert
David and Karen Paxton
Jim and Vicki Woods

Silver

Allen Behbehani
George and Pam Boland in memory of Ed and Barbara Hough
Steve and Anita Bright in memory of Irving Bright, Jr.
Jamey and Jordan Brown
Dr. Keith H. and Jan Crawford
Bob and Barbara Day
W. David and Ann Denton
Edward and Lisa Hely in memory of Norman Hely
Gene Hipp in memory of Edna and Gene Paul Hipp
Chris and Vicki Hunkler
Larry and Roxie Jarvis
Dan and Claire Key
Bill Metzger
The Michelson Family
Bill and Lucy Paxton
George and Lana Sirk
George Sullivan in honor of George Goodman's contributions
Tommy Thomas in memory of Ward and Ruth Thomas
Renee and Steve Tilley in memory of Ed and Gerry Tilley and Ed and Barbara Hough
Dr. William and Joanie Walden
Dick and Kristie Wilson in memory of Royce and Doris Gregory
Mike and Cindy Wyatt
The Ladies Golf Association

The Early History

The sun was shining on a warm summer day. The sound of a tugboat was heard in the distance by the Market House vendors. The gentleman boarded his carriage among the hustle and bustle of the busy river town, and tipped his hat to passers-by. It was a perfect day to play a little golf on the outskirts of town, a perfect time to discuss the politics of the day, and play some cards with friends.

Would this be the day the decision was made to form a private country club in Paducah? Perhaps it was.

The gentleman pulled in at Wallace Park and took his mashie and his putter to the little sand green. He dreamed of a golf course where champions were crowned and important tournaments were played. He yearned for a place where his children could swim in a pool and play tennis, a place where he could dine and dance with his wife. He embraced the idea of a home away from home where life-long friendships were cemented.

Today was the day he would finally share his thoughts with his group.

The official records show that The Country Club of Paducah was incorporated in 1913, not as early as some thought, but newspaper articles regarding the formation of a country club appeared about seven years earlier.

Wallace Park was the most likely the place where our founding fathers gathered to pursue the idea of the Country Club of Paducah. Their desire for a nicer, longer private golf course and more amenities was a frequent subject of dreams and discussion after the turn of the century.

Historian Fred Neuman wrote that LaBelle Park, as it was first named, existed from 1890 until about 1904 on the outskirts of town. It featured rolling hills, a lake for swimming or canoeing, apple trees, a dance pavilion, and a casino.

The property then became known as Wallace Park, which was owned and developed by the Paducah Traction Company to encourage the use of its 11 miles of trolley lines.

Encompassing 75 acres of land, Wallace Park was located in the west end of Paducah between what is now Buckner Lane and Alben Barkley Drive, formerly Blandville Road. It was referred to as a "resort" on several occasions.

Nurseryman John Schneidman remembered playing a small golf course at the park when one of the sand greens was located at Sycamore Drive and Blandville Road. Only a large oak tree remained after the course was eliminated, according to *The Fairhurst Essays* by Richard E. Fairhurst.

Fred Neuman was told that the little golf course located in this area "is one of the little-known items of recreational history, but the authentic story comes from one man who played golf there; one who kept the greens; one caddie; and one man who watched his father play golf there." He said the course was eliminated in the 1940s, but others say it was eliminated years earlier.

Material on microfilm in the Paducah Public Library, mainly from Paducah newspapers, reveals that the efforts to form a country club started several different times throughout a seven or eight-year span before a small group of men finally saw it to fruition.

The earliest written account of an effort to form a country club was in the *Paducah Evening Sun* on July 27, 1905. The headline said "Country Club to be Incorporated." The story that followed said that "promoters of the country club will likely perfect organization this afternoon. The requisite 50 names having been secured for the articles of incorporation."

"The object of the club is to build a fine club house down in the country and make runs to it in automobiles, have lunch, and make it a sort of pleasure 'resort.' The

Above: Postcard depicting the lake at Wallace Park in Paducah.

capital stock is to be fixed at $25,000, divided into shares of $100 each." This description fits with stories and postcards that circulated in 1910 that show a clubhouse or "casino" near the lake in Wallace Park.

In subsequent issues, the newspaper does not mention that any action actually took place "that afternoon" or any time soon after the July story ran. Perhaps the reference was to Wallace Park itself and not to a private country club.

If the 1905 article was referring to the Country Club of Paducah, the club remained an idea or goal for at least seven months. On March 5, 1906, The Sun announced in another headline "Country Club will be Organized Early This Spring. A Preliminary Meeting will be held at the Commercial Club Tomorrow."

(The Commercial Club, probably similar to today's Rotary or Kiwanis Clubs, was where city leaders and professionals gathered on a regular basis for meetings on the topics of the day.)

The 1906 story continued: "Preliminary steps will be taken at the Commercial Club headquarters toward the organization of a country club—an organization committee (is) composed of Given Campbell, Cook Husbands, Gus Thompson, Louis Rieke, Jr., E.P. Noble, Saunders Fowler, W.L. Brainerd, Edwin J. Paxton and M.F. Fitzpatrick." (Records are unclear as to whether this was the precursor to the country club since their names were not mentioned in subsequent publications, but it is likely.)

The newspaper article said, "It is proposed to organize the club and then solicit the membership and consider propositions for sites, and the details of the organization will be perfected at the meeting tomorrow night (March 6, 1906)." Images of this newspaper were provided by the University of Kentucky, Chronicling America, The Library of Congress. For the next three years the newspaper archives do not include any coverage of club activity.

Moving along to *The Paducah Evening Sun* as it was called in 1909, readers of the December 11 issue find the following information under the headline "Country Club Plan with Good Prospect:"

"At the suggestion of a number of gentlemen in social and business circles, Mr. Wallace Weil is attempting to form an organization to establish a country club on the site of the Bloomfield home in Arcadia.

Mr. Weil started on the work a few days ago, and has met with so much encouragement that it looks as if the club will be formed. There has been an ever increasing demand for a club of this character and efforts have been made before to organize one." This reference might explain the gap in time between the first organizational efforts and 1909.

"The Bloomfield home is one of the prettiest sites around Paducah. It is not far from the city and the car lines to the grounds are ample for the usual country club play grounds, and the house can be transformed into a county club house with few changes."

"Country Club is Now Probability" said the front-page story of March 8, 1910.

"Negotiations are now underway for purchase of a site" is the subhead. The story concludes that the deal was not yet closed, but "it is thought it will be consummated." The reporter again referred to property as one of the "prettiest around Paducah, and if it is purchased, it is the intention to make it one of the most attractive places in the Purchase."

"A handsome new club house will be built, and every convenience arranged for the pleasure and comfort of the members of the country club, which already has a large membership," the story said.

President Charles K. Wheeler

On the following day, March 9, 1910, the *Sun* said the country club purchased the Bloomfield property on March 8.

"Late yesterday afternoon the Bloomfield home, located on the Blandville Road a short distance from Wallace Park, was purchased by members of the Country Club. The deal has been pending for several days, but the sale was not completed until yesterday. The club will erect a new modern clubhouse. Golf links will be laid out and other arrangements made for amusement of the members in athletics."

On March 19, 1910, *The Paducah Evening Sun* noted that the Paducah Country Club or "The Country Club of Paducah" elected its officers—Charles K. Wheeler, president; J.D. Mocquot, vice-president; and S.D. Sinnott, secretary and treasurer.

The article states that the "organization of the Country Club of Paducah has been effected. There is an initial enrollment of 30 names while the club membership will be limited to 60 members."

The newspaperman covering this sequence of events goes on to say that the location for the clubhouse has not been definitely decided, "but it is likely that the Gregory home in the Gregory Heights addition will be leased." Perhaps we have the Bloomfield property and the Gregory property combining to form the proposed Country Club of Paducah site for the golf course and clubhouse?

Questions regarding this organizational process are also complicated by a few references in other publications. The *Kentucky Magazine* in 1917 said a country club had existed for 13 years with an active membership of 158. A spokesperson with the State library in Frankfort said not to assume the reference in the old *Kentucky Magazine* was correct or that the reference was to the Country Club of Paducah, since it was definitely incorporated in 1913.

Another reference appeared in Caron's Paducah City Directory 1912-1913, "Paducah Golf Club" was listed as South of Broadway, West of Lovelaceville Road. The 1914-1915 edition of Caron's Paducah City Directory refers to "The Country Club of Paducah" listed at the same address with Charles K. Wheeler as president; Calhoun Rieke, treasurer; and E. Douglas Bagby, secretary.

This appears to be an accurate listing, since Mr. Bagby and Mr. Wheeler are the secretary and president listed on the "shares" certificates of 1913. Wheeler presided until 1916.

(The club has used the year 1902 on the logo for decades, but there is no written record, newspaper article, or State records in the archives that indicate the club existed at that time.)

While the original clubhouse was under construction around 1912, a dwelling nearby was converted to a temporary clubhouse. Pictured left to right: Joe Friedman, Stewart Sinnott, Saunders Fowler, J.D. Mocquot, Luke Russell, Mr. Sherrill, Wallace Weil, Louis Rieke, Sr., J.T. Donovan, unknown, another Mr. Sherrill, George Wallace, Charlie Rieke, J.C. Utterback, and J.W. Keiler.

In historian Fred G. Neuman's "The Story of Paducah" (1927), he refers to the Paducah Country Club as built in 1912 and skirting the city on the western boundary.

The contractor who built the beautiful frame clubhouse in 1912-1913 was William Karnes at a cost of $16,000. He worked with the architect who designed it, W.L. Brainerd. All of the trees on that first 9-hole golf course were planted by Herb Wallerstein in 1935.

"Access to the first Country Club of Paducah was initially provided by a large field at the back of Wallace Park where families in buggies and on horseback could leave their hacks for all day fun at the club," the historian noted.

A few years after the private club opened, Neuman wrote, "It appears that Wallace Park will succumb to the city borders expanding and the building of homes," which is exactly what transpired.

Wallace Park was platted and sold in 1924, according to an Arcadia Methodist Church publication. J.C. Utterback, W.F. Bradshaw and J.S. Brinkley under the name Park Realty Company transformed the park into a residential subdivision.

Mike Livingston, a life-time club member, and his sister, Peggy (Conyer), who was about nine years old when their parents joined the club, grew up in one of those homes. For many years, Ginny Ann and Rick Coltharp lived at the top of the hill on Cedar Lane in the Wallace home, which was built around 1858 by Phillip Wallace. It is believed that he was the person who called the surrounding property LaBelle Park.

The Paducah Country Club quickly became a recreational haven for its members.

The Paducah Country Club quickly became a recreational haven for its members. It did not take long for the founders to file the paperwork in Frankfort and declare the club a corporation.

Articles of Incorporation

On January 10, 1913, a letter was sent to the Secretary of State for Kentucky in Frankfort from the Law Offices of Wheeler & Hughes, City National Bank Building, Paducah, Ky. G.K. Wheeler, D.H. Hughes, and J.G. Wheeler were the principals on the letterhead.

Dear Sir:

We hand you Articles of Incorporation of the Paducah Country Club together with check of our Mr. Wheeler for $3.00 recording fees. Under Article 8, Chapter 32 of the Kentucky Statues, as we interpret it, no corporation tax is acquired.

Respectfully,
Wheeler & Hughes

The Articles of Incorporation were filed and the charter issued on the 13th day of January, 1913. (A copy of the document obtained in 2015 from the State of Kentucky, Office of the Secretary of State, Alison Lundergan Grimes is pictured at right.)

Within the Articles of Incorporation was this statement: "Be it known that George C. Wallace, Joseph L. Friedman, Charles F. Rieke, Muscoe Burnett, and Charles K. Wheeler, herby associate themselves together to become a body corporate, under and by virtue of Article 8, Chapter 32 Kentucky Statutes, and being the Act of the General Assembly of Kentucky of March 22nd, 1892."

The name of this Corporation is "THE COUNTRY CLUB OF PADUCAH, KENTUCKY."

Article IV states in part: "The object of this association is to encourage manly sports and open air exercise, and, to this end, the company may acquire by purchase or gift a sufficient quantity of ground upon which to establish golf links, tennis courts, and other outdoor athletic games. It may erect upon grounds so acquired any building or buildings to further or accomplish the objects names: it may issue notes or bonds in payment for ground purchased, or buildings erected thereon, and secure the same by pledge or mortgage on said real property, and shall have power to do or perform any other act not inconsistent with law to carry out the purpose of the company."

Article V states in part: "The affairs of the company shall be managed by a President and Board of Governors, consisting of not less than four, nor more than seven members, and a Secretary and Treasurer....The Board of Governors shall be appointed by the President."

It goes on to explain about the duties and authorities of the appointed officers, and concludes by

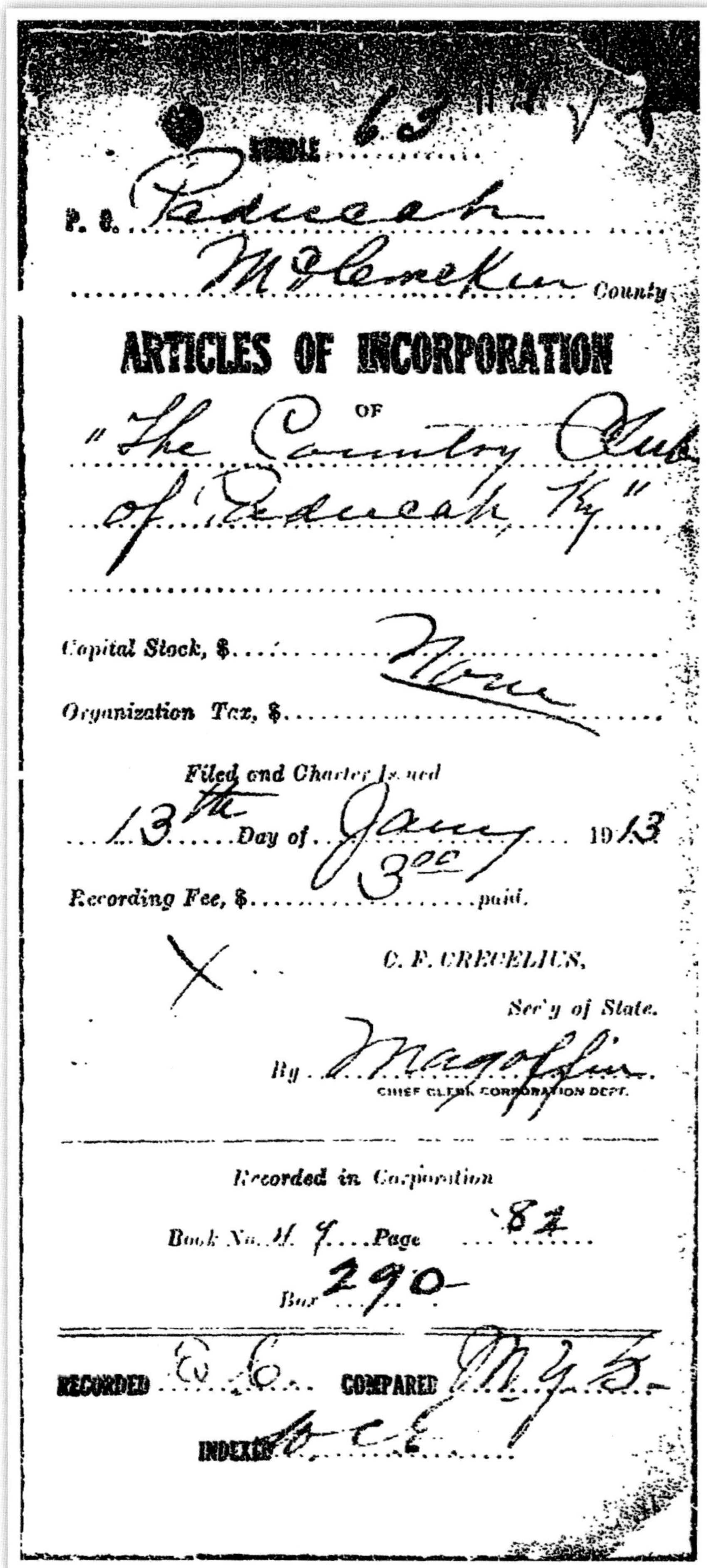

P. O. Paducah

McCracken County

ARTICLES OF INCORPORATION

OF

"The Country Club of Paducah Ky"

Capital Stock, $ None

Organization Tax, $

Filed and Charter Issued

13th Day of Jany 1913

Recording Fee, $ 3.00 paid.

C. F. CRECELIUS,
Sec'y of State.

By Magoffin
CHIEF CLERK CORPORATION DEPT.

Recorded in Corporation

Book No. 4 Page 87

Box 290

RECORDED … COMPARED …

INDEXED …

The Articles of Incorporation, January 13, 1913.

saying, "This company shall continue for fifty years from the first of February."

The notary public McCracken County who witnessed was Mattie Thompson on January 9, 1913.

E. Douglas Bagley was the agent on the Statement of Corporation of April 21, 1913.

The club's founding fathers quickly began to "sell" certificates of membership for $100. George Sullivan, George Goodman's grandson, has in his possession today two of the original documents—one issued to Goodman's good friend, W.J. Gilbert, and one to Thos Haden. (Gilbert was a local druggist and long-time friend of Irvin S. Cobb.)

In May of 1913, Gilbert was issued one share, No. 68, of the capital stock of The Country Club of Paducah, Ky. It was signed by Charles K. Wheeler, president, and Douglas Bagby. Haden's was No. 114 with the date listed as August, 1913. Eight years later W.J. Gilbert was the club champion, a year after George Goodman won the title.

INCORPORATED UNDER THE LAWS OF
No 68 THE STATE OF KENTUCKY Shares ONE
THE COUNTRY CLUB
OF PADUCAH, KY.
This Certifies that [illegible] is the owner of ONE Shares of the Capital Stock of The Country Club, of Paducah, Ky.
transferable only on the books of the Corporation by the holder hereof in person or by Attorney upon surrender of this Certificate properly endorsed
The holder of this Certificate will not be entitled to the privileges of this Club until duly elected a member by the Board of Governors
In Witness Whereof, the said Corporation has caused this Certificate to be signed by its duly authorized officers and to be sealed with the Seal of the Corporation at Paducah Ky.
ATTEST: Sec'y Pres.
SHARES $100 EACH.

INCORPORATED UNDER THE LAWS OF
No 114 THE STATE OF KENTUCKY Shares ONE
THE COUNTRY CLUB
OF PADUCAH, KY.
This Certifies that Thos Haden is the owner of ONE Shares of the Capital Stock of The Country Club, of Paducah, Ky.
transferable only on the books of the Corporation by the holder hereof in person or by Attorney upon surrender of this Certificate properly endorsed
The holder of this Certificate will not be entitled to the privileges of this Club until duly elected a member by the Board of Governors
In Witness Whereof, the said Corporation has caused this Certificate to be signed by its duly authorized officers and to be sealed with the Seal of the Corporation at Paducah Ky.
ATTEST: Sec'y Pres.
SHARES $100 EACH.

Copies of the "shares" given to new club members in 1913. Courtesy of George Sullivan.

J.R. Wallerstein and Melvin Wallerstein putt for the hole on number five in 1919. In the background is the old clubhouse that burned in 1955. Paducah Sun-Democrat *photo.*

Thus began the History of the Country Club of Paducah and the story of the men and women who have been its driving force through the years and the generations of families who make up its legacy.

Social Life and Club Business

This chapter is primarily devoted to the social life at the club from the 1930s to 2017, but also to the happenings of the day. Major events that impacted the club, such as the fire of 1955, the election of presidents and board members, the opening of the clubhouse in 1984, and the ice storm of 2009 are just a few "moments" in history covered here. Let's begin our walk down memory lane.

In the 1930s, the Country Club of Paducah was quite the social venue. Events that took place at the club were covered extensively in the newspaper with dozens of attendees' names listed, floral decorations described with a flair, and many other details of the happenings of the day included.

In the scrapbook of Miss Sara Kathryn Fergerson are dozens of references to the parties and weddings, horse shows, and swimming meets and golf events that took place at the club.

In 1932, for example, one clipping noted that the wife of club Governor Charles K. Wheeler and Miss Elizabeth Sinnott hosted a bridge party and breakfast at the club. Among the guests was Mrs. Muscoe Burnett whose husband's name appears on the club's Articles of Incorporation in 1913.

"One of the prettiest affairs of the Thanksgiving season was the continental supper and dance given at the Paducah Country Club for members and their out-of-town guests on Wednesday evening," one entry said. The year was 1935.

"The club house was attractively decorated with a profusion of autumn leaves and spiders and the lamps were draped with vines and leaves. Oak leaf decorations were placed over the doors and the mantle held silver urns of red haw berries. Supper was served buffet style in the dining room where Mrs. Hobart Massey and Mrs. William F. Paxton presided at the coffee services."

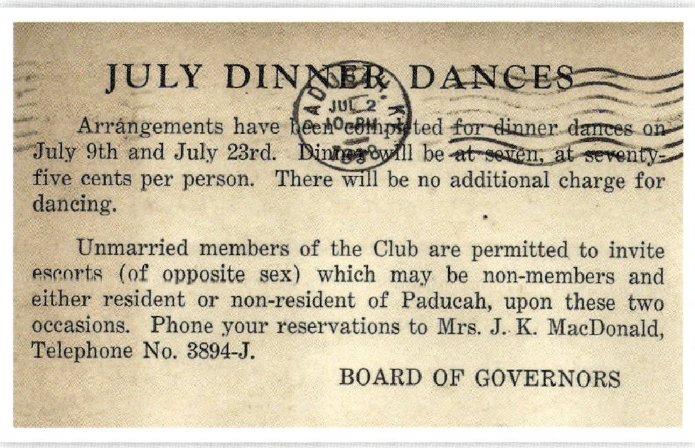

JULY DINNER DANCES

Arrangements have been completed for dinner dances on July 9th and July 23rd. Dinner will be at seven, at seventy-five cents per person. There will be no additional charge for dancing.

Unmarried members of the Club are permitted to invite escorts (of opposite sex) which may be non-members and either resident or non-resident of Paducah, upon these two occasions. Phone your reservations to Mrs. J. K. MacDonald, Telephone No. 3894-J.

BOARD OF GOVERNORS

"The guests were seated at three large tables which held glowing ivory tapers in crystal candlesticks and sprays of red haw berries and ivy down their length. After supper dancing was enjoyed to the music of Harry Ware's orchestra," the writer noted. Parties such as this were well attended and thoroughly enjoyed every time the club opened its doors, or so it seemed.

On December 29, 1935, the club had its annual dinner-dance "in an elaborate setting of holiday decorations" consisting of red cellophane bows, streams of icicles, hundreds of red balloons over the dance floor for over 250 party-goers. Mrs. Fred Lack was the chairman assisted by Mrs. Hermon Toof, Mrs. Neil Kruger, Miss Elizabeth Sinnott, Mrs. Warren Sights, Mrs. Allen Shemwell, Mrs. James Wheeler, Mrs. Melvin Cornillaud, Mrs. Lanson Ditto, Mrs. Jesse Loeb, Mrs. Stanley Petter, Mrs. James Rose Smith, Mrs. William Paxton, and Mrs. Leo Keiler.

In the spring of 1936, a journalist described social life at the club: "A fitting welcome to spring was the tastefully arranged luncheon and bridge party given at the Paducah Country Club Friday, April 17, with Mrs. James Glauber, Mrs. Edson Hart, and Mrs. C.E. Kidd hosts for the Hospitality Department of the club."

The creative description said the clubhouse was "brightened with a profusion of early spring blossoms and the tables held white vases of bush honeysuckle and jonquils." These ladies-only socials kept Paducah women busy and the club on its toes.

In July the writer noted, "Outstanding among the Fourth of July celebrations in the city was the beautifully arranged dinner and dance given at the Paducah Country Club." All of the major holidays celebrations at the club are "over the top."

The swimming pool was always an active spot on the old country club grounds. Children walked and road their bicycles to get there, and sometimes they swam, jumped, and played all day long. It was not just a spot for entertaining the youngsters—adults joined the fun and sat along the concrete wall that lined the back side of the pool or lounged in the chairs on the lawn.

Shelton Wins Golf, Aquatic Honors At Country Club

Versatile Youngster Shoots 75 To Win Flag Tourney, Captures Free-Style And Diving Events

Beaten By Shelton In Handicap Meet, Fairhurst 2nd In Flag Affair

In 1936, Johnny Shelton, the 18-year-old son of Mr. and Mrs. George H. Shelton made the headlines after his performance during the Country Club's Fourth of July swim meet. "Shelton Wins Golf, Aquatic Honors At Country Club."

"With the skill and stamina of an Olympic decathlon champion (he) sandwiched a dazzling exhibition in the swimming meet between one of the most spectacular rounds of golf played in Paducah this summer. He captured the free-style swimming race and the diving contest in the pool. He barely nosed out Robert Pence and Lanson Ditto in the junior division of the free style aquatic competition."

Tom Stahl, Jr., took second place in the fancy diving contest after he won the breaststroke competition. In the children's division, Warren Sights, Jr., finished first. "A large crowd gathered around the country club pool to watch the events," a tradition that continued for decades. A silver loving cup went to each of the winners.

Miss Sara Fergerson penned below the newspaper clipping that she had a date with Mr. Shelton for the club picnic that evening. (Miss Fergerson and Mr. Shelton later married. She was the mother of Sally Crowe and the aunt of Genie Drossos.)

As the club continued to grow and prosper in the 1940s, new chairmen were appointed, improvements were funded, and members continued coming to the club for a host of social functions.

Golf has been the main focus from the time the club was formed, but during the thirties, forties and fifties, the social scene shared the limelight.

H.R. "Bunks" Dallam became the official secretary-treasurer of the club in 1941. His minutes of meetings are one of the main sources for this history. Members of the Board of Governors in 1942 were Victor Speck, Sr., C.J. Carney, Henry Weil, Tomas Paxton, Ransey Martin, J.R. Smith, and W.M. Carson.

The club was the venue for stag parties which usually included a full fare of fun—golf, dinner, and cards. Sometimes gentlemen enjoyed the crap table a little too much and it was finally removed in 1948. The basement of the club housed slot machines, a jukebox, bingo, and an ice chest since members could bring their own liquor at that time.

Mrs. John Welsch was appointed the chairman of hospitality in 1942, and Mrs. B.A. Washburn and Miss Jane Shelbourne were the ladies' golf committee chairmen in 1943. The board considered hiring a club hostess.

A humorous comment included in the board minutes said someone needed to find out the cost of putting in an outside entrance to the basement card room and another place "where ladies could drink their Coca-Colas! That way they won't have to crowd into the vestibule leading to the locker room!"

In the January 16, 1942, "Bunks" Dallam entered in the board minutes a "Detail of subscriptions for $7,000," which one might assume was for memberships. Names listed were Jack Fisher, Warren Sights, Luther Carson, R.J. Martin, Jesse Weil, Milton Livingston, and Leo F. Keiler.

In another listing, the names of H.A. Teef, H.R. Dallam, Gov. Rosenthal, C.J. Carney, Henry Weil, Victor Speck, R.V. Green, W.M. Carson, E.C. Hawkins, Stanley Petter, and Luther Carson were included. "Also members as of this date are Roscoe Reed, Lanson Ditto, Floyd Sperry, David Reed, H.L. Wallerstein, O.L. Boren, and Jesse Loeb," Dallam penciled.

In the spring of 1942, Mrs. Carrie Rudy, Miss Elizabeth Sinnott, and Miss Elizabeth Anderson were

Mr. and Mrs. Wyatt Bell, Mr. and Mrs. Bill Paxton and friends.

Party in the old dining room.

associate members accepted into the club. R.E. Peters, Roy Shelbourne, H.L. Roberts, W.F. Paxton, R.E. Claussner, Irving Bright, Sr., and George Katterjohn became new members.

When the Board of Governors met on July 21, 1942, Jack Fisher was president. It is not possible to list everyone who has ever served on the board of directors, but it is noteworthy during certain years when changes were taking place.

The following year when Palmer James was president, he declared the tennis courts must be put in playable condition. The board approved $100 to make improvements. John Jordan was hired as a porter at $12 per week and C.J. Carney was taking care of the golf course and grounds until Mr. Ben Bolte was employed as caretaker.

The birth of the Member-Guest Golf Tournament was probably in the spring of 1942. Membership Chairman W.M. Carson suggested that the club give a stag dinner with golf contests in the afternoon and that "each active member be allowed to invite some friend who was a prospective member as his guest." The minutes also said that this would be an ideal way to get new members. By the time the event was on the calendar, the board decided that ladies would have the same privilege.

The "Governors of Golf" in October were C.J. Carney and H.L. Wallerstein. Irv Bright was thanked for his generosity in having the new "Tap Room" painted and decorated.

In 1943, several ladies were listed as associate members: Christine Alliston, Sara Burnett, Anita Flournoy, Lillian Hobson, Philippa Hughes, Pauline Kruger, Carrie Rudy, Ruby Rankin, and Elizabeth Sinnott.

Ed Hough remembered the trolley coming out to the original club site. "My grandfather drove one of the trolleys for several years after he retired. I remember that one went out Jefferson to the club and turned around on the side of the hill that was No. 9 fairway—that's why the ground was so hard. During the war, the trolley went back down Broadway to downtown. They took those tracks up when I was a child. They were dug up during the war for steel."

By 1945, the 19th Hole was deemed too small for the large increase in members, so it was moved into the locker rooms, which were more spacious.

Activities which took place at the Country Club of Paducah in those days were considered newsworthy and received prominent headlines in the social section of the *Sun-Democrat*. Just the kick-off for the summer made the news. In 1945 a headline announced "June Opens Season for Golf, Swimming at Country Club."

Diane Michael, daughter of Mr. and Mrs. Ed Michael, was in charge of the swimming pool and gave lessons.

The annual Easter Egg Hunt was a popular function for the children of the club for decades. Photos furnished by current member Dr. Rob Robertson and former member Barbaranelle Paxton McClennahan include over 100 children dressed up on Easter Sunday with baskets in hand, many wearing Easter hats and sitting on the steps at the old club.

Search the photos from 1945, 1946, and 1948, and perhaps you will find a familiar face or two.

Easter Egg Hunts in the late 1940s drew large crowds.

Children flocked to the Easter egg hunts for one of the most popular events at the club.

On September 10, 1946, W.F. Paxton was elected president of the club. The club by-laws were revised, possibly for the first time since the incorporation of the Country Club of Paducah in 1913.

One year later the active membership was 200 with a total of 484 members. President Paxton said, "We've enjoyed the greatest revenue in the history of the club," in his 1946-47 annual report. "And we've spent more for member benefits."

The board spent $11,477.07 on equipment and improvements. In 1947, the estimated value of 40 acres, the clubhouse, caretaker house, truck and tractor was $40,000. Improvements done in 1945 included repairing the wiring of the clubhouse, which President Paxton said was in very bad condition. Also during the Paxton presidency, cash was no longer accepted.

In 1947, the total number of members reached 484 with 200 of those being active regular golf members. For many years, up to five local ministers were given club memberships.

Moving into the late 1940s, the Charity League reserved the club for the annual Snow Ball, a tradition that existed for at least 60 years.

Those were invited to join the club, were Dr. James Ward, Dr. Charles Billington, Pat Turner, C.V. Henderson, A.B. Fendley, and Admiral Eugene Paro.

When E. Palmer James was president in 1948, the club had 496 members with 214 of those listed as active and six non-residents. Lady members totaled 192, juniors 58, student 4, ministerial 4, visiting 1, and associate 17. The 1949 annual meeting was held on October 27 with 50 members attending. Sixty-two attended in 1950.

A new ballroom floor was installed and a remodel of the 19th Hole took place that year. James said, "The greater part of the improvements was made possible by the voluntary contributions given by the membership, all of which funds were spent solely and exclusively on the improvements of the kitchen, dining room, ballroom, ladies' powder room and men's card room upstairs."

He goes on to mention that general revenues were used for the erection and remodeling of the barn and for the resurfacing of the apron to the entrance of the club.

When Eleanor Crounse graced the dance floor, she was clad in the latest fashionable gowns. She strikes an elegant figure with her handsome dance partner, Dr. Charles Billington.

"The Board of Governors experimented with the idea of a full-time club manager…and we still think that a full time manager is a matter that is going to be absolutely necessary to inaugurate." (This experiment did not work out at that time.)

President James concluded his letter to the membership by saying that the outgoing board realized that necessary improvements, such as reconditioning of the swimming pool and tennis courts, and possible replacement of the clubhouse roof, were not completed.

Space does not permit the inclusion of financial information for each year, but the board's statement to the members in 1948 was as follows:

The initiation fee in 1948 was $2,245. Gross receipts from the 19th Hole were $17,055.75. The golf course wages were $3,242.75 and the lifeguard at the pool expense was $131.67. The slot machine taxes were $960. The total operating expenses were $29,519.40.

Around that time, two of the ladies who frequently used the club for dining as well as sports were Mrs. Edwin (Florence) Paxton, Sr., and her daughter, Patricia, (now Pat Brockenborough).

One of the best stories Pat tells about those fond memories was a day when the club bill fell into her father's hands.

In the Words of Pat Brockenborough:

I came from a tee-totaling family. My father, Edwin Paxton, was the tee-totaling parent. My mother, Florence Paxton, would have an occasional drink, but concealed it from my father.

The summer of 1950, I was a recent college graduate from the University of Kentucky and had returned home to work at *The Sun-Democrat* and WKYB radio. I turned 21 in June, when my mother announced that she was going to treat me to my first legal drink. And so, after work one day in June, I picked her up and we drove out to the old Country Club—the original clapboard building of which I have fond memories—and ordered a drink from the bar. The bartender was Leroi King, a gentlemen we senior members remember as a genial fellow who was a first rate mixologist.

Pat Brockenborough addresses lady golfers in 2015.

We both enjoyed my rite of passage so much that we decided to make it a regular routine. And so, every evening that summer, I would drive home after work, pick Mother up, and we would go out to the club for a libation. It was customary for some members to take their drinks outside to number nine green and watch golfers approach the green and putt in. Lawn chairs were provided for our comfort and convenience.

"Bunks" Dallam, Dr. Henry Dallam's father, was the club bookkeeper. As was customary, members signed itemized checks that Dallam totaled each month, sending the total amount due to members.

One month, the bill was unusually high, due to a luncheon I hosted, but failed to notify my father. When the bill arrived, he told Mother and me that he felt there must be a bookkeeping mistake and had asked "Bunks" to send him all the charges. OMG, the bar bills would show up and we would have a lot of explaining to do!

Now, Leroi was a great bar man, beloved by all. But he was either lazy or uneducated, because he would abbreviate the items for his convenience. When the bill arrived, my father summoned Mother and me and said, "Can you two explain these? There are several checks with T.C. written on them and several with H.B." The T.C.s were Tom Collins and the H.B.s were high balls.

"Oh, that Leroi," Mother laughed, "the T.C.s stand for toasted cheese sandwiches."

"And the H.B.s are hamburgers," I offered. That seemed to satisfy him and he paid the bill.

Today, I wonder. My father was a bright man, naïve to a point, perhaps, but not easily taken in. In any case, the matter was settled to his satisfaction."

Pat recalled other memorable times at the club. "One summer afternoon, Mother and I sat in lawn chairs behind number nine green when a gentleman, a local doctor, hit my mother in the stomach with his approach shot. "Oh, did I hit you?" he asked Mother. "You certainly did," she replied. "Damn!" he said, "I haven't had a decent shot all day."

According to Pat, "The club's young people experienced great times at the old location." She would catch a bus at 14th and Broadway near the family home and ride with friends to Central Avenue near No. 4 tee. They would spend the day playing tennis, swimming, and, in the evening, playing hide and seek.

The McMurry twins, Pelham and Fletcher, were among the group. "Sometimes when we played hide and seek, they would trick us because we couldn't tell them apart," Pat said. "I also remember their mother, Lucille, making them a special costume. They won the Halloween costume contest at the club when they dressed as a horse—one was the rear and one was the head!"

(Pelham was a prominent attorney in Paducah until his death. Fletcher was the uncle of Fletcher Schrock, a partner in the same firm today, McMurry & Livingston, which Pelham founded with Mike Livingston.)

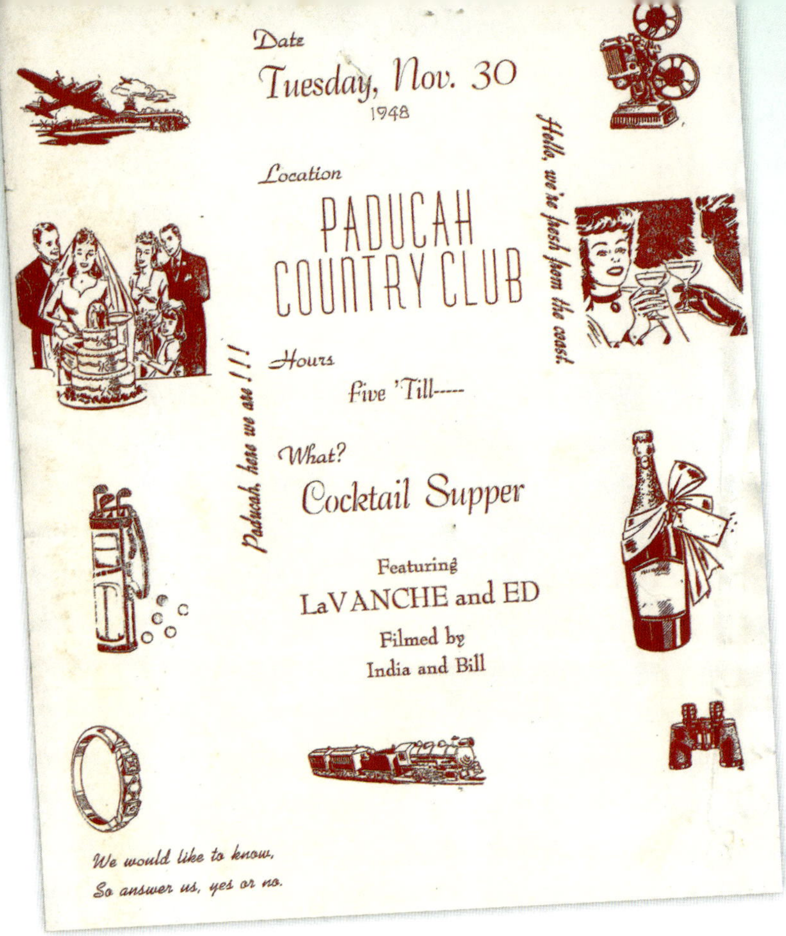

A large invitation in red and white advertised a cocktail supper at the Paducah Country Club on November 30, 1948. The party was in honor of LaVanche and Ed Simmel and hosted by India and Bill Paxton.

In a 1948 letter to the membership, Palmer James wrote: "The membership is at one of its highest in history with 214 active, 192 lady members, 58 juniors, etc., for a total of 496. The revenues of the club are now at an all-time high." James also mentioned that the tennis courts and pool still needed numerous improvements. (In modern times, only the year 1999 has exceeded 496.)

Olivia Cave was named the hospitality "chairlady" in 1950. (She and her husband, "Hawk," were active club members for decades. Olivia was still dining and swimming at the club in her nineties. She provided a few photos for this book.)

The manager, Bert Wilde, began having organized bingo parties at the club, an idea that was well received; Mr. Wilde, on the other hand, must not have been because he was replaced after a short time by Dave Tosh.

Long-time members recall the days when dining at that club on Saturday night was a coveted invitation for guests of members. The Paducah Country Club, as it was sometimes called, was the venue for many civic and social events at its first location.

For example, a Citizens' Dinner honoring Edwin J. Paxton for 50 years of community service was held at the club on June 30, 1950. (He had been a club member since 1925.

Some of Kentucky's most prominent residents attended, including civic-minded Paducahans and club members. Heading the guest list, which was printed on the program, were Vice-President and Mrs. Alben W. Barkley.

Others on the list included Harry, Lee, and Sam Livingston; Fred Neuman, Edwin Paxton, Jr., Frank, Fred, and Patricia Paxton, and W.F. Paxton, Mr. and Mrs. Henry Weil, Mr. and Mrs. Henry Ward, Charles, Dalton, and Howard Woodall and their spouses, and 100 more.

The menu included "Chicken a la Country Club" and "Old Kentucky Apple Pie." Songs were sung by The Gay Nineties Four with Thomas S. Waller serving as toastmaster. Mayor Robert Cherry paid tribute to Mr. Paxton as the "JCC Best Friend," while Fred Wahl addressed the group about Mr. Paxton "Our Boss." The "Veep," Kentucky's favorite son, was the main speaker.

In November of 1951, the board had a choice to make—raise the dues or raise the number of members to 350. The Governors voted to raise dues 30 percent under Jack Piers leadership. At the same meeting, board member John McDonald said he thought the club would be more attractive to single members if they could bring guests of the opposite sex. Rule 11 was amended to accommodate this idea.

Potter Smith presented drawings for a new dining room and bar to be built off the porch at an estimated cost of $7,500. This became an agenda item for many future meetings.

Members of the Board of Governors in 1952 were Bill Backus, John McDonald, Jr., David Clark, H.R. Dallam, and Potter Smith, with President Jack Piers.

In the summer of '53, Piers presided at a special meeting regarding a liquor license for the club. Was it advisable to ask the City of Paducah to take the club into the city limits? "This would eliminate our present unsatisfactory method of operation," the minutes read. "And, the taxes would be offset by a savings in insurance, water rent, etc."

The issue was whether the club should obtain city and state liquor licenses making the sale of alcoholic beverages legal or continue operating as usual.

The board meetings focused on this possibility of annexation for several months. One vote was to move forward with it, but when some opposition was voiced by a small number of people, the board tabled the move and closed the club bar. This did not last long because a large number of members wanted it open.

If the board ran into a problem, an occasional drastic measure was taken. Such was the case in 1953 when complaints were filed with the board about the crap table and games in the basement of the club; the board voted to have the manager burn it.

The club president in 1954, Louis Kirchoff, saved the club some money when he bought 10 tons of refrigerator equipment from the Cobb Hotel at a cost of $1,000 for air conditioning the 19th Hole.

In March of 1954, Grace Livingston and Marie McClure appeared at the board meeting to explain improvements and share ideas for the club ballroom. Mr. and Mrs. George Weitzel were contacted in regard to the decorating

Between 1949 and 1952, the club pool drew members of all ages. Jack Piers, young Bill Paxton, and teenagers Gretchen Oehlschlaeger, Denny Sullivan, Barbaranelle Paxton, and her mother, India Paxton.

job and also about new furniture. At that same meeting, the board voted to place two jukeboxes at the club from Central Novelties Company.

Raymond Roof said the swimming pool should have a new reinforced bottom and that the fence should be removed and other improvements made. He was authorized to spend $2,500.

Also during this meeting, the board passed a rule that "ladies and children under 16 cannot use the golf course on Saturday, Sunday afternoons, or holidays between noon and 4 p.m. Motion made by Dalton Woodall and carried unanimously by Kirchoff, A.E. Boyd, Jr., Tommy Whittemore, Frank Sawyer, Ramsey Marin and Raymond Roof.

A building program that could cost as much as $80,000 was considered in October. The board was leaning toward a $25,000 renovation instead.

Little did the members and management know what was coming next.

The Fire of February 28, 1955

In the wee hours of February 28, 1955, the neighbors who lived along the perimeter of the club property at Pines Road, Central Avenue, Country Club Lane, and North 36th and 40th Streets were awakened by the popping and crackling of burning tree limbs and raging flames. Fire engulfed the clubhouse that sat at the top of the hill for more than 40 years. It burned to the ground…a sad day that shook the community.

Pat Tilford whose family lived at the corner of Pines Road and North 36nd Street said she and her siblings went out on their porch and gazed in amazement at the fire. Others remember the smell of smoke that soaked the neighborhood. Embers danced in the air and dotted the early morning sky.

Only the foundation walls and chimney were standing when the sun came up. The fire was discovered by the night watchman, Mr. Cissell, around 12:30 a.m. in the kitchen on the main floor. He had made two rounds and was in the process of making his third inspection when he heard a noise upstairs.

Thinking someone may have entered the club, he rushed upstairs and was met by flames coming from the kitchen. He attempted to fight the fire with a fire extinguisher, but was forced back and out of the building by the flames.

It was out of control by the time a civil defense fire truck from Station No. 4 answered the call and reached the scene. No city water supply was available since the club was located outside the city limits at that time; and since it was February, the club pool was dry.

According to the front page story by *Sun-Democrat* staff writer Jim Phillips, "They covered the water from their one tank to protect the nearby home of Ed Verplanke, manager of the club. Firemen remained until 2:17 a.m."

Verplanke had checked the outside of the club before retiring for the night with no indication of problems. When he was awakened by the crackling flames, he rushed the short distance to the clubhouse and urged Mr. Cissell to get out of the building. When flames scorched the large trees, it cast a light that could be seen for miles.

Photos provided by Jay Davidson, and the Sun-Democrat *archives.*

A meeting had been held the evening before the fire. The last social events held in the old club were the junior and adult Mardi Gras balls. The next scheduled event was the Patty Berg golf clinic on March 23, which joined a long list of cancellations for the remainder of the year.

Members' golf clubs, which were stored there for the winter, were lost as well as new merchandise in the pro shop, but that was minor compared to the structure itself. The tennis courts and pool were not harmed by the blaze.

Louis Kirchoff was president when the club burned. He estimated the loss at $200,000 in the *Sun-Democrat* story. Insurance did not cover what the club was worth.

After the Fire, Re-Building the Clubhouse

A called meeting of the Board of Governors, the Building Committee, and the Finance Committee was held on May 20, 1955, at the Cobb Hotel, to discuss the proposed clubhouse to replace the original one that burned on February 28.

Present at that important meeting were President Kirchoff, A.E. Boyd, Stanley Melvin, Jack Keiler, Dewey Payne, Morris Lee, Raymond Roof, Tommy Whittemore, Jack Watt, H.R. Dallam, W.F. Paxton, Jack Piers, Harold Sullivan, Fred Nagel, and architect Lee Potter Smith.

Paxton presented sketches and plans for the proposed clubhouse and explained them in detail. Fortunately, architect Smith was ready to turn the plans over to contractors for bids; the board voted to accept the plans and specifications.

By August, Kirchoff had worked tirelessly talking to members, trying to persuade them to come on board and buy $300 debentures so the building of a nice clubhouse could proceed. Unfortunately, his goals were not met.

Plans from the United States Steel Company for a pre-fabricated clubhouse were discussed, along with the possibility of buying the home and property of Walter Hougland if it proved suitable for a clubhouse.

They met again to discuss the Hougland property and finally decided since they had no definite price at which it could be purchased, and that it lacked the necessary space needed for the clubhouse, it should not be considered any longer. At that point, the Board of Governors decided to go with a much less expensive facility.

John Cassidy Construction Company was selected to build the new clubhouse, which he did in a relatively short period of time. (William Karnes built the first clubhouse, and B.H. Green & Son, Inc., built the current facility.)

Members celebrated Labor Day of 1956 with a new club on the old site. The dedication was held on the first Sunday in September with golf matches being played the next day.

Above: The new clubhouse in 1956.

Left: Golfers pictured with the facility in the background were Jim Dunn, Mary Russell, Tom Whittemore, Sr., Sam Livingston, and Vic Speck, Jr.

Records indicate that Labor Day weekend was one of the biggest weekends at the club. Men's club championships were won and lost that weekend and almost all members of the club and their families participated in everything the club had to offer—tennis, swimming, dining, and golf.

The Paducah newspaper ran a full page on the grand opening of the new clubhouse written by Paducah resident and *Courier-Journal* reporter Harry Bolser. In the story, he said the clubhouse would be dedicated at 4:30 p.m. with the board and Club President James Rieke hosting a reception.

Other items of interest that occurred in 1956-58 and were either reported in the club minutes or newsletters:

During the July 1956 meeting applications for membership were extended to Jack Wilson, who went on to be president; Ralph McRight, who had served as the golf pro/manager several times; John Decker, and Brooks Jones.

The Board of Governors for the 302 members in 1957 were President Richard Smith, Tommy Whittemore, Sr., J.C. Rieke, Dalton Woodall, W.C. Backus, Robert Hougland, and H.R. Dallam.

Fertilizer was purchased at a cost of $59.75 for a pet ton, and 100 pounds of Bermuda seed at 50 cents per pound was also approved by the board.

One of the most well-attended, exciting events at the old club was the annual Men's Calcutta party, which was held the evening before the Men's Member-Member

One of the most popular spots at the club is the swimming pool, about 50 yards from the clubhouse. At the table are Tom Paxton, Phil Mengel, and Janet Woodall. Sunbathers are Sarah Russell, Pat Mabry, Julie Nichols, Greta and Linda Woodall, Kay Culver and Nell Taylor.

Mrs. Hughes Garvin, Mr. J.E. Dunn, Mrs. Walker Turner, Mrs. Melvin Cornillaud, and Mrs. Rieke in the ballroom "lounge."

Golf Tournament. Ladies and gents were decked out in their best club attire as they prepared for a fun night of commentary by Dalton Woodall and Hawk Cave, very popular auctioneers. The only people who ever complained were the neighbors, according to Ed Hough, who joined in 1958 with his wife, Barbara, and their daughters, Pam and Renee.

"We were fun people back then. Everything was a celebration!
—Ed Hough

Hough said it was the most popular night on the social calendar with lots of cash and cocktails flowing. "I remember that Evelyn Bailey enjoyed bidding on her husband, Jack, and their son, Jackie, during those years when they both played golf. Sitting on opposite sides of the main dining room at the old club, Evelyn didn't realize that she was bidding against her family as the bids went higher and higher!"

Ed Hough

"It was great fun back then! We raised over $25,000 sometimes," Hough laughed when he was interviewed in 2014. (The club still hosts a casual get-together for the Calcutta team bidding. Former board member and past president, John Williams, has served as the "auctioneer" several times.)

Hough also said the annual Christmas dance and the annual Board of Governors or President's reception were wonderful events enjoyed by the members. They were both black tie, formal affairs. "The president's reception was a big deal. The board and the new president and spouses were in a receiving line. It was early in the year and the first event and the club picked up the tab. We felt like the club owed that to the membership…one big blowout a year. Everyone would come," Hough remembered.

He pointed out that the "waiters" were excellent, singling out "Pick" Patterson, and Leroi King. "The club started having really good food when we hired Bill Newcomb. He was the best. And then came Ruby." Hough said, "She raised all the kids!"

"We were fun people back then. Everything was a celebration! It seemed like the veterans were all like kids turned loose after the War," he continued.

"I asked Lee Warren to be in charge of golf and other social activities when I was president and he did a fine job! We started the member-guest. It was a club staple for many years." (Both men served as club president. Hough passed away in 2015 at age 94, and Warren died in 2016 at age 91.)

The club newsletters are a valuable source of information for the club history; they include activities not always mentioned in the board minutes. In the sixties, seventies, and early eighties, photographs verify that the Country Club of Paducah was still the center of social activities for many of its members.

Many swim competitions were held in the club pool in the 1960s. In a 1964 clipping taken from the *Sun-Democrat*, young swimmers named included Shelby Lawley, David Paxton, Jimmie Wooldridge, Mary Hays Render, George Gould, Buzzy Peel, and Scott Stryker; Mark Curtis, Tina Lund, Barry Pfanstiel, Connie Koven, and John Harris.

LABOR DAY WINNERS—Labor Day is always a big one for sports at Paducah Country Club. Pictured above are, from the left, Glenn Noss, Labor Day Golf champion; Jim Musgove, runner-up; George Sullivan, handicap winner; Mickey Romer, fifth flight winner in the spring handicap match tourney; Tom Whittemore, spring champion; and Ed Hannan, Labor Day handicap runner-up. Not pictured were Dr. C. M. Blanton, Jim Curtis and Jack Kerr, second, third and fourth flight winners in the spring match tourney. Pictured below are the winners in swimming and diving contests. They are, from the left, front row, Shelby Lawley, David Paxton, Jimmie Wooldridge, Mary Hays Render, George Gould, Buzzy Peel and Scott Stryker, and, back row, Marty Render, Tim Stryker, Mark Curtis, Tina Lund, Barry Pfanstiel, Connie Koven and John Harris. Winners in tennis were Nancy Backus, Allen Kleet and John Harris. 1964

Spectators gathered for a swim meet at the old pool.

The country club pool was a busy place that drew swimmers of all ages. Having a great time in the summer of '69 are Karen Lund (green bathing suit); Bill Conyer (center), Jimma Grimm (yellow suit), and Tim Stryker (yellow trunks). Inset: The same group of swimmers practiced their "water ballet" moves at the original club pool.

In June of 1966, the board informed Hubbuch's of Louisville to proceed with a contract for decorating the club foyer, bar, blue room, and ballroom. The swimming pool committee noted that golf balls in the pool were out of bounds!

In February of 1967, members were saddened when it was announced in the newsletter that Robert Koven, Pierce E. Lackey, and Dr. James Harris had passed away.

The Superintendent of Paducah Public Schools, Dr. Newman Walker, became a new member in '67 along with Bob Grimm, and Dr. Bill Chumley.

Specials for the month included cocktails on Thursday evenings at a cost of 40 cents each, a 12-oz. steak was $2.50 per person, and the seafood platter on Fridays was $2.75.

"As of today, we have a stereo record player for the cocktail lounge and will have the dance floor down every Friday, Saturday, and Sunday," the minutes said.

Members of the 1968 Board of "Directors" were Vic Speck, Jr., Dr. Henry Dallam, Russell Shelton, Jack Bailey, Jack Kerr, Bill Usher, Lee Livingston, and Gresham Hougland, president. Since the club's incorporation, the board members had been referred to as Board of Governors.

Commenting on the change from governors to directors, attorney David Denton said the board re-stated the Articles of Incorporation and filed them with the Kentucky Secretary of State in 1973.

"Corporations sometimes do that when the 'old' articles are believed to be antiquated or outdated," Denton explained. "My best guess is the modern term 'directors' was being used and the old-time term 'governors' was dropped. The state statutes in 1973 were referring to corporations having directors, not governors."

Mary Jane Harris was asked to be the activities director of the club. New active members approved by the board were Jules Samuels, Royce Gregory, Jon Wallner, W.J. Brockenborough, Lane Peck, Rev. Paul Donner, and Benjamin Huey Green.

At the annual meeting on January 20, 1976, outgoing President Lester Myrick noted that in 1975 the initiation fee was increased to $2,000 since there was a waiting list. Twenty new golf carts were purchased for operation by the club, and capital improvements totaled $52,508.

In 1977, the initiation fee went to $2,500, provided the regular membership reached 450 on or before Sept. 1, whichever came first. Directors were Joe Whedon, David Denton, Bob Bell, Joe Harry Metzger, Patrick Kerr, Joe Rinella, and Henry Dallam, Jr., and Bill Usher, president.

In 1979, the board was composed of President Henry Dallam, Jr., Larry Barnett, Irv Bright, Jr., William Pfanstiel, Vic Speck, Jr., Jack Wilson, Tom Ezzell, and Jim Curtis. Harold Leonard was the club manager.

(The transition from the Country Club Drive location to the Blandville Road site between 1979 and 1984 is covered in Chapter 3.)

"A picture is worth a thousand words."

Photographs from the 1970s and early 1980s showing life inside the clubhouse.

Row 1, from left: Grayson Lee Harralson, Danny Key, and Bill Paxton, 1981; Pat Parrish, Bill Black, Sr., Henry Dallam; Carol and Bo Bell with Gretchen and Dr. Henry Dallam at a wedding reception, 1981; Mary D. Rieke chatting with Sam Livingston.

Row 2, from left: Bainey Ladt and Mary Ann Barnett; Just for fun! Costumed members are LaNelle Boyles, Beaulah Mae Futrell, Imogene and Louis Igert, Clyde Boyles; Sherry Shadle and Dr. Paul Grumley; Beth Garey and Sally Michelson.

Row 3, from left: Dick Fairhurst and Mary Jane Hart, 1979; Bill Paxton, Cynthia Pfanstiel and Janice Grace at a party in the ballroom in 1972; Alene Livingston and Grace Murt in the early 1980s; Julie Rieke, Mary Barker, and Jim Rieke with Gretchen Dallam; Dot and Bob Ely (front) with Gene and Alice Fisher and Harry and Gloria Livingston in the old clubhouse bar in the late 1970s; Harold and Jane Sullivan with Eleanor Crounse, 1979.

Row 4, from left: Ward and Ruth Thomas with grandson, Ward, in 1979; Eleanor Crounse, Mary Lalla and Walker Turner, 1979; Woody Hook and daughter Susan Sloan; Crissy Paxton, Carrie Speck, and Kathleen Washburn; Ruth Friedman, Gloria Livingston, Grace Livingston, Mickey Romer, Derby Day Party, 1979; Tom Paxton, Dorothy and Charles Billington, 1979; Joanie and Bill Walden.

Row 5, from left: Don Hartline, Jimmy Curtis, and Harry Livingston at the Derby Day party, 1979; Ward and Ruth Thomas (background) and Dawne Robertson; "Mix" and Micky Romer, Carol and Allen Bright and Alene Livingston in the early 1980s; Dr. Clyde Peel, Bill Usher, Dwain Lowry; Ann and Vic Speck and Carol Croft, 1981; Anne and Dr. Jim Gwinn with Mark Whitlow and Bill Paxton, 1981.

From left: Phil and Betty Higdon; Dr. Keith Crawford (right) with Dr. Charles and Gail Ransler; George Sirk, Tony and Kayla Page.

Enjoying the Easter bunny with Ashley Shadoan (left) are Libby Shadoan, Kaki Shadoan, Molly Pugh, Parker Shadoan, Ripley Pugh, grandchildren of Beverly and Rip Pugh.

The Sabel sisters: Pat Wooldridge, Peggy Paxton, and Ginger Usher.

Board members Tony Page and Louis Michelson said the board is considering closing the dining room Tuesday through Friday except for private parties and luncheons and asked for members' input. The annual Easter egg hunt and holiday buffet were staged in April of 1990. The pool was a busy place as always.

The annual tracking fee for private carts was $400 annually when the season kicked off. Cart fees were $7.35.

The September newsletter said that the golf pro shop will soon be under construction.

Club members mourned the loss of Mr. H.R. "Bunks" Dallam, who passed away in the fall of 1990.

On the dining scene, Ruby's beans and turnip greens and John's catfish were the highlight of Stag Night on November 15, 1990.

The golf season drew to a close in November with Jim Marvin winning the Senior Club Championship, Bill Crabtree reported.

The Long-Range Planning Committee was considering the remodeling of the existing golf pro shop and changing it into an adult lounge. One schematic expands the 19th Hole bar into a children's' room; the other constructs a new and separate bar in lounge, keeping the children's' room where it is.

The new monthly dues structure included $125 for regular members.

In January of 1991, the adult lounge construction was underway. Greens committee chairman Jack Weitlauf said a program had begun to clean out the roughs in order to achieve the goal of complete Bermuda grass cover by the end of July.

President Banks said, "The past year has proved to be one of our best years ever with all the improvements at the club—such as the new look in the 19th Hole, the new golf and tennis pro shops, and the new Kentucky Room."

In the summer newsletter, Jackie Nackley mentioned that President Bush declared July 4 as the official "Welcome Home Day" for all our military troops who served in Desert Storm. The club extended thanks to members Dr. Andrew Kim, Dr. Brad Mutchler, and Mr. and Mrs. Semeraro for their service.

Golf course Superintendent Larry Schmitt resigned, and Mark Spire from the Country Club of Brookline, MA, was hired. Fred Schwan succeeded Brian Martin who had been the Director of Tennis for six years. With PGA professionals Larry Mullen and Todd Trimble also coming on board in 1991, the year proved to be one of major over-haul in the club's key positions. (*See related stories in chapters on golf and tennis pros and superintendents.*)

Gus Van Sant, Sr., applied for regular membership at the club. Van Sant, the brother-in-law of Jane Ann Nall, who was an outstanding lady golfer from Mayfield for decades, assisted Ryder Cup Captain Tom Watson in all selections of the team's wardrobe in 1993.

The Christmas dance that Ed Hough referred to as "one of the most fun events held at the club" in the 1950s was held in 1991.

When 1992 rolled around, Burton Banks' term ended as president and John D. Williams was the new president. Williams was vice-president and general manager of WPSD-TV at that time, having been with Channel 6 for 27 years.

He announced in May that Gary Robertson and Steve DuPerrieu would supervise the new fitness center, which had just opened. In January of 1992, the board was still comprised of nine directors and the president. Jim Brown was appointed to the greens committee for a three-year term. The purchase of 20 new Club Cars was given the go-ahead, and the tennis committee reported that a fitness center might cost between $50,000 and $60,000.

By-law changes were passed. The changes said the club extends membership to qualified persons without regard to race, color, creed, national origin or disability and that the use of the male pronoun "he" would be for convenience only and such use included the use of the female pronoun. A regular member description change stated that a regular member shall be at least 18 years of age.

At the February meeting, the board passed a motion to proceed with the development of the fitness center once costs were secured.

Attorney Rick Straub reported on behalf of the by-laws committee and the board approved the following amendment: "Non-members who reside in any county, any part of which lies within 85 miles of the City of Paducah, may use the golf course at the guest of a member no more than three times in any calendar year."

In May, a new membership category was established and called a "house member" with a $2,500 initiation fee and dues of $70 per month with no voting privileges. This would also include use of the fitness center as well as food and beverage.

The initiation fees were raised from $7,500 to $10,000 and jackets were still required when eating in the dining room and lounge; this changed the next year for bar attire. Members were enjoying the special events that Jackie Nackley scheduled—from a clambake to Monte Carlo night to Breakfast with Santa.

Rick Straub became the secretary-treasurer of the club, replacing Ray Carlson, and in January, the new superintendent, Larry Hantle, instituted the six-quadrant hole location chart.

Straub's stint as secretary-treasurer was brief because he was elected president in January of 1994. John Golliher took his place. In the March newsletter, President Straub remarked about the state of the club saying, "The Country Club of Paducah has come a long way in a very short time. The foresight, dedication and hard work of the leadership during the past several decades has resulted in an outstanding facility."

Straub said the financial picture looked good, too many more members might result in serious overcrowding, the tennis program compares with any in the state and the bubble has lasted longer than most thought it would. He also said, "I was quite disappointed to see that our golf course had dropped from the Golf Digest listing of the top five courses in Kentucky."

On the social scene, a group called "Jumpin' Jive" entertained a sell-out crowd—Pat Lynch, Cheri Paxton, Al Knudsen, April Cochran, and Chris Black were a huge success at the September and November dinners and shows. Another crowd pleaser took the stage much to the delight of the members—the club's own Conrad Trogolo and his band. Connie is one of the most talented pianists who entertained at the club.

In April, Straub told the membership that the most immediate concern is the prospect of a permanent indoor tennis facility. The board's second concern was related to the lack of use of the upstairs dining room and bar and options were being considered. The third concern was the use of private carts.

In the summer of 1994, members returned 210 surveys sent to them by the board. The main response was that the members did not want an assessment and also a formal dining area is still desired, and more covered tennis courts are needed.

Straub announced the remodeling of the upstairs bar, which will be called the Paducah Room. After the August board meeting, Straub told the membership that the board was not ready to spend the money for an indoor tennis facility. Ed Hely was thanked for his work on the proposed project.

"Jumpin' Jive" entertained a sell-out crowd—Pat Lynch, Cheri Paxton, Al Knudsen, April Cochran, and Chris Black.

The Cruisers (John Craft on guitar and Jim Long on saxophone) have played at many club events.

Wally Bateman applied for membership in the club. He served as president and remained a member until moving to Florida some 20 years later.

On the social front, Dr. John Craft and "The Cruisers" were back by popular demand for the New Year's Eve Gala.

In 1995 new board members were Jim Harris, Edward Hely and Hal Sullivan. President Straub commented on the fact that 140-plus members voted, which was a record number for several years. He announced that the club upstairs dining room would be closed on Tuesdays, Wednesdays, and Thursdays.

Early spring news included the tennis courts resurfacing, mats being placed on the driving range, and the implementing of a special children's menu with art by Alice Fisher. Tina Terrell was hired as a massage therapist for members. Liz Bozarth also held this position.

Grandparents Day was held at the club, Jackie Nackley reported, plus National Children's Day was celebrated in the Paducah Room. Soloist Richard Abraham, long-time city commissioner, entertained members along with pianist Jeff Clark.

On the social front, the Paducah Symphony Orchestra League hosted its first annual Father-Daughter Dinner Dance at the club. The black-tie affair is still a hit.

Edward Hely was elected club president in 1996 with Jim Harris as secretary-treasurer. In his first "President's Corner," Hely noted that granite yardage markers were being placed on the tees and fairways; the pool areas will be expanded and improved; and the newly remodeled golf pro shop was complete.

Dr. John Colgan, Chris Bell, and Robert Petter, Jr., applied for junior memberships.

Hely announced that the board decided "to complete a project that has been in the planning stages for over two years on the golf course…re-doing all the bunkers on the course, re-contouring them, re-doing the drainage work, and replacing the sand. It has not been done since the course opened in 1979."

Leroi King, a long-time employee of the old club, passed away. "Leroi was somewhat of an institution greeting members," President Hely remembered, "always showing his wry sense of humor talking about who he had 'visited in jail' that day."

The club hosted the Bird Shooter's Ball, a casual party with members clad in camouflage, jeans, and hiking boots and dancing to John Craft and The Cruisers.

Chef Nick Cerbonne arrived at the Country Club of Paducah from New Jersey. Dr. Ted Borodofsky and his band were a sell-out and Chris Black and Jumpin' Jive were back by popular demand. After 12 years, Linda Carroll made a career move and left the club.

The fall of 1997 was a busy time at the club with the still new GM Charlie Lopez planning events for the member's enjoyment. "The Crypt Keepers Halloween Ball" and Oktoberfest Week with German and Bavarian specials pleased the attendees, the manager said in the newsletter. The American Indian and Pilgrim buffet was also a hit.

At the end of the year, Hal Sullivan and Ed Hely were commended by Manager Lopez for the positive changes in operations of the club. Hal Sullivan served as tennis chairman while he was a board member from 1995-97.

Hely, who is both a golfer and tennis player, completed four years on the board and two years as president. His roots are deep when it comes to the Country Club of Paducah. Edward's mother, Sue, and father, Norman, were both golfers, and Ed grew up near the old club on Country Club Lane.

James A. Harris, Jr., was elected president for 1998, while his brother, John, was named secretary-treasurer. Both Jim and John were active at the club for many years. They swam and played tennis and golf starting in the 1960s when their family moved to Paducah and joined the club.

In March of 1998, Jim Harris told the membership in his "President's Comments" column in the newsletter, "New to the board's structure this year is the Long-Range Planning Committee. Pat Cvengros will ably chair this committee, the purpose of which will be to develop and prioritize the club's overall capital expenditure program."

In September, the membership survey concerning capital dues and clubhouse renovation/remodeling was the topic of Charlie Lopez' forum. The survey revealed that the clubhouse renovation as the No. 1 priority and the golf cart paths a close second.

The board approved McMahon Group from St. Louis to assist with strategic planning which would culminate in a clubhouse renovation proposal. The process might take 18 months to complete.

On the turf front, Larry Hantle said that Virginia Tech University studied samples of our greens and reported that a disease named Take All Patch was prevalent in the root system.

Labor Day weekend 1998, faces in the pool crowd: Emily Frampton; Kim and Steve Keiler, and Jeff Holland; Jim Woods and Beth and Burton Banks; Rachel Caksackkar, Emily Owens, and Alison Albritton.

The golf committee asked the board to institute a tracking fee for any golf cart used on the club property. This motion passed.

Charlie Lopez accepted a position as GM at Vestavia Country Club in Birmingham, while Richard Centenni was welcomed as the second GM after serving in that position in Murfreesboro, Tennessee. Mark Evans returned to the club as food and beverage manager director.

Jim Harris was re-elected president and John Harris was re-elected secretary-treasurer in 1999.

In June, the board approved for the McMahon Group to move to Phase II of renovations of the club.

Manager Centenni reported the opening of the Bistro where dress is casual. The last social function of the year was the New Year's Millennium Celebration." Members welcomed the new year for the 87th time since it was incorporated.

Stilley, Cates, Kight—the assistant golf pros—along with Todd Trimble—were all listed in the newsletter with their email addresses, something new at the club. Trimble said they were not ready for an automated tee sheet yet, but members will be able to dial into a web page for starting times in the fall of 2000.

Dick Walker was elected president for the year 2000 and Dana Curtis was the new secretary-treasurer. The newly formed House Committee Chairman Bob Garey began working in earnest with staff to help improve food and service. (*See his comments in the Presidents' Chapter.*)

Other board members were Dr. Mark Gillespie, Bob Wagner, Tom Whittemore, Dick Wilson, Connie Trogolo, Frank Shelton, and Butch Bradley.

In May, the board approved $20,000 for interior upgrades recommended by the decorating committee.

In July, President Walker appointed a long-range planning committee consisting of the president, secretary/treasurer, three staff managers, and the last four past presidents. Thirty days later the results of the membership survey on improving the club were published.

A few of the results provided by the written questionnaire were as follows:

- Golf and dining are the two most important activities at the club.
- 86 percent feel clubhouse improvements are needed.
- Pool bathhouse/restrooms received low satisfaction ratings.
- Golf operations and the golf course received high ratings.
- Tennis facilities and operations received high ratings.
- Fitness facilities received average ratings.
- Clubhouse interior décor, Kentucky room décor and size, the 19th Hole, the kids' room, and the men's locker room received low ratings.

The highest priorities for potential future improvements included upgrading the kitchen, providing a casual bar/lounge, improving access to member dining, improving the clubhouse interior décor, and providing more space for casual dining with a view of the golf course. A new rear exterior with a traditional architectural style was pictured. The report noted that the clubhouse was designed for 300 members, and the club now has 600 members.

The project cost would be $2.8 million as stated in the materials given to the membership. In 1999, the total membership was 608, an all-time high.

The Club Improvement Program of August, 2000

When Richard "Dick" Walker was president, the Country Club of Paducah Improvement Program was created after the results of the 1999 membership survey were compiled.

After reviewing the survey results, the board decided to come up with a plan for this "Club Improvement Program."

The club's Mission Statement was updated at that time and both the program and the statement were included in a presentation to the members. That Mission Statement was as follows:

> "The Country Club of Paducah shall be a full service, family-oriented private club that serves as the primary social and recreational center for its members. The club shall provide high quality facilities, services and programs with an emphasis on dining, golf and tennis."

The Improvement Program was addressed in a letter from Walker on behalf of the board, which stated, "The satisfaction of our present members and the ability to continue to attract new members rely heavily on the quality of the facilities we provide. We have important areas of our facilities which are below the quality levels we need to meet and the capacities we need to serve our members."

Walker also pointed out that the clubhouse was built for 300 and was now serving 600 members.

"The most important components of the Improvement Program are a new casual dining room and lounge overlooking the golf course and a new traditional clubhouse exterior appearance. Other improvements include the expansion of the kitchen and the replacement of equipment, plus the replacement of outdated interior furnishings and mechanical systems and equipment."

An outdoor deck with a golf course view and a lounge adjacent to the casual dining room (Kentucky Room) were part of the program.

"The board of directors feels strongly this project is in the best interest of our club and unanimously recommends that you vote for approval."

The cost of construction, furnishings, fees, and contingency were estimated at $2.8 million. The schedule of events said construction would begin January of 2001 and complete that summer. The regular/corporate member contribution was estimated at $6,300 with $3,000 refundable when the member resigns and a new member joins.

The vote failed by a narrow margin, according to a September 28 letter. Some board members thought that the membership did not understand that they were not only voting on facility improvements, but also on ways to pay down the large debt owed by the club. The board halted plans for improvements, but an assessment was looming.

In a letter to the 565 members dated October 6, 2000, the following points were made regarding an upcoming assessment:

- The assessment is a step towards much improved fiscal responsibility.
- Conservative management will no longer fix the problems facing the club.
- Golf course projects such as a new cart barn and new practice facility are on hold.
- The club is in need of approximately $250,000 for overdue maintenance and repairs.
- This marks a change in fiscal policy of the club.

After much agonizing discussion and deliberation, an assessment was passed on September 26, 2000. Life at the club fell back into regular rhythm for the loyal members, while others gave up their memberships in frustration.

The calendar flipped to 2001 with Walker as president and Butch Bradley secretary-treasurer. Manager Centenni said, "The club has been a busy place with fixing, painting, and maintenance going on. The Kentucky Room was painted, re-arranged, and new chairs were on their way."

Dues were $192 for regular and corporate members and the food and beverage minimum was $35 per month, according to the manager. "In an effort to balance our budget, some tough decisions had to be made to control our expenses," he explained.

In October, Centenni announced that the new membership program brought in 65 new members and 13 returning ones. "Our goal was to replace the members who resigned last fall," he noted.

One newsletter mentioned "that the clubhouse underwent a dramatic change and we owe the decorating committee a debt of gratitude." Serving on that committee were Beth Garey, Jane Gamble, Joyce Paxton, Jean Reed, Alice Morello, Jane Bright, and Carol Bell. "A very special year-round thanks to the tireless efforts of Beth Garey who has spent countless hours at the club. We appreciate all you do for us!" the newsletter said.

Terry and Ozie (Bohle) Carlton, Lucy Paxton, and Julie DuPerrieu were also thanked for decorating during the holidays in 2001.

Moving on to the year 2002, Dr. Bob Garey was elected president.

Linda Carroll was listed as manager under "Clubhouse News." She wrote that the business offices of the club are now located downstairs just off the 19th Hole. A Centennial Celebration was on the schedule to allow members to celebrate the club's 100-year existence. Now it is clear that the anniversary of the club's incorporation slipped by in 2013.

"As we reflect on the great times we have had in the past at the club, this is the time to make memories for future reflections," Linda said. She also mentioned that dancing was a big part of the old club.

The Friday night buffets were becoming more and more popular; the Mother's Day brunch continued to sell out, and the annual Easter egg hunt was conducted much to the delight of the club children. Men's Night was a "happening" on one Wednesday per month following golf.

Memorial Day continued as one of the most widely participated days at the club along with Labor Day weekend when members use to mark the culmination of the golf season with the club championships, barbeques, and pool activities. Jon Wright was the head lifeguard in 2002.

2003

Bob Garey was re-elected president of the club and Butch Bradley was re-elected secretary-treasurer. Tim Lambert was appointed golf committee chairman with Bill Usher serving as green committee chairman. Dr. Jim Woods was finance chairman, an invaluable asset, Garey noted; he has also served as secretary-treasurer of the board.

New lockers are under construction in the clubhouse and on the tennis front, a new ball machine was purchased.

The year came to a close with a flurry of parties.

Newlyweds Elizabeth (Key) and Bryan Kaegi, on October 11, 2003, leaving the club.

2004

John Golliher had served on the greens committee for 10 years, according to Larry Hantle. "I want to publicly thank John for his support and service." He and his family moved to California.

Linda Carroll thanked Bob Garey profusely for the leadership he provided during some difficult, but productive, years of service as president.

She also said, "The club has changed in many ways and these gentlemen (Tim Lambert, Pat Morello, and Jim Woods) were instrumental in the good changes that have taken place."

Garey did find time to record a double eagle on No. 18 on January 16!

Gorman "Butch" Bradley was elected the 2004 club president with Dr. Ron Kupper, Jr., elected secretary-treasurer. Kupper will also serve as golf committee chairman.

The board solicited the services of Ed Henderson of Master Club Advisors to assist with planning the club's future needs while meeting membership desires within our financial capabilities, the newsletter said. MCA was a national firm that works with private club management and directors. The firm conducted an operational audit for the Country Club of Paducah.

In other business, the board mentioned contacting Stinespring Homeowners Association about constructing a cart path along Holt Road on the north side of No. 8 green. This had not been built as of 2017.

Long-time employee Ruby Petty with Mark Curtis on New Year's Eve, 2004.

At the end of 2004, Linda Carroll resigned and the board began a search for a club manager, according to President Bradley. Jonathan Bennett was hired in March of 2005.

2005

In a letter to the membership dated February 1, 2005, President Bradley addressed questions about the club debt, possible improvements to the clubhouse, and the employment of the new manager, all topics discussed at the annual meeting with just a few members in attendance.

The debt has been reduced to $133,000. If there are no unforeseen expenditures, and the committee feels the funds are available, the debt may be paid in full earlier, the letter noted.

The board's goal is to move all dining from the Kentucky Room and 19th Hole to the main floor, but keep the downstairs kitchen open with a grill menu to provide service to golfers making the turn, members using the pool, and those with small children. A patio, children's room, and other items were included in the reconfiguration.

To accomplish the move, the upstairs kitchen will require complete renovation and expansion and the dining facilities will be expanded. The building committee has been meeting with an architect. Bradley said that plans should be submitted for bids by early April.

Bradley said approval from the voting membership was necessary. He estimated a $1 million expansion project, including the parking lot. "The board is absolutely committed to completing the project with no assessment and no increase in the current debt retirement."

"It is the goal of the building committee to complete the year without any interruption in the club house operations. The club house should be able to re-open around March 1, 2006."

The building committee consists of Chairman Tim Farmer, John D. Williams, Pat Kerr, Jane Bateman, Gorman Bradley, Bill Usher, Cindy Wyatt, Darla Sims, Andrew Coiner, David Hutcheson, Sr., and Beth Garey.

In other business, the board purchased 12 Club Cars and traded in used ones, a four percent dues increase was installed, and the superintendent took over the upkeep of the clubhouse grounds.

Ward Thomas resigned at age 99 on January 31, 2005, after 48 years of membership, as did another long-time member, Gene Fisher.

2006

Wally Bateman was elected president and Tim Farmer will serve as secretary and vice-president of the board, a new position. Bateman appointed Oscar Gamble greens committee chairman. *Renee Tilley became the first woman elected to the board.*

Brian Hershey was named Executive Food and Beverage Director.

A&K Construction Company began work on the kitchen project, and the existing deck needed replacing, according to the board minutes.

In March of 2006, a resolution was passed to cap the senior membership to 40. Twenty years of continuous membership at the club and having reached the age of 70 were the two criteria for this classification. "All seniors who meet the criteria will be put on a waiting list available upon written application on a first come, first serve basis, and will be eligible only after a current senior member leaves the grandfathered membership class," the resolution stated.

The board voted to make all interior facilities at the club smoke free for the first time in its long history, Manager Jonathan Bennett announced. The membership is awaiting the much anticipated grand re-opening this spring.

As Wally Bateman bid the membership farewell as president, he gave a re-cap of 2006. The club opened the new dining areas; a successful membership drive netted 42 members; and No. 5 pond has a new rock retaining wall.

2007

Tim Farmer was elected president with Oscar Gamble as vice-president, and Sam Thompson, secretary-treasurer. Gamble also was the greens and tennis committees' chairman.

Social activities were in full swing with Valentine's Day, Derby Day, wine tastings, cooking classes, and a clam bake under the direction of Brian Hershey. Pilates classes, Father's Day brunch, and the opening of the 19th Hole Pub downstairs were newsworthy.

The pool is always a busy place during the summer months at the club. In 2007, President Farmer noted, "The pool is in terrific shape this year. It was pressure washed and painted. Other improvements include new pool furniture, gates, and spruced up changing room."

The Capital Improvement Fund was voted on at the annual meeting. Future projects expected included the parking lot, the lakes, cart paths, bunkers, greens, and the tennis building totaling over $1.7 million.

2008

Tim Farmer, the outgoing president, was thanked for leading the club through the building renovations in 2007. Dr. Rosemary Shiben became a member of the board, and attorney Andrew Coiner was the new vice-president nominated by incoming president Oscar Gamble.

The current clubhouse in the 1990s, before the remodel of the Kentucky Room.

Hurricane force winds damaged the golf course and the tennis facility on September 14.

Brian Hershey welcomed James Hunt as assistant food and beverage director.

The year drew to a close with a flurry of holiday social events.

2009

January of 2009 kicked off with a business meeting and long-term goals for the board with Andrew Coiner elected president.

The three long-term goals at that time were to replace the greens, replace indoor tennis court structures, and update the pool.

Board members Mike Wyatt and Dr. John Colgan initiated discussions about a golf membership for "singles."

The ice storm hit in late January wreaking havoc across the course and grounds.

At the March 2009 board meeting, Larry Hantle discussed course clean-up progress after the ice storm and said the quote of $130,000 from an arborist should stand. The finance committee chairman, Mark Curtis, recommended a "Member Assistance Payment" of $400 to help with the cleanup. By opening day, April 18, the golf course was ready for play despite losing 170 trees just on nine holes.

Once business at the club resumed, Gary Zakutney was assigned the job of handicap chairman, according to golf committee chairman Jeff Torbett.

It was suggested that the off-season operating hours for the clubhouse and golf shop change and also close on Mondays and Tuesdays, but no action was taken by the board.

On April 8, President Coiner announced a by-law change. House and tennis members may now play up to five rounds of golf a calendar year, during non-peak hours, upon payment of greens fees.

President Coiner, a Paducah attorney, addressed the membership in his newsletter column, "From the President" in May when life at the club was back on track. "Last month we strolled down Memory Lane, better known as Turnberry Drive, with thoughts about family and friends at the Country Club of Paducah. Every time you set foot in the clubhouse, the golf course, the tennis court or the pool, you have an opportunity for an event you'll never forget. This month I want to share with you additional recent memories about the quality of your fellow members," he wrote.

"It's no secret Mother Nature body slammed the club's property. It's also no secret after considerable consideration, the board called upon the membership to financially assist in the cleanup. The support the club is receiving is overwhelmingly positive and immediate," Coiner continued.

He praised the 226 members who have contributed so far, and said "If you don't think there are Golf Gods carrying Karma Scorecards consider this: Every winning team on open golf day and the first men's night contained at least one raker (who helped with the course cleanup). To those who participated, may you get a kick back into the fairway on every rare, crooked shot this summer."

In the July newsletter, President Coiner challenged members to appreciate the value the club offers and to recruit a new member. "Our club is a significant recreational value for the initiation fees and offered membership categories. Dining at our club is also value."

He pointed out that we have a Robert Trent Jones designed golf course, a recently renovated clubhouse, a beautiful patio with views; a swimming pool with renovated dressing rooms and a grill, and a tennis facility which includes indoor, outdoor, and clay courts, a tennis center and a workout area.

2010

Mike Wyatt became president of the club in January of 2010 and the new secretary-treasurer was David Denton, who was appointed to the board to fill the vacancy created when Rex Smith resigned to run for public office.

Kurt Kuebler of Kopplin & Kuebler was hired to search for a Chief Operating Officer/General Manager for the club. Kuebler was a successful GM at the Loxahatchee Club in Jupiter, Florida, for many years.

In other business, the idea of replacing the greens was tabled for the near future and the board agreed to establish a valet service for the members.

In the April newsletter, Wyatt told members about financial stress that a number of natural "disasters" have placed on the club—the straight-line wind of April 2006, remnants of Hurricane Ike in October of 2008, which took the roof off of the tennis center at a cost of $116,524; the ice storm of 2009 with a price tag of $338,000 to start; and the 500-plus stumps which must be ground.

In a concerted effort to improve the club's finances, the board approved a Rainy Day Fund Assessment and a dues increase of 10 percent.

Moving into spring, President Wyatt announced that Tim Straley was the new General Manager. Straley continues to serve in that capacity in 2017.

A new club logo was introduced.

Mike Harlow was named the club's executive chef. Harlow worked with Manager Straley in Illinois. Members are still enjoying his expertise as he prepares and leads his staff.

New and different types of entertainment are now on the club social calendar. "Funny men" comedians are an example. For decades, the Charity League of Paducah has hosted its annual Snowball at the club; the group's "Winter Wonderland" party was held on New Year's Eve.

The Higdon Development Project planned on property adjacent to the club on No. 3 and No. 4 fairways was discussed in new business during the August meeting. Today several duplexes and a small pond with fountain are "home" to several club members. The board discussed building tees with the dirt obtained from the project.

House chairman Denton introduced the Sponsored Reciprocal Dining Plan, a new plan for the club that offered dining to local reciprocal country clubs in an effort to increase food and beverage revenue.

Membership promotions, a Reservation Rewards Program, and other incentives for dining at the club continued to be offered.

Wyatt, Denton, and the rest of the board worked on aggressive plans to improve the club's financial situation while they were in office. Membership drives were conducted and capital projects deferred in some instances. It was a time of budget cutting and tightening the belt at the club.

Manager Straley summarized all that was accomplished during the year by saying, "We have embarked on freshening up the Country Club of Paducah in many areas. From the landscaping at the front entrance, to painting the clubhouse, to new china, silverware and uniforms, we have set a new tone for our members and guests that embodies the culture and feel of a private club."

"We have addressed and improved the overall food quality…we are well on our way to bringing the 'best dining available in Paducah' back to the club," Straley added.

The final newsletter of the year 2010 paid tribute to H. Burton Banks, an excellent golfer and a club member since 1964, who was also president in 1990-91. Burton had passed away unexpectedly.

2011

By 2011, the board under the leadership of President Mike Wyatt, realized that financial problems needed to be addressed and action taken. The board's letter to the membership said "Tough times call for tough measures… We would have preferred to end the year with no increases, however, as business people, we realize that is simply not feasible." A 2.5 percent dues increase and a small food and beverage minimum were implemented and a new membership promotion was offered.

A membership promotion was published in January whereby regular memberships were $2,500 (initiation) and $285 per month. Many incentives in all categories were offered as the drive to entice members continued.

Finance Chairman David Denton introduced the "Club within a Club" concept, which would bring people with common interests together for functions. He also presented the board with the idea of "The Turnberry Club," an exclusive club to fund special projects for the golf course.

According to the minutes, the group's sole interest would be to improve the course. The benefit of being a member would be pride in helping to improve the golf course, and a plaque would be displayed in honor of those who joined the Turnberry group.

At the April board meeting, a by-law change was made regarding junior membership—an applicant would only need to be under age 40 at the time of application. Junior dues were set at $150 per month with a $1,500 initiation fee.

The following change, in part, regarding non-resident membership was passed by the board: After May 15, 2011, any person whose primary dwelling is beyond a 35-miles radius from the club shall be eligible for non-resident membership. A person whose dwelling is in close proximity to the 35-mile radius may still be approved for a non-resident membership upon a vote of two-thirds of the board.

In January, Larry Hantle reported that tee and hole location charts were being revamped to include six areas.

Seventy-four people joined the club, proving that the membership drives and incentives were paying off. This brought the total membership to 577.

A host of social activities crowded the calendar with Family Night, Mardi Gras and St. Paddy's Day buffets, a Murder Mystery Dinner Show, Comedy Night, and an Indoor Golf Tournament providing fun for the members.

Since its renovation, the old "Kentucky Room" needed a new name. Members voted and decided not to get too creative—it was re-named The 19th Hole. The 19th Hole downstairs was officially opened in early 2011.

Other news flashes were as follows:

President Wyatt nominated David Denton for club president 2012; tennis pro Kerns returned from a trip to Saudi Arabia; Christina Haynes was hired at the tennis shop; the Turnberry Foundation had $145,000 in pledges; and Jamey Brown was chosen secretary-treasurer for the coming year. Brown also assumed the chairmanship of the membership committee in January, 2012

As 2011 was drawing to a close, the finance committee proudly reported that by year-end, the club will be in good standing, the balance sheet was continuing to strengthen, and revenues were showing a healthy trend, the minutes reflect.

Tim Straley reported to the membership that "great strides were made toward getting us back onto a solid financial base. 2011 has definitely shown itself to be the year of a beginning turnaround for the club as a whole."

2012

In January, outgoing president Mike Wyatt happily reported that the club's line of credit balance was zero for the first time in several years. "The board made some very difficult decisions in 2011," he explained, and went on to say that the club's turn-around came in part to Tim Straley's excellent cost controls and a very aggressive membership drive."

"We can now start planning for the future rather than paying off the past. Thank you for your support," he added. Wyatt commended the 2012 incoming president and 2011 finance chairman, David Denton, for being another reason for the turn-around.

In the February newsletter, Wyatt said, "The club has changed a lot in the last 110 years…To ignore change is to issue our club a death sentence. The new board must continue to find new ways to bring in revenue." He urged members to continue to support the club and embrace the board's concepts. "That support will guarantee our longevity and hold our dues in line."

Food and beverage operations continued to be a work in progress for Straley and the board with emphasis on new ways to increase banquet sales. Anthony Hunter was the new banquet manager and Kristie Ison the new dining room manager.

Denton, the new president, addressed the membership saying that the club is underutilized and urged members to take advantage of what all the facility offers. "I'll confess I cannot walk around the grounds without having an increased sense of pride in our multi-purpose complex. There is a renewed recognition of how lucky we are to have such a facility. Through my mind runs a quote by

Pam Boland and Christy Meisenheimer

In 2012, Olivia Cave (left) and Mary Jane Park celebrated more than 50 years of club membership.

Life-long member Mike Livingston

The family of Peggy and Bill Bob Conyer (right), preserving club traditions.

the Irish poet Oscar Wilde. Paraphrasing, it goes: 'The best way to appreciate your (club) is to imagine yourself without it.' Think about it!" Denton suggested.

In June, President Denton wrote, "I am developing more and more admiration for the individuals who, in years past, served as directors, officers, and committee members on behalf of the multitudes. For 110 years, they advanced the cause against a vast array of challenges ranging from natural disasters to those that were man-made. I believe that keeping our membership united under the arc of one organization ranks as one of their most significant accomplishments. Certainly, conflicting opinions have led to the split or demise of many private clubs, yet our club, for all its diversity, survives and flourishes."

In other business, board member Jeff Holland proposed a by-laws change that would allow the spouse of a voting member to be eligible for election to the board of directors. The motion passed.

Another year was underway with dozens of social activities and golf and tennis season just around the corner. Dates and offerings will be published on the club's website (www.ccofpaducah.com) which is free to members.

In the minutes of 2012, golf committee chairman Chris Hunkler researched plans to replace golf carts and create a storage area for them. Club Car was chosen as the provider of the carts.

Greens chairman, Kurt Averill, said the committee's challenge was to increase golf play through outings and guest play as well as more member play.

The membership campaign saw a major spike in junior memberships with more total members at the club since 2006 when there were 456. In 1999, the club had 519 members and in 2010 there were 358. By the end of 2012, the total was 417.

The Turnberry Foundation

Acting on David Denton's idea in 2011, several club members voluntarily contributed a total of approximately $170,000 when the Turnberry Foundation was established.

"What a phenomenal start to a very worthy cause which will guarantee a legacy for the golf course here at the club, President Mike Wyatt commented. In 2012, the Turnberry Foundation's first project was to construct decorative stone walls on No. 1 and No. 2 ponds at an estimated cost of $85,000.

Jim Brown was president and Ed Hely, Jason Siener, Kenny Hunt, and Wally Bateman were serving as directors when the May newsletter gave an update. By-laws and Articles of Incorporation were adopted Brown said, "Our sole purpose is to improve, enhance, and foster an appreciation of the Country Club of Paducah's Robert Trent Jones course as a championship course, which is second to none in the surrounding area.

"Our goal was to create a pool of funds, separate from the operating budget of the club, to be used for capital projects over and above those that would normally be the responsibility of the club itself," he added.

Today, the Turnberry Foundation's contributors are listed on a bronze plaque on the back wall of the golf shop building.

The membership committee emailed a survey to the 560 members with the board stressing the importance of the results; by October the results were in with a 46 percent response rate. Members indicated they recognize how vital the golf course and programs are to the success of the club even if they do not play.

The Country Club of Paducah extended condolences to the families of Jimmy Curtis and Edna Hipp, who passed away. Mr. Curtis had been a club member since 1954, serving on many committees over the years. Mrs. Hipp had been a member since 1965 and was known for her love of tennis.

At the November meeting, the board nominated and elected Tom Greene to serve as president in 2013 and Jamey Brown to serve as secretary-treasurer. At the final meeting of 2012, the Long-Range Planning committee had KRW Strategies give a presentation analyzing the results of the survey of the membership done earlier.

Striving for quality, maintaining and creating tradition, cultivating a family friendly environment, and demonstrating value for all members were listed as four objectives the board and management should use going forward.

2013

Ushering in another new year at the Country Club of Paducah, new President Tom Greene said he would like for us to become "one of the ten best country clubs in Kentucky." Stan Eckenberg, head of the Long Range Planning Committee, was commended for his leadership.

The "Rainy Day Fund," which was instituted as a result of the ice storm in 2009, is fully funded and will be discontinued. The "Facilities Enhancement Fund" was approved by the board for maintaining the status quo of and improving the facilities of the club. This is a capital fund that will be used to address some deferred maintenance as well as for making improvements across all areas of the club, according to the February newsletter.

Work during the winter months paid off as the pond walls at No. 1 and No. 2 are almost complete. Spearheaded by the Turnberry Foundation and co-sponsored by the club, this work will greatly enhance the golf course.

The membership noticed a large increase in the number of activities happening at the club. The Father-Daughter Dance in February, for example, was certainly a night to remember. The men were handsome in their tuxedos, while the girls of all ages glittered in their party dresses.

Katheryn Joyner, chairman of the social committee, became a driving force as she and her group worked with Manager Straley to find activities that would increase member participation. Among the items on the March calendar were couples' tennis, indoor golf, St. Patrick's Day dinner specials, the annual Easter egg hunt; and in April, wine tasting, Ladies Night Out, a fishing tournament and a day for children to make Mother's Day gifts.

The month of May featured a Polynesian buffet and Margarita Madness on the patio. Remember when Ed Hough said, "We were fun people back then?" Perhaps today's members have reclaimed that feeling of having fun while at their club.

The Children's Fishing Derby was a huge success with 34 youngsters catching 109 fish on the club property. Katie O'Neill, Spencer Cates, Christian Anderson, Virginia Walsh, Ben LeBuhn, and Grace Denton were the winners!

One of the best ideas the social committee had in 2013 was the family campout on the driving range. Those who enjoyed the fun grabbed tents, sleeping bags, and blankets, played ping pong, pool games, watched movies, ate s'mores, and stuffed themselves with pancakes the next morning!

Back to board business, Pat Kerr will act as the club's architect in designing the new entrance to the club as well as the cart storage facility.

Later in the year, the entrance to the clubhouse has a new and improved look thanks in part to Doug Edwards, who donated the new American flagpole. It now stands with the Kentucky and Country Club flags at the entrance.

Doug had been a member of the club since 1975 when he passed away in 2013. He served on countless committees and as club president.

Another member loss occurred in 2013 with the passing of David Hutcheson. In 1970, David and Barbara Hutcheson joined the club. Dave's name was very familiar to those who were members when the club relocated from its first site since he bought and sold property along the golf course. He lived at Meadow Links until he passed away in the spring. Dave supported the club both as a member, golfer, and businessman (Florence & Hutcheson) for over 40 years.

David Hutcheson

In June, the golf course suffered a flash flood with over five inches of rain in three hours.

Social activities packed the fall calendar as members attended Ladies Night Out, a very popular addition with "A Chocolate Affair" as the theme; a wild game dinner with bourbon tasting, a family Halloween party, a cooking class for kids, and the member appreciation mixer. Membership Appreciation Night was a hit with wonderful food stations from "Around the World" from Chef Mike Harlow.

The year 2013 came to a close with the rejuvenation of a New Year's Eve party.

2014

Jamey Brown was elected president of the club when the board's focus was on a host of projects that were projected to cost approximately $820,000.

As Greens Committee Chairman, Kurt Averill updated the board on the Forward Tee Project, which includes relocating six tee boxes and thereby reducing the yardage.

Golf Chairman Chris Hunkler said the cart storage project was almost complete; and Tennis Chairman Adam Chustz noted that the fitness center renovation project was underway. House Committee Chairman Jeff Holland announced that $14,000 had been raised so far to start the Playground Project, which would be located by the pool.

An intensive marketing campaign was underway with Membership Chairman Mark Chambers reporting on new brochures, folders, and other marketing materials that will be used for membership promotion.

In the minutes, the board voted to have a much-needed history of the club compiled, written, and published since many records and photographs have been lost over the years. Vicki Hunkler, who first became a member in 1979 and has a master's in journalism will be asked to take the job," Tim Straley said.

President Brown mentioned the 2012 board survey of the membership regarding "What You Want from your Club" in the newsletter. "While you haven't heard much about it recently, behind the scenes we have been working diligently to turn the results of those surveys into an action plan," he said.

"The result is the club's first strategic plan whose purpose is to help guide decisions, prioritize investments, and focus the board, our management team, and the staff's efforts towards doing the things that you deem most important to your membership

By the conclusion of 2014, the major projects were completed; in addition, the updating of the entrance signs, the installation of an ice machine at the golf shop and hitting mats at the driving range, and cart path repairs were all finished.

Louis Michelson's 70th birthday party in 2014 in the Board Room. Sally and Louis Michelson (left); Harry and Alecia Alvis with Louis.

The club began paperless billing for monthly statements. The newsletter will be available by email and online with only a limited number of printed copies available. Also in keeping with the surge of technology usage by practically everyone, President Brown announced that the club will now have an "app" for cell phones.

Members thoroughly enjoyed the "Welcome Back" party held when the club re-opened after its January break.

Manager Tim Straley announced many fun activities for children at the club. A first ever "Junior Culinary Academy" was one of those that would raise funds to help pay for the playground by the pool. A day camp for those age five to 12 was held at the club for a five-week period with many thanks from parents.

The spring social calendar was packed with a spring golf and tennis fashion show; a junior tennis pizza party, indoor mini golf, the Mardi Gras buffet, a French wine dinner, and other events too numerous to list.

The new fleet of Club Car golf carts arrived at the newly built cart storage facility. The hunter green carts are a much-needed welcome addition to the club's golfing members, according to golf committee chairman, Chris Hunkler.

The opening day scramble in May kicked off the golf season along with the Ladies Spring Tournament and the Men's Two-Man Open.

The biggest news on the golf course in 2014 was replacing of the fairway grass with Meyer Zoysia after they were lost. President Jamey Brown said the course "would be returned to an even more favorable condition than the golfers have ever experienced before." Members do not relish the idea of "cart paths only" for a lengthy period of time, but the long-term results of having Zoysia fairways is something golfers plan to enjoy for years to come.

The Fairway Renewal Project received much needed financial support. In the August newsletter, Brown noted that more than 90 members generously contributed. "We escaped what could have been a financially devastating event for the club. There are not too many clubs in the country that could have sustained the hit by Mother Nature that we took and actually have had the ability to come out on the positive side of the situation."

Attending the Welcome Back Party after the club's annual January break in 2014 were (clockwise from left) Sue Roberts, Phyllis Curtis, Judy Shepherd; Jim and Brenda Brown, Jordan and Jamey Brown; John and Sherry Shadle.

The board approved member Gene Hipp's request to install a teak bench behind the back tee box on No. 1 to honor the memory of his wife, Edna, and his son, Gene Paul.

The year 2014 was one of the most eventful in the history of the club. The change from Bermuda to Zoysia fairways was a monumental undertaking, both physically and financially. The addition of a golf cart storage facility, a children's playground, a remodeled fitness center, new forward tees, a new front entrance, and a new fleet of golf carts were additional accomplishments.

Without member support and the leadership of President Jamey Brown and the board of directors, the Fairway Renewal Project and others might not have been completed by the end of this memorable year. Hats off to board members Jason Siener, Jeff Holland, Mark Chambers, Chris Hunkler, Adam Chustz, and Kurt Averill as well as Jamey Brown.

Members also tipped their hats to Superintendent Larry Hantle and his crew and GM Tim Straley as they also helped steer the club through a difficult, but very rewarding year.

2015

The new year was marked with the release of a full schedule of social and dining events at the club. Banquet and Events Manager Katie Graves set as her goal to offer new creative events. From elegant international wine dinners to theme parties like Super Bowl, UK games, Dueling Pianos and the Membership Appreciation Mixer, the 2015 list was designed for member enjoyment.

Kurt Averill was the new president. The board continued to introduce programs and incentives to promote membership.

Ladies Night Out was held in February with attendees painting with the theme celebrating Paducah's Dogwood Trail. The Second Annual Junior Culinary Academy was the highlight of the March calendar.

The March newsletter featured a photo from the *Paducah Sun* of Jamey and daughter, Milly Brown, dancing at the Father-Daughter Dance held at the club and sponsored by the Paducah Symphony Orchestra. "This is a perfect example of how traditions begin at your club," the headline read.

Tim Straley attended the Club Manager Association of America's 88th Annual Conference and brought home ideas "to keep the energy and excitement alive at the club," he reported.

On the deck during Ladies Night Out in 2014 are (from left) Jordan Brown, Mykala Brown, and Adrienne Yaeger.

In April, the board honored those who have been supporting the club for 50-plus years by waiving the monthly food and beverage requirement. President Averill thanked the following members: Jane Bright, Bill Bob Conyer, Mary Dyer, Sue Hely Fendley, Benny Green, Gene Hipp, H.E. Katterjohn, June Keiler, Mike Livingston, Jr., Jerry Page, Frank Paxton, James Paxton, Jr., Peggy Paxton, Bill Paxton, Robert Petter, Sr., Joe Powell, Richard Roof, Vic Speck, George Sullivan, and Bill Usher, Sr.

Membership milestones with 40 or more years at the club were recognized in the newsletter and included Dr. Hilary Hunt, Dr. Harry Brigance, Elizabeth Edwards, Dr. Bob Garey, Dr. Jeff Johnson, Robert Milford, and John Williams.

In 2015, Jim Brown gave an update on Turnberry Foundation projects and reported approximately $34,000 was in the foundation's bank account. One of the first projects was the forward tees; another was to hire a consultant

The 2015 Junior Culinary Academy class members learning from Chef Mike Harlow and Jason Fritts were Spencer Cates, Ryan Jones, Bella Rose Brown, River Stilley, Lexi Straley, Caden Kern, Kip Siener, Addison Hart, and Tage Edwards.

Above: Dueling Pianos is a member favorite on the social calendar. Right: Jamey Brown dances to the beat with daughter Milly in 2015.

to provide a conceptual improvement plan for the practice facility, although this was tabled due to the fairway "crisis."

In August, President Averill declared the membership drive officially over. Fifty-eight new members were added to the club roster.

As the golf, tennis, and pool activities began their annual fall wind-down, former board member Louis Michelson submitted a letter that was published in the newsletter.

Above: Randi Stovesand on the treadmill with Claire Key in the background. Right: Dan Key on the recumbent bike in the refurbished tennis center.

A club member for almost 50 years as of 2015, Michelson stated, "During these years I have seen many challenges occur form moving our club 'out to the country,' the construction of our golf course, the clubhouse expansion, the destruction of our tennis bubble, the recession of 2008, the ice storm of 2009 with the loss of 600-plus trees and last, but not least, the loss of our fairways in 2014."

Michelson praised the "miraculous recovery" the club made without levying an assessment on the membership and added, "I am most grateful and appreciative to all who have given so much to continue the traditions of the Country Club of Paducah. It is through these efforts we have the status as being one of the premier country clubs for a community of our size in this great country!"

Frank Paxton had been a member of the club for 67 years when he passed away. For many years at the old club, Frank chaired finance committees, advised boards and politicians, and initiated the Julian Carroll golf event to raise funds and recognize Paducah's favorite son, the Governor of Kentucky. In the final newsletter of 2015, condolences were extended to his wife, Joyce, and the Paxton family.

2016

Kurt Averill concluded his term as club president and welcomed Adam Chustz as the new president. Chustz is a tennis player and chaired the tennis and fitness committee during his tenure as vice-president.

June Keiler was recognized in the newsletter for being a member of the club for 70 years! Bill Bob and Peggy Conyer and Vic and Anne Speck reached the 60-year mark. Peggy Livingston Conyer and Vic Speck, Jr., were children of club members before the 1950s.

Manager Tim Straley published a slight increase in monthly dues bringing the premier membership as it is now called to $397, recreation to $310, and social to $203. The non-resident membership is $131 monthly with a $500 promotional initiation fee.

The fitness center can now be accessed 24 hours a day with a key card.

Guest golf rates from October 1-March 31 were lowered to $30 during the week and $40 on weekends for 18 holes in hopes of attracting more prospective members to the course.

A full page in the February newsletter reminded members that "The Best Sunday Dining in Paducah is at the Country Club of Paducah!" Those who attend seem to agree. Where else can you find an omelet "action station," an "action griddle" for French toast or pancakes, a carving station, plus luncheon entrees on the menu?

In an effort to increase the attendance at the Board of Directors' Annual Membership Meeting, the board moved it to April 19.

In March, Dr. Mark Gillespie filled the seat left when director Tommy Owen and his family moved to Louisville.

Bill Usher, past president and long-time chairman of the greens committee, passed away. His influence and input in club-making decisions for more than 50 years will long be remembered.

Usher told many interesting stories about life at the club during an interview for this history. He respected and enjoyed being with employees as well as his golf partners and singled out a few like Bob Patterson and Edgar "Deacon" Stratton, Bunks Dallam, Bill Newcomb, and Ruby White.

Usher was one of the leaders of the movement to relocate the old club to the present site. "All of those who had been against it came out like they'd been shot out of a cannon to play golf once it opened! They were very happy to be back on the golf course," he laughed.

Usher was assertive and not shy about offering an opinion, but he was a good politician and businessman, an avid pilot, and knowledgeable about golf, according to his friends.

Manager Straley recognized Leon Mason, one of his valuable employees in the kitchen who celebrated 10 years with the club.

In May, President Chustz announced that membership has grown to 504, up from 490 at the beginning of 2014.

Karen Marvin, Jane Bright, and Peggy Paxton.

"Doc" Craft at a card game.

Golf guest rounds are up 88 percent in the past year, and the line of credit was paid off. Members may now download the free Smartphone App for the club.

Ruby Petty's memory lives on with her special fried chicken back on the menu! "Many members have told me that the fried chicken takes them back in time. We are honored to be able to use "Miss" Ruby's recipe and produce a product that she was known for. Thank you, Sissy, for sharing…so that we can pay tribute and remember her for the wonderful impact she had on our club," said Executive Chef Mike Harlow.

"Looking back as the club goes forward" seemed to be the theme in the May newsletter. On the tennis front, Chris Dallas said the two "Country Club Classics" are being brought back, the Men's Singles Ladder and the Ladies Doubles Leagues, plus club championships.

On the golf course, men who want to play from the forward or red tees will now be able to post scores from them. Pro Stilley also noted that new scorecards are available with new combo tee ratings (black/blue and red/white).

The Turnberry Foundation selected architect Drew Rogers to design an improved practice facility that would significantly enhance the golfing experience of our club, Jim Brown reported. "We are currently working with the architect to create a plan for how we might move forward."

Projects completed thus far by the Foundation are six forward tees on holes 3, 7, 9, 10, 15, and 17, with a contribution by the LGA, and the rock walls on No. 1 and No. 2, which were done as a joint project with the club. Those who have served on this "board" are Kenny Hunt, Jason Seiner, Ed Hely, Wally Bateman, David Denton, Lyn Foster, and Brown.

The Spring Fishing Derby was held with Luca Taleban winning the 7-and-under category with a 14.5-inch catch.

Bob Grimm, Dick Wilson, (top), Larry Barton, Larry Jarvis, Harry Alvis, Tommy Thomas, Tommy Whittemore, Scott Ware, Louis Michelson, Gene Hipp, Bob Day, Bo Bell, and Bill Ragland enjoy cards and comradery just as dozens of other groups have in the history of the club.

Olivia O'Neill and McCoy Gregory were second and third. Carter Wyatt caught a whopping 24-inch fish to win the 8-and-up division. Spencer Cates and Alec Darnell were second and third.

Natalie Broster was introduced as the new Banquet and Events Manager. Natalie is a Murray State graduate who hails from Albion, Illinois.

Ladies gather for afternoon Mahjong, a relatively new activity at the club. Bunco has also been initiated as a night-time game.

As the summer of 2016 progressed and fall arrived, members enjoyed dueling pianos by the pool, bunco and mahjong, the Member Appreciation reception, glow golf, "White Wines on the Patio," and a host of other social activities.

The pool drew not only children, but a group of ladies who tread water several days a week. Regular members of the group are Barbara Livingston, Genie Drossos, Phyllis Russell, Sandy Massey, Leigh Smith, Susan Hancock, Ana Sredl, Reva Harper, and Carol Donner.

When high-stakes card games were played at the old club, stories were rampant about the wins and losses. Today, the card players who usually gather for gin games play more for fun.

In keeping with the club traditions ongoing since the early 1900s, the current calendar is filled with special dinners, the Sunday buffets, wedding receptions, the Easter egg hunt, and a host of other social activities.

Kevin McEwan and Jason Goins (right) joined a host of other members for the corn hole social in May of 2016.

"The Swim Club"

John Anderson and Chris Dallas, Allen Behbehani, Tom Garrett, Sam Thompson, and Amy Anderson, survived the cold temperatures to finish the first ever 5K held at the club in 2016.

Members continue to build memories and establish traditions at the Country Club of Paducah.

The Move

In the words of an unnamed philosopher, "A small body of determined spirits fired by an unquenchable faith in their mission can alter the course of history."

The Uphill Climb from Country Club Lane to Turnberry Drive

The struggles and triumphs the Country Club of Paducah and its Board of Directors experienced from 1963 until the club moved to 6500 Turnberry Drive are carefully outlined in the meticulous minutes prepared on a typewriter by H.R. "Bunks" Dallam, board secretary.

As one reviews the history of the club through these detailed documents, volumes of interesting information are presented in chronological order, the majority of which is in his own words. From the land acquisition to the hiring of Robert Trent Jones, from the golf course construction to the opening of the clubhouse, Dallam's notes offer a thorough trip through this significant time in the history of the club.

George Crounse presided at the first meeting in 1963 with directors W.F. Paxton, Russell Lund, William Reed, W.M. Carson, Victor Speck, Jr., Tom Whittemore, Sam Livingston, and Dallam in attendance.

Wilson Gunn and Bill Bone will be in charge of golf tournaments, and Channing Hale, assisted by C.C. Gould and Bill Bone, will be in charge of the pool, the president announced. Those approved for active membership were Ben Lookofsky, Nolan Fisher, John Ellis, Dr. Eli Khouri, and Hogan Mitchell.

Manager Ed Verplanke was advised that he had the authority and the responsibility to operate the bar and the restaurant.

"Governor Russell Lund gave an excellent report regarding his investigation of the crowded conditions at the certain times of the golf course…and also the possibility of a classification of club membership that would not include golf privileges," the secretary noted.

Tommy Whittemore was authorized to purchase a spiking machine for $398. George Sullivan was extended a membership application.

Sam Livingston advised the board that the men's regular club championship would be held as usual on Sunday and Labor Day and the entry fee would be $5. The salary of the club manager was voted on and remained at $675 per month.

It was business as usual as the club approached its 50th year of incorporation, an event that was celebrated in the local media.

The Club's 50th Birthday

On September 8, 1963, the *Sun-Democrat* ran a full-page feature with the headline "Paducah Country Club Passes the Age of 50" by Gene Ruoff. Four photos feature the board members, Bob Hassman, H.R. "Bunks" Dallam, W.F. "Bill" Paxton, Tommy Whittemore, Sr., and Dr. Clyde Peel. Ed Cave, Jr., was president.

The original clubhouse, as it was in 1919, shows J.R. and Melvin Wallerstein putting on No. 5 near the structure that burned in 1955. The "new" clubhouse built in 1956 showing the 25x45 foot patio outside the 19th hole is also featured in the spread.

Bunks Dallam putting near the original clubhouse.

The Board of Directors of the Paducah Country Club in September of 1963 was composed of (left to right), Bob Hassman, H.R. Dallam, Ed Cave, Jr., president; Bill Paxton, Tommy Whittemore, and Dr. Clyde Peel.

A photograph of boxcars taken in 1955 was entitled "JUST WAITING." The two boxcars served as an emergency clubhouse for the club between the destruction of its old building in '55 and the completion of the new one the next year.

Jack Mike Wilson, son of Virgie and the late Jack Wilson, was pictured "slapping a hefty drive off number six tee" and described as "one of the country club's outstanding young golfers."

The newspaper writer began his story by saying, "The Paducah Country Club, celebrating its 50th anniversary this year, is not an organization that the casual observer would accuse of growth." He said membership remained static at around 300 full members with 1,000 people enjoying the facility.

He goes on to explain his initial comment and points out that expansion has been in the extent and quality of services offered to the members. "Strangely enough, the real growth of the club seems to have coincided with its greatest disaster: the $200,000 loss it suffered when the old clubhouse, built in 1913 when the club moved from Wallace Park, went up in flames early in the morning of February 28, 1955," Ruoff reported. (*See related story in the Social Life and Club Business Chapter.*)

He said the first clubhouse erected in 1913 cost $16,000. "It's replacement value was many times that amount. The building had been insured at $70,000, the most insurance that could be obtained on the 42-year-old structure, and the contents had been insured for another $10,000 or more."

Ruoff mentioned the proposed expansion of the crowded clubhouse and an addition to it, which became a moot point with the fire. He said the board and members decided to go ahead and build and furnish a structure that would serve for years to come at a cost of "a whopping $240,000."

About $90,000 of this could be furnished by insurance and earnings, and 10-year bank loans could provide another $75,000, he quoted. Members would be the source of another $75,000.

"They were asked to buy $300 debenture bonds which would in turn be purchased from them by new members who might be admitted. By August 3, 1963, the financial plans had been completed and the bid of John Cassidy Construction Company of Paducah was accepted. A few revisions in the plans brought the final building cost to $199,992."

And the rest is history, he added. The modern, well-equipped boxcars where members gathered during the winter of the construction were hauled to the top of the hill and the members moved into the new facilities in the spring of 1956.

Ruoff did a thorough job of interviewing and researching this extensive story on the club. He said that Bill Bone, the golf pro, had overseen the rebuilding, enlarging, and seeding of the greens with 328 Bermuda grass. "The greens are now smooth as carpets and are gently contoured," he said. (He also referred to the many trees that had been hit hard by elm blight in 1963.)

Ruoff tipped his hat to some of the original incorporators of the Country Club of Paducah, Wallace, Burnett, Friedman, and C. Rieke, making a note that the location they chose "has proved fortunate and unfortunate."

"Out in the country when it was built, the city has gradually encompassed it, making it much more accessible to most of its members. But at the same time, the expansion of the city has prevented expansion of the club grounds."

He concluded with the prophetic statement that rumbles are heard about the possibility of moving the club.

Relocation…A Long Process

In 1964, the minutes stated that there were 136 male adult golfers in the club with 80 women and children also playing some. The crowded course, especially on the weekends around noon and again around 4 p.m., was discussed again.

Four new water lines were installed in the golf course. "Two members playing golf in a cart picked up 87 paper cups in one nine-hole round recently. The two members are to be commended, but it is obvious that a number of other members are being very thoughtless."

The governors agreed to proceed with estimates for remodeling the lower floor of the club to improve the pro shop and enlarge the 19th Hole…for card playing purposes.

The initiation fee was increased to $600, plus taxes. Bill Bone's contract was renewed for 1965. Louis Kolb, Ray Mullen, Jr., Neville Stone, and Dalton Woodall were elected to two-year terms on the board at the January 19, 1965, annual meeting. Russ Lund was elected president and membership requests were accepted from Gene Hipp and Joe Mitchell.

Vic Speck, Jr., who joined in 1965 after growing up at the club under his father's membership, played an active role for more than 30 years on the golf and greens committees. Soon after he joined, the governors asked Speck for advice about the golf course. He is quoted in the minutes as saying it was necessary to purchase a new greens mower costing under $500 and a roto tiller for $80. The go-ahead was given.

(An addressograph machine was purchased at that same meeting.)

The club will begin accepting social memberships, the minutes said. A non-resident member is a male or female who lives more than 25 air miles from Paducah.

James Mitchell's salary would be given a bonus of $100 per month for the extra duties he is doing until a new manager arrives. Some junior members were suspended for a period of two weeks for their recent misbehavior.

Howard W. Newcomb was introduced to the directors at the November 2, 1965, as the new club manager.

Limited social memberships were approved for Dr. Robert Colgan, Dr. Robert Miller, Howard Gray, and Raymond Savignac.

The secretary advised the board that the space for storing office records was limited and that the new manager needed additional storage space. Unfortunately, the board authorized and instructed Dallam to destroy all records earlier than 1962. Fortunately, some notebooks full of early board minutes are still intact and were incorporated into this history.

In the spring of 1966 with Dalton Woodall at the helm, the board once again employed Robert Osteen as lifeguard at the pool. Others who served as lifeguards were Sally Nemer and Kyle Katterjohn.

The business of the club went on as usual.

It was 1966 and the talk about the need for a new golf course was at high pitch. The "rumored" move mentioned in the *Sun-Democrat* story in 1963 was now more than a rumor; it was becoming the board's main focus.

A committee composed of James Rieke, Dr. Merle Fowler, and Sam Livingston was instructed to look into a suitable property for an 18-hole golf course. Rieke told the group that he had purchased land that was formerly the Stahl Farm, 146 acres, which adjoined 15 acres owned by Harold Sullivan and 31 acres owned by M.S. Barks.

Rieke said he would sell the land to the club at what he paid for it if the club wanted it. The property was located on the north side of Blandville Road. Attending a special called meeting to review the property were Woodall, Louis Kolb, Russ Shelton, Ray Mullen, Jr., Gresham Hougland, and Dwain Lowry, plus the golf chairman, Vic Speck, Jr.

The board then issued a letter to the membership on March 24, 1966, regarding the purchase of the Blandville Road property. The infamous battles that started around this time are still discussed today.

Sam Livingston, Jack Tick, and Herb Wallerstein in front of the original clubhouse.

The letter read in part: "This is to inform you as a member of the Country Club of Paducah Incorporated, that the president and directors request your presence at a membership meeting…."

"Your officers have been working and…deliberating on the future of our club. There has been much work and searching to find enough property for an 18-hole golf course…. We must act now if we are to think of the growth of Paducah, and the future of our youth…. This proposal does not anticipate an assessment on the membership whatsoever…Your officers that you elected to represent you have the power under our by-laws to purchase this property; however, we think it should be a club effort; therefore, we request your presence at this very important meeting…." Dalton Woodall, President.

In a subsequent letter (April 2, 1966), the members were told that there was no intention to sell the clubhouse or ground, to assess the membership, to increase dues, to vote on the purchase of any one specific piece of land, and no intention to purchase any land for a golf course without the concurrence of a professional golf course architect.

The resolution was approved by a vote of 202 to 48 at the membership meeting. This permitted a standing committee to investigate several locations for the possible purchase of property suitable for an 18-hole golf course and other club facilities in McCracken County.

Speck, Lee Powell, Dr. Eli Khouri, Jim Musgove, and Ed Hannan were appointed by Woodall to serve on the property committee.

Speck reported to the board that three pieces of property were being discussed for a proposed golf course. He said the committee had been in touch with Robert Trent Jones and other architects and that Mr. Jones would come to Paducah and go over the various sites. The committee was unanimous when it voted to authorize the committee to proceed and have Jones come to Paducah.

"When all of this started, I was asked who I would suggest to build and design our new course. I thought we might as well shoot for the moon, so I said Robert Trent Jones! He was THE guy then," Speck said.

Robert Trent Jones

"I wrote him in 1966. That board with Russ Shelton as president got it all moving. Trent Jones flew down here when Chicago Southern was still flying here. I went and picked him up at the airport. He had an old moth eaten sweater and some khakis on and a brief case. The only thing he had with him was an airline schedule in the brief case."

"We rode around the periphery of the property because he said he didn't need to walk it. He just wanted a topo board and he said he'd get us a layout, which he did."

"During construction, Pete Dye told me that he'd like to come down and watch Trent Jones and Jones agreed. He was shaping No. 12 and 13 and Dye watched him. Jones came back and came before the board and gave them figures and signed the contract," Speck recalled.

It was an exciting time for the serious golfers at the Country Club of Paducah.

Russell Shelton was elected president of the club. He retained the present golf committee (Vic Speck, Eddie Hannan, Jim Musgove, and Dr. Eli Khouri) and asked each director to give serious thought to some of the problems that might be incurred in getting the new 18-hole golf course.

RUSSELL SHELTON DALTON WOODALL

Russell Shelton New PCC President

Russell Shelton, Paducah industrial executive, was elected president of the Paducah Country Club at a meeting of the board of directors Tuesday evening. He succeeds Dalton A. Woodall as president.

Under Mr. Woodall's leadership during the past year, a new wing was added to the clubhouse, and the building was air-conditioned and redecorated completely.

Four new directors for the coming year elected were:

E. M. Bailey, Lee Livingston, William Usher and Edmund Tilley.

The four holdover directors are: Gresham Hougland, Dwain Lowry, Ed Cain and Shelton.

Retiring directors are: Louis Kolb, Ray Mullen, Neville Stone and Woodall.

Howard W. Newcomb has been appointed club manager for the ensuing year.

(Members who served on the board during these important decision-making years were Jack Bailey, Sr., Lee Livingston, Bill Usher, Ed Tilley, Ray Mullen, Jr., Ed Cain, C. A. Wahl, Louis Kolb, Gresham Hougland, Dwain Lowry, plus Dalton Woodall and Shelton.)

Robert Trent Jones had visited the club. He met with the board on February 25, 1967, for long discussions and recommended that two pieces of property would be necessary for making the best golf course. The board voted to exercise options on both pieces of property for $850, and to have Jones draw up preliminary plans for the golf course at a cost of $1,500.

The property was owned by Herman and Virginia Yopp, Joe and Aimee Rosenfield, and Edwin and Mary Michael. Grace and Lucille Thompson owned additional property.

In March of '67, the board said that the $1,500 covering preliminary plans for the golf course by Jones was a one-time expense and that if the club decided against a new golf course, these plans would be returned with no further obligation to the club.

This is the course layout illustrated by Robert Trent Jones around 1967, which Bill Usher rescued and preserved for the past 50 years. The original measures about four feet square. Courtesy of Ginger Usher.

At the June meeting, the drawings and map detail on the proposed new course, which was received from Jones, was presented by President Russ Shelton.

By August with the golf course plans proceeding, at least in the minds and hearts of many club members, especially the most avid golfers, the board decided to renew the two options on the property for a period of six months. It also decided to put together information required by lenders, and to secure a model from R.T. Jones of the proposed new golf course, which he had mentioned to Vic Speck the year before.

For many years, this model was staged at the club for all to see. In recent times, it was tossed by employees not realizing its importance and sentimental value. The late Bill Usher, and now his wife, Ginger, owns the large-scale drawing of the original layout.

In September of 1967, President Shelton advised the board of the progress that had been made in regard to finding a way to finance the new golf course. He thought Prudential Insurance Company might be interested in loaning the money for a 20-year period at a rate of about seven percent.

At the December 1 meeting of the board, Shelton presented a copy of "Report of Feasibility Study of Financing New Golf Course" that had been prepared by Lee, Freeman & Smiley. On December 4 at a meeting of the entire membership, this would be presented.

When the membership convened, the following motion was made by Ed Cain with the unanimous approval of the Board of Directors:

"The Board of Directors of the Country Club of Paducah be authorized to purchase property on the Blandville Road…for the purpose of developing additional golfing facilities, and further, that the board be authorized to proceed with the necessary steps to arrange proper financing and for the building of the initial nine holes; both of these to be done without an assessment, an increase in dues, or a change in the present facilities." It was seconded by Gresham Hougland. President Shelton requested a roll call vote, which resulted in the motion being carried 148 "yes" and 18 "no."

At the December 12, 1967, meeting a loan amount of $290,000 was discussed. The board also "abolished the category of limited social membership, and transfer all… to active membership." The by-laws were amended "to the effect that the number of active members be 550" with some exceptions.

The year 1968 rolled in and the newly elected directors from a field of eight were Dr. Henry Dallam, Jr., Dr. Merle Fowler, J.P. Kerr, and Victor Speck, Jr. They joined Bailey, Lee Livingston, Tilley, and Usher.

When President Shelton addressed the new board, he suggested that the board might appoint a lady as an ex-officio member of the board. He also suggested more activities for junior members, new netting for the tennis courts, and a new diving board at the pool. "In looking over my term as president, the board and I have been busy for the past year with the expansion program. Maybe the next board will want to pay more attention to the entertainment and social activity for the membership."

The board tried to re-elect Shelton as president, but he declined saying he would have considerable travel related to his own business. The board praised him for "all the work he had done, the time he had devoted to the club work for two years." Gresham Hougland was elected president at the next meeting and asked to establish the Office for Promotion, Financing, and Expansion of the club."

Shelton continued service as finance committee chairman. He talked with the son of Robert Trent Jones, Reece Jones, about land clearing specifications that might be completed in the spring of 1968. With that, President Hougland said he would send a letter to the property owners that the club would exercise its options to purchase the Blandville Road property on advice of counsel, Dwain Lowry.

The time and work that was devoted to this project, even at this stage, was extensive to say the least. Today's membership should be thankful that Vic Speck, Gresham Hougland, Russ Shelton, and others persevered when resistance began. Because of their efforts, the Country Club of Paducah and the Robert Trent Jones Golf Course are here today at this location for all to enjoy.

Returning to the details of the proposed "move" to this site, one finds surveys being done and deeds being prepared in March of 1968. The price for the 103.288 acres (Thompson) was $70,000. The Michael-Rosenfield-Yopp acreage totaling 155.015 acres was $108,510.50, for a total of $178,510.50.

The low bidder for clearing the first phase of the ground for the new golf course was Loren Jones at $13,000.

In June, Cabot Robertson, an engineer from R.T. Jones, attended the board meeting and answered questions. He had spent two days with contractor Loren Jones, outlining the clearing of property and lines of various fairways, greens, etc.

Four months later, the second phase of land clearing for the new golf course was completed. Hougland informed the board that the club was ready to proceed with the next phase, the moving of dirt to get the proper levels and fills as outlined in the specifications that had been prepared by the office of the architect. The group decided to request bids for Phase 3.

Those bids received were from Loren Jones, Solomon and Company, and John Smith in order of the bidding amounts. Jones was again chosen. An employee of the excavation company was approved to live on the new club property during the completion of the project.

By March of 1969, Jack Bailey was president and Dr. Merle Fowler, Russ Shelton, Henry Dallam, Irv Bright, Hal Brown, Jack Kerr, George Sullivan and Vic Speck, Jr., were on the Board of Governors. At that meeting, the group recommended the ladies lounge be renovated and redecorated and that J.T. Davidson, Homer Thompson, Bill Reed, and Steve Reed be given pay raises as employees working on the golf course.

Interest rates were high and Shelton told the board that borrowing to complete golf course construction at that time was not feasible. He offered two alternatives: sell the excess land and go to the membership for money.

In June, Joe Sanders made a presentation of what Sanders Brothers Nursery could do to

Club President Gresham Hougland (left) on the patio at the old club with (clockwise) Jack Shadle, Shelby Cave, Olivia Cave, Genny Hougland, A.B. and Sue Fendley.

complete the new course. The $140,000 cash plus surplus land, Sanders would agree to seed 100-120 acres, build tees not built by Loren Jones, put in an automatic sprinkler, be supervised by Robert Trent Jones, put Bermuda on the greens and fairways, sprig the tees and greens, and spend $4,000 on an air compressor. Or, for $228,000 cash with NO surplus land involved, Sanders would do the itemized work.

No decision was reached by the board at that meeting.

Members continued to play golf on the crowded 9-hole facility and utilize the clubhouse at the Country Club Drive location while factions continued talking about the upside and downside of moving to the Blandville Road location.

In August of 1969, Shelton advised the board about his communications with R.T. Jones and said that a pond might need to be built near the 16th hole. He said the next visit would entail staking off and marking all boundary lines of the golf course, at which time "we could determine just what property the club would have for sale."

Invoices from R.T. Jones, and also from Loren Jones, totaling over $70,000 were due while the board waited for its loan at the bank to be increased. Jack Bailey offered to help with this situation.

In the fall, Shelton told the board that progress had been made on the golf course, namely, that Eddie Hannan & Co. was finalizing the boundaries and when he was finished, "We can determine just what excess property the club will have to sell." A few months later, the board authorized Bailey to sign a contract with Hannan not to exceed $1,300 for a survey of the club property.

At the December meeting, Vic Speck was asked to contact Buddy Clymer to determine if and under what conditions he would accept the greenskeeper position. The last meeting of 1969 was important in that the board received the printed survey of the Blandville Road property that indicated which tracts of land would not be needed for the new golf course. The best and most profitable ways to sell it were discussed at length.

Hal Brown said that once again Jim Musgove was interested in talking to the board regarding the possible purchase of this property. The group still did not know how many lots would actually be available and asked that Hannan draw up a proposal.

On November 10, 1972, a letter from President Ed Hough and the board was sent to all club members to give them an update on the Blandville Road property and suggest a possible plan of action. (It was signed by Jim Curtis, Nolan Fisher, Lee Warren, Jack Wilson, Jerry Page, Harold Gilbert, Ed Hough, and Mike Livingston, Jr.)

In summary, the letter said the club had spent a total of $347,512 to date on the site/golf course, but that no money had been spent since 1969. The additional cost of completing the new course could be anywhere from $200,000 to $600,000. It said, "There is a very real and sincere difference of opinion among our members on the course the club should take. One group, many of whom play golf seldom or not at all, would like to concentrate the resources on major improvements at the present site. The other group...would like to complete the new course as soon as possible, spend little on improvements at the present site, and possibly sell the present site..."

In this letter, the group proposes a plan to create a new golf club that would take title to the Blandville Road property and assume all debt. It would have no legal connection with the present club, except that all its original members would be persons who are members of the Paducah Country Club.

Any current member could come on board for a small initiation fee or choose not to join and have no voice in its management. Those who joined could remain members of both clubs if they chose to. The letter included many more details and explanations, but it concluded by asking for the advice of the members by November 22, 1972.

When 1975 rolled in, Lester Myrick was president with Bill Dyer, Hal Brown, D.L. Boucher, Henry Whitlow, Don Hartline, and W.R. Reed on the board. In his exit letter that year, Myrick said the Blandville Road property indebtedness was reduced to $13,546. Twenty new Melox golf carts were purchased and will be operated, rented, and maintained by the club, he mentioned.

Finances continued to be a concern. A.B. Fendley discussed the need to have financing for the new clubhouse, tennis courts, and golf course on the Blandville Road property. At the May meeting, it was decided that a permanent building committee be appointed.

Myrick was designated to send a letter to members requesting they approve the building of the clubhouse or approve selling of the Blandville Road property.

At the first meeting in 1976, Bill Usher was voted in as president. Bob Bell, Joe Whedon, A.B. Fendley, Bill Reed, Pat Kerr, and Bill Dyer were on the board. Governor Julian Carroll of Paducah was given non-resident membership while he was Kentucky's Governor.

Finally, a meeting of the general membership was held to give power to the Board of Directors to enter into contract with persons wishing to purchase the excess acreage at the Blandville Road property. The group would be known as Country Club Investors (CCI).

"Proceeds from these sales will be used to develop the golf course," the notice of official meeting stated. The Advisory Committee that made this proposal to vote on August 19, 1976, was composed of Pat Cvengros, Jack Bailey, Norman Greenberg, Gene Katterjohn, Russ Lund, Royce Gregory, and Frank Paxton.

At that meeting, nothing definitive happened and the vote of 150 to 58 instructed the powers that be to get more information to present to the members.

This group of 70 investors (CCI) put up $5,000 each and were given certificates that entitled them to one of two things—use toward the purchase of a lot, or hold the certificate and eventually be paid back the money, possibly with interest. This $350,000 would be to purchase five tracts of land on or near the new golf course from the club so it could proceed with the golf course construction.

In February of 1977, directors Joe Rinella, Bob Bell, Pat Kerr, David Denton, and Joe Whedon met with President Bill Usher. (Joe Harry Metzger was also on the board.) Usher said the April 4 membership meeting would be held to vote on the selling of the excess property on Blandville Road (approximately 105 acres).

At the April 4th meeting, architect Pat Kerr showed slides regarding the development and operation of the new golf course.

Frank Paxton, on behalf of the development company CCI, read the name of 72 members who have paid $5,000 to join said company. Paxton then proposed the following:

"On behalf of the afore-mentioned members, I hereby propose that this valid offer of $350,000 to the Paducah Country Club...be accepted, provided that these funds be ear-marked with the additional dollars necessary to assure the completion of the 18-hole golf course."

Dr. J.D. "Denny" Noonan and Dr. Hilary Hunt moved and seconded that this motion be accepted. By a standing vote, Noonan's motion carried 158-3.

Royce Gregory then offered an amendment, which stated that the "Board of Directors is further authorized to borrow up to $150,000 to complete construction of the 18-hole golf course." It was unanimously approved.

Following the membership meeting, the board met and took action on several important items. Charles Sanders' proposal was declared "best for the club," provided that R.T. Jones' details be followed. The president was authorized to arrange a $150,000 line of credit for construction of the golf course and related facilities.

"We couldn't afford to make a mistake. We could sell the remaining property to Dave Hutcheson or investors, or we could do it ourselves. We sold it to the investors," Bill Usher said.

A short time later, CCI sold the property to Florence and Hutcheson (Bob Florence and David Hutcheson) who had agreed to subdivide the tracts, complete infrastructure, and sell the lots to buyers who wanted to live at the club. Hutcheson had a meeting with the investors and by a show of hands asked for commitments from those who would buy a home site. An estimated 15-20 investors raised their hands.

And the rest is history. (Lots which were purchased at $40,000, for example, have been sold for more than $120,000 in more recent times.)

Howard Gardner, who became superintendent, continued working on the course development and "growing in" process. The *Sun-Democrat* newspaper said full-scale construction of the course is now underway.

The "new" golf course, in the minds of the Country Club's avid golfers and core members, had been "underway" since 1967. Ten years later after much planning, purchasing, discussing, and waiting, the dream course was finally going to be a reality.

Pat Moynahan, *Sun-Democrat* Sports Editor, covered the golf course work in a lengthy feature that ran on April 19, 1977. "Bulldozers and earth movers began rolling again Monday on a 250-acre plot of ground west of Paducah which has borne the faint outline of a golf course for the past nine years," Moynahan said.

"The shadowy silhouette in a woods lot off U.S. Highway 62 across from Sunshine Dairy will be shaped and landscaped into a plush, 18-hole championship golf course in another year—the culmination of a project begun in 1967 by the Country Club of Paducah."

He described the club's plans as being "little more than scrub brush and skinned topsoil for the last nine years." Today's club members who carefully watched the site for more than a decade remember how it developed.

Bill Usher was quoted in the story saying, "It will be a championship course, the kind the pros play on every weekend. Our objective is to make a course the average golfer can play from the middle tees and have a decent score. A championship course is long, but it doesn't have to be too difficult for anyone but the pros to play."

"The combination of terrain, trees, and water in a picturesque and playable course is what makes a championship golf course," Usher explained.

Usher went on to describe the course for Moynahan: "The shaping is what gives the course its character. That's where the architect expresses himself—in the shape and contour of the greens and the traps and hazards around them. It is laid out for the best type of course we can carve out of the 250-acre plot."

The *Sun-Democrat* said The Florida Golf Corporation will shape the trees and greens under the supervision of Robert Trent Jones of Montclair, New Jersey. In that article, Usher said the cost for the project is nearly $650,000, and he expects no further delays. "The initial project halted when land price and prime interest rate increased drastically while the course was still in the planning stages," Moynahan reported.

Usher said in April of 1977 that he expected the course to be completed by August 15. "After a year allowed for growth and maintenance, it should be playable by July or August, 1978." (Thirty-seven years later, Usher said the Robert Trent Jones course is proof of what members can do to "raise the bar" at their country club.)

(On July 27 of 1978, the newspaper ran an aerial photo of the golf course by photographer Barkley Thieleman and said it was approximately 95 percent complete. President Irv Bright was quoted as saying it might be ready for limited play later that year and then more likely in 1979. "The planting of fairways…was completed this week and the greens are to be planted next month. The fairways will be of Bermuda grass, while the greens will be bent grass," he said.)

Continuing with the business at hand, on May 12, 1977, the following resolution was adopted by the board: "Be it resolved that the Country Club of Paducah sell and convey to Country Club Investments, Inc., all of the excess land not needed for the construction of the new golf course…" It went on to say the price for the approximate 105 acres would be $350,000. "The officers of this club are hereby authorized to enter into a contract for sale and to execute a general warranty deed to the purchaser."

At the last meeting of 1977, President Usher explained the need for a Greens Committee. It was unanimously voted to adapt under Section 11, Part F, the provision for a Greens Committee. Jim Flynn, Bill Reed, and Jim Musgove were appointed to the first one. The Greens Committee has continued working with each superintendent on behalf of the membership for almost 40 years. Some of the chairmen of that key committee are mentioned in other chapters.

In March of 1978, Irv Bright, Jr., was president of the club with Henry Dallam, Joe Rinella, Charles Metzger, and Vic Speck still on the board and David Denton, Jack Wilson, and Bill Paxton joining as newly elected directors.

Some focus was on tennis, with Dallam presenting a proposed budget of $4,633. Bill Bone, golf professional, had his contract renewed and tennis pro Paul Rowton was given another six-month contract.

Jack Wilson presented Howard Gardner's proposed budget for golf expenses at the new and old clubs. In other board business, it was decided that the 15 percent gratuity members had to pay would be evenly distributed between employees.

At the April 17, 1978, board meeting, restriction on new club property was discussed. A meeting with CCI (the group of investors who purchased the excess property around the golf course) was urged.

President Bright appointed a committee of the following to make recommendation on the future of the Country Club of Paducah: Jerry Page, chairman; Jack Piers, co-chairman; and members Fred Paxton, Barbara Livingston, Allan Rhodes, Russ Lund, Helen Garrett, Tom Ezzell, Bill Pfanstiel, and Dr. Bill Chumley.

Pat Wathen was hired as head supervisor and lifeguard at the pool and a sweeper for the tennis courts was approved. Margaret Johnson vacated the rental house at the Blandville Road property.

The board discussed the results of the meeting of the boards of the club and CCI with Joe Rinella presenting a drawing of the proposed road at the new golf course. Conversation took place about who would pay for the road, and the board decided to get an estimate of the costs with Jack Wilson taking the lead on that.

Also at the May, 1978, meeting, W.C. Backus, Jr., Hardy Roberts, and Jack Watt submitted resignations. Membership was at an all-time high. By September, Harold Leonard was on board as club manager. (*See related story in the Manager's Chapter.*)

From left, Harry and Gloria Livingston, Harold Leonard, former club manager; and Alice and Gene Fisher in the old bar at the clubhouse in the late seventies.

In the spring, Jerry Page presented the Long-Range Planning Committee's most recent report. He explained the plans from the architect with the location of the tennis courts, parking, and pool. A discussion was held about how much money the club would get from the sale of memberships.

At the June 18, 1978, called membership meeting, a vote was taken on relocating the clubhouse to the Blandville road site. Of the 317 votes cast, 214 voted against it and 103 were in favor.

Club business continued: Yardage signs for the new golf course were not purchased. Bob Robinson was authorized to hire an operator with a machine to lay cart paths. And, the desire to open the course on August 1, 1979, was discussed.

The board minutes of August, 1979, listed President Henry Dallam, Jr., and Vic Speck, Jimmy Curtis, Tom Ezzell, Larry Barnett, Bill Pfanstiel, Irv Bright, and W.F. Paxton III in attendance. Bob Robinson and Jim Musgove of the Greens Committee were also present.

Robinson informed the board that the cost to install asphalt cart paths at the new course was $36,500 or $34,000 for five inches of gravel after excavating, or $23,000 for placing two inches of gravel on the ground. The Greens Committee recommended the asphalt, but members were asked to obtain additional bids.

In other business, a computer service from Hal Brown was discussed, and board member Barnett said a used computer could be purchased for $4,000.

President Dallam read a letter from Jack Piers of the Planning Committee regarding Theodore Christner of the Christner Partnership, an architect he was working with on plans for the new clubhouse. After much discussion, the board cast a majority vote to go with local architect Rick Coltharp.

Prior to that meeting and the vote, other meetings had been held with the out-of-town architect. In an extensive memo dated April 13, 1979, it says that Jack Piers, Jerry Page, Ted Christner, the architect; Hanno Weber, and members of the Building Committee and club staff were in attendance to discuss the presentation of a schematic site and clubhouse plans.

The descriptions of that proposed clubhouse included an arcade and porte-cochere, a circular stair connecting three levels, a fourth layer to the west overlooking fairways, courtyards, covered terraces, no flat roofs, and all the amenities and facilities desired. The building cost was listed at $2,140,000.

(This became a moot point when the board eventually voted to hire Rick Coltharp to build the new clubhouse.)

"The Report of the Long-Range Planning Committee of the Country Club of Paducah" dated April 17, 1979, was the result of countless hours of work and dedication by those who compiled it, especially Jerry Page. The committee members were appointed in 1978 by President Irv Bright after the club voted in 1977 to construct the new golf course.

The findings pointed out that the present club structure is archaic, inadequate, and in poor condition. The tennis courts were inadequate, the facility was overcrowded, and two golf courses could not be maintained due to the cost. "The clubhouse kitchen is a nightmare! The swimming pool is all but gone…the club facilities are deteriorated to the point of requiring major expenditures…."

As a result, the committee recommended relocation to Blandville Road in an orderly fashion. Many recommendations were also offered on memberships.

Tom Ezzell, in June of 1979, wrote a formal letter to the members in which he incorporated his sense of humor with the realities at hand as he called them. "The new golf course is a fact of life. (Ezzell was very much opposed to the new golf course when he was asked to serve on the board by Irv Bright.) The problem was simply this: We have a club in debt, a clubhouse too small…a pool just barely north of condemnation, too few tennis courts…and two expensive golf courses."

Ezzell stated that he finally swallowed a second bitter reality—the inevitability of the moving of the club to the Blandville Road site. "This wasn't easy, since in my 35-40 years of membership I have loved the present location." Calling his letter a monologue, Ezzell added that "my money and dues will help the younger members build a marvelous facility for the future."

Ezzell urged his fellow members to "give it your very thoughtful consideration" and accept the plan of action. "And good or bad, it was drawn up with a sincere effort to keep in mind the best interest of not just one group, but every single member of the Country Club of Paducah."

Hardy Roberts, Jr., offered another letter to some members totally opposing the proposal by the board and urging them to vote against the move. Other pro and con letters circulated during that time.

At a special membership meeting on June 18, 1979, the proposal was voted down 213-104.

Then on July 2, twenty-five members called a special meeting of the club membership to consider the disposal of the Blandville Road site among other items. The elected board of directors informed the members that they did not approve nor endorse such a meeting, but its consent was not needed.

Club business concluded in 1979 in a state of flux.

Jerry Page was thanked by President Henry Dallam in a letter dated January 12, 1980, for all his work toward the Blandville Road site proposal. "We were disappointed at the membership's rejection of the proposal...." and he went on to give his deepest personal thanks for all Page had done for The Country Club of Paducah.

Enter the "Club Division Committee."

Signed by Bill Backus, Dr. Charles Billington, Joe Frampton, Pat Kerr, Jerry Page, Fred Paxton, Jack Piers, Richard Roberts, Robert Robinson, and Bill Usher, a letter to club members dated February 26, 1980, stated that a revised plan has been prepared and submitted for review, a much simpler version of the first plan to divide the club heard on February 21.

The letter urged every member to participate in discussion at two more called meetings in March. The plan was in support of the formation of a new club, which would take title to the Blandville Road property.

Meetings were occurring on a regular basis in hopes of settling the issue once and for all. A special committee met; the Greens Committee met; the Planning and Financial Committees met. A variety of solutions were proposed and the membership was asked numerous times for its input.

For example, on January 11, 1980, Joe Framptom, secretary of the committee, was appointed to prepare a plan for a division of the club; he wrote to the members: "In order to properly devise a plan, the committee believes that each member of the club should have an opportunity to express his opinion regarding the division. Thus, the committee encourages each member to submit in writing his ideas for consideration."

Dr. Billington was chairman of the committee and Bob Robinson was vice-chairman. Fred Paxton served as financial coordinator for the group.

In 1980, President Bill Howerton conducted a meeting that included club manager, Paul Stolle, and greenskeeper Howard Gardner, and the board members.

Florence and Hutcheson, Inc., was mentioned in regard to the construction of the entrance road from Holt Road at the March meeting.

Requests from Jim Flynn of the Greens Committee were as follows:

- Do not open the old golf course on Pines Road.
- No putting green or practice area at old club.
- Remove some of top soil from old greens and use on the tees at the new course.
- Close new course on Mondays.
- Purchase new airifier and verticut mower.
- Dredge No. 2 pond in the fall.

On March 6, 1980, the letter to the membership said that 215 members voted on the question of whether to divide the club with 11 voting "no" and 104 voting "yes." Two-hundred did not vote. The remainder of the letter pointed out the pros and cons of moving totally to the Blandville Road site or staying on Country Club Lane.

In the club newsletter, the board included a questionnaire for the members, and on April 10, 1980, Howerton published the results with over 300 members participating.

As for the future direction of the club, 56 percent wanted the clubhouse, tennis courts, and swimming pool at the old site for 10-15 years with golf on Blandville Road.

The under 35's wanted to move quickly to the new site.

Older members resented an assessment, while the majority of members expect to continue the $25 assessment until the club was out of debt.

Howerton said he could not recommend the sale of part of the club site because the current market is depressed. It was noted that "at this time we still have no definite direction as to the ultimate best future for this old club site."

Howerton recommended that the old course be closed with mowing to continue. "Finally, the questionnaire asked about the operation and use of the new golf course. We received a few more pleas to sell it, but the cries are becoming fewer and fainter."

Also in that newsletter, the board recommended that the Greens Committee find a suitable location for a double-wide trailer for the 19th hole at the new site, that the cart paths on the front nine holes be completed immediately, and the old golf course not be reopened.

The board approved approximately $10,000 in expenditures to open the pool, wading pool, and bath house, and said they should all be ready by Memorial Day.

In August, J. Anthony's, Inc. (Tony Page) went into contract with the board to operate the club restaurant and bar. Margaret Johnson was still employed as the bartender.

Bill Bone announced, "The new golf shop is open and Christmas merchandise is arriving."

President Bill Howerton "talked" at length to the club members in the newsletter discouraging them from having negative attitudes.

The new year rolled in with some new business at the Country Club of Paducah. Bill Howerton was elected president and Marshall Nemer was re-elected secretary of the club. Bruce McAbrey would serve as assistant secretary.

It was decided that three board members would serve two-year terms and three would serve three-year terms. Frank Paxton, Bill Usher, and Dr. Clark Hall were the two-year directors, and Ray Carlson, Bruce McAbrey, and Robert "Bo" Bell were the three-year directors.

The initiation fee was reduced to $1,500 in May of 1981.

The *Paducah Sun* ran a story on July 16, 1981, about an exclusive alcohol rehabilitation center deciding not to bid on the 33-acre Pines Road property. The firm, called MMI, said the decision was based on fear that opposition from local resident could upset its timetable for opening the facility.

The story said the club was split between two sites, the new site where the golf course opened and the Pines Road facility where only a clubhouse, tennis courts, and swimming pool are open. Howerton said the club eventually plans to sell the Pines Road site and build new facilities on Blandville Road…but will wait until it is financially feasible.

"It (the rehab center) would have been a private hospital," according to club president, Judge Bill Howerton. A.O. Wynn and his son also offered to buy the property that summer, and in August a meeting with the Elks Club representative took place.

The Elks Club wanted to purchase 4.7 acres of the Pines Road site for $300,000; this would leave 40 acres. A story in the *Paducah Sun* on July 24, 1981, said the Elks' lodge is basically a gathering spot that offers lunches and a reading room. Exalted Ruler Dick Brown said the offer was "a quarter-million-dollar-plus" offer in that story.

By September, Howerton presented a "starter plan" for a new clubhouse that would cost in the neighborhood of $750,000 from the St. Louis architect. Grace Murt was suggested as the person to take over the operation of the 20th hole at Blandville-West.

In other news at the club, lights were installed on the new tennis courts and 80 players participated in the Labor Day tennis tournament. Jerry Marlett of the National Golf Foundation was hired to aid in the planning of a new clubhouse and Johnny Box was hired for the food service.

On October 4, 1981, a 98-21 vote was cast in favor of selling the Pines Road property.

Also in December, Pines Investments (Johnny Box) cancelled its food service with the club; Florence and Hutcheson Engineers were completing the irrigation system at the golf course, and Barbara Brownell was recognized by the board.

Bill Howerton was thanked for "his good work and dedication…in a period of turmoil and unrest and advancement in the club," Marshall Nemer said.

Some of the meetings were still held at the Country Club Lane clubhouse, where Harry Livingston was elected president in February of 1982.

The new president appointed Sue Fendley to act as a liaison between the board and the women members as one of his first action items. Grace Murt became the acting club manager and Hula Wilson was kitchen manager.

Permission was also granted to the LGA in 1982 to hold an invitational known as the Sue Haley. The LGA provided money for two shelters to be erected on the golf course.

Plans to build a new swimming pool at the Blandville-West site were discussed with pool chairman Louis Michelson. Pat Kerr presented his design concept for the pool and the tennis courts, which had been done in 1979. It was decided that the construction of a Junior Olympic size pool begin as soon as possible at a cost not to exceed $150,000. (The old pool on Country Club Lane needed to be closed, according to the State Department.)

In October of 1982, Rick Coltharp of Architectural Design Associates, was asked to work with the membership and board representative, Jim Brockenborough, toward the design of a suitable and functional clubhouse.

In December, Marian Widener was named chairperson of the committee to handle the interior design and furnishings of a new clubhouse once it was nearing completion, and Livingston signed the contract for the architect's services. (The building was supposed to measure about 15,850 square feet.)

Meanwhile, the clock was ticking and the club had no new clubhouse.

In July of 1982, President Harry Livingston gave the nod for the club to secure additional property from CCI at the new club site between the fairways of No. 9 and No. 10 and back to Holt Road.

The board noted that Realtors Dwight Swann and George Sirk have the contract for the club to sell the property on Country Club Drive to a group of investors (Gary Graham). The board passed a motion to accept the "option to purchase" agreement on August 10. The board attorney was Herb Melton. Later Graham said his long-range plans were to develop the property as a health club and athletic facility.

In other action at the August 1982 meeting, Livingston brought up annexation of the Blandville Road property: "Be so resolved that the request of the Country Club of Paducah to have its property at the Blandville-West site be annexed into the City of Paducah be written and sent to the Mayor and City Commissioners at once."

Joe Walker, *Sun* staff writer, covered the Paducah City Commission meeting the night final action was taken to annex the new country club on Blandville Road. Mayor Penrod opposed the annexation because the state attorney general and corporate counsel Jim Utter said it was illegal.

"According to an attorney general's opinion, a mile-and-a-half section of Blandville Road right of way to be annexed must have some economic value for the plan to be legal. The highway could not be annexed just to provide access to the club property," the story read.

More coverage of this opinion was done by the *Paducah Sun* on February 11, 1983, in Jack Paxton's "Notebook."

(Edwin J. "Jack" Paxton III was Editor of the *Sun-Democrat* from 1977 until his tragic plane crash in 1985. He worked for NBC News, covering stories in Viet Nam, Ireland, and in the States, before returning to his hometown in the late seventies. Paxton took the reins from his father, Edwin Paxton, Jr., and quickly changed the newspaper's name to the *Paducah Sun*, a more conservative connotation.)

A Country Club of Paducah member, Paxton explained in his column that the opinion from the attorney general was purely advisory and carried no weight in law, but "attorney generals do tend to specialize in legal matters and this opinion is based on precedent," the editor commented.

"If the city annexed the new club it would take in about $20,000 a year more in taxes. To annex the club, it would have to annex the stretch of Blandville Road...which has no intrinsic value to the city, but it has a real and factual annual value of $20,000, because without the road the city doesn't get the club."

"The city wants the club, the club wants the city—whether for fire, police and insurance purposes, as club officers say, or to serve liquor without question of legality, as some charge, or both. The point is, nobody's about to be annexed who doesn't want to be annexed," Paxton *pointed out.*

"So, you've got a proposition that would help both parties and every Paducah taxpayer. But you've got a judge and an attorney general saying that, though this annexation might be the good and right thing to do for all parties and all taxpayers, it probably isn't legal.

"The real-life probably course is that the commissioners will vote for annexation and anyone who wants can take it to court...There is respectable historical, moral and legal precedent in this country for breaking a law in order to test its rightness---if one is willing to take the consequences.

"In this case, I'm told by lawyers, there almost certainly would be no penalty should a judge rule annexation of the new club illegal. The annexation simply would be declared invalid. Meanwhile, rulings, appeals and more rulings take time, during which the annexation would remain in effect. Sadly, for adults and children, law, like life, has gray lines in it," the editor concluded.

Anyone who knew Jack Paxton would testify that he is missed for his civic leadership, his direct manner, and his skills as a writer and reporter. When Tom Brokaw of NBC heard of Paxton's death, he referred to him as a "go-anywhere, do-anything risk taker," according to a story by the *Sun* staff writers Bill Bartleman and Joe Walker.

The club was annexed by the City of Paducah and again..."The rest is history."

Prior to the construction of the new clubhouse, club business went on as usual.

In 1982, the board members expressed their sympathy in the deaths of former board member Royce Gregory, past president Russell Lund, and Martha Backus, three long-time members of the country club.

The board finally entered into a management and purchase agreement with Gary Graham for the Country Club Lane facility. A new class of membership known as the "Westwood Country Club Membership" was established as long as the club continues to use site.

(George Sirk, Jr., eventually sold the property to Bob Jones and Tim Jones and it became Westwood Country Club. Dwight Swann had the listing agreement.)

The New Clubhouse... Construction Began in 1983

The spring of 1983 found the club accepting bids on the new clubhouse, which was designed by local architect Rick Coltharp.

B.H. Green and Son, Inc., submitted the low bid and received the nod to build it.

On June 14, *Paducah Sun* writer Joe Walker wrote a news story about officials turning over the first shovel of dirt "where a $1.2 million clubhouse will stand by early next year."

He quoted Benny Green who said construction would begin right away on the 16,000-square-foot complex and would take about nine and a half months to complete. "The clubhouse will stand at the crest of a hill overlooking the club's golf course, etc.…between Holt and Olivet Church Roads," Walker reported.

Harry Livingston, club president, said the clubhouse will bring the entire facility's value to more than $3 million. The golf course was built for $700,000, and the pool, which opened in 1982, for $150,000. He added that the clubhouse could not have been built without the assistance of Paducah's three banks, which underwrote it (Paducah Bank, Citizens Bank, and Peoples First National).

At the ground-breaking ceremonies, the president said, "This is the greatest honor I've ever had with the club." Ed "Hawk" Cave, a building committee representative, who had been a member of the original club for more than 60 years, was on hand as well as Club Secretary-Treasurer Marshall Nemer, John D. Williams, Marian Widener, Charlotte Woodall, Nolan Fisher, City Commissioner Jim Flynn, and other members.

In August of 1983, the club had 514 members, 39 of whom were non-resident; this included many more tennis members than the club has today. The club gained about 45 new members and lost about 26 after the old club property was sold. Discussions continued about the desire to purchase more of the Country Club Investors (CCI) land.

Cart path paving was almost complete, and four clay courts were mentioned as a desirable option once the club could afford to build them. Eight hard surface courts had already been built. The cost would be about $10,000 per court compared to the

President Harry Livingston with club officers and members at the groundbreaking for the new clubhouse.

B.H. Green and Son, Inc., constructing the clubhouse in 1983.

$20,000 per court for the existing ones.

In September, all outstanding bonds were called, and Roger Schmitt's contract as golf course superintendent was renewed. The pool closed on October 2; and lastly, discussion was held to raise the initiation fee once the new clubhouse opened.

Randy Marcum was hired as the club manager on November 15, 1983. D.J. Henderson Interiors received the bid to furnish the new clubhouse with furniture. Members were told they could not use the Westwood Country Club after December 31. The clubhouse was at 41 percent completion by the end of November.

Doug Edwards was elected president in early 1984 when the clubhouse was 63 percent complete and on schedule. Twenty-four new members were approved.

Jim Brown, chairman of the greens committee and a director of the KSGA, notified the organization that the golf course would not be ready for the scheduled State Amateur Championship and that the club would like to host in 1985.

Bill Bowland presented a proposal to lease and operate the pro shop when the new club opened. Other proposals were presented later, but in March the board accepted Bowland's proposal.

The board approved the following items: Don Schrack as club manager; the building of four clay tennis courts at a cost of about $60,000; and the purchase of a portable dance floor for the new clubhouse. The much anticipated grand opening of the clubhouse was scheduled for May.

The new clubhouse opened on Memorial Day weekend in May of 1984 much to the delight of the members. A sense of relief and accomplishment was felt by all who had watched the move from the club's original home to the present one. A return to normalcy was welcomed.

COURSE
RULES
CARTS IN FAIRWAY
REPAIR BALL MARKS
HOLE LOCATION
6

Men's Golf

Since the 1913, the Country Club of Paducah has evolved from a place where a few men gathered to play golf on a short, nine-hole course with small sand greens, to a club rich in tradition where golf is played on a Robert Trent Jones championship golf course.

Located outside the city limits in the early days, the clubhouse was built first, and then the golf course. Some accounts say it was 1923 before the course was actually in good condition, which was also the year that the club changed from sand to grass greens.

The best golfers at the club in those early days may have putted their way to the championships, since they were playing on sand greens. George H. Goodman's name was etched on a tall silver trophy as the 1920 Club Champion. He may not have been the very first, but he was one of the first.

Another golfer who won on sand greens was Goodman's good friend, W.J. Gilbert, the 1921 winner of the President's Trophy. Goodman repeated in 1925, 1926, and 1934, and also took the handicap tournament in 1933.

Finding reports of other tournaments in those days is a rare occurrence. However, in 1937 a sports reporter wrote that Johnny Shelton and Jimmie Rieke were setting the pace as they played a qualifying round in the Paducah Country Club's Spring Handicap Golf Tournament. Richard Smith was in third place in early qualifying. Jimmie English, Jack Fisher, J.W. Kern, Rev. George Heaton, and Roy Shelbourne also participated.

"From the start its golfers have made this season, the country club apparently is planning to win the Paxton Cup for the first time next September. In addition to Shelton, Rieke, and Smith, when Tommy Whittemore, "Buzz" Hassman, Lanson Ditto, Herbert Wallerstein, George Shelton, and some of the club's other stars get going, the club will be a tough one to beat!"

Will J. Gilbert and George H. Goodman (right) in 1952, more than 30 years after they won numerous golf tournaments at the first club.

Governors' Cup winners received sterling silver cups in the 1920s. At left is George Goodman's 1920 trophy, and below, W.J. Gilbert's 1921 trophy.

Original Golf Course Club Champions
A partial list from 1920-1978

1920 George Goodman
1925 George Goodman
1926 George Goodman
1934 George Goodman
1921 Will J. Gilbert
1944 Charles Mechamer
1945 Dr. Harry Wolfe
1946 Bill List
1947 Pete Smith
1948 Jimmy Stewart
1960 Vic Speck, Jr.
1963 Vic Speck, Jr.
1969 Vic Speck, Jr.
1970 Vic Speck, Jr.
1974 David Paxton
1975 George Sullivan
1978 George Sullivan

The Men's Club Champions
From 1979-2016

1979 Tommy Thomas
1980 Kenny Hunt
1981 Jim Brown
1982 Jim Brown
1983 Jim Brown
1984 Jim Brown
1985 Jim Brown
1986 Mike Shelbourne
1987 Jim Brown
1988 Jim Brown
1989 Jim Brown
1990 Jim Brown
1991 Jim Brown
1992 Jim Brown
1993 Mark Knecht
1994 Jim Brown
1995 Jim Brown
1996 Jim Brown
1997 Mark Knecht
1998 Mike Shelbourne
1999 Jim Brown
2000 Jim Brown
2001 Jim Brown
2002 Jim Brown
2003 Will Cox
2004 Will Cox
2005 Case Cochran
2006 Jim Brown
2007 Ric Webster
2008 Ric Webster
2009 Ryan Cochran
2010 Jim Brown
2011 Ric Webster
2012 Jim Brown
2013 Jim Brown
2014 Joey Mayo
2015 Jim Brown
2016 Jason Siener

Winners of the Senior Club Championship
From 1980-2016

1980 Hal Brown
1981 Charles Earhart
1982 Jim Flynn
1983 Jim Flynn
1984 Jack Pedley
1985 Hilary Hunt
1986 Jim Flynn
1987 Vic Speck
1988 Jack Pedley
1989 Jerry Shepherd
1990 Jim Marvin
1991 Jerry Shepherd
1992 Vito Canonico
1993 Jerry Spepherd
1994 Tommy Thomas
1995 Vic Speck
1996 Jim Marvin
1997 Jerry Shepherd
1998 Bill Metzger
1999 Tommy Thomas
2000 Tommy Whittemore
2001 Tommy Thomas
2002 Tommy Thomas
2003 Ronnie Brown
2004 Tommy Whittemore
2005 Tommy Thomas
2006 Tommy Thomas
2007 Bob Garey
2008 Jim Brown
2009 Tommy Thomas
2010 Jim Brown
2011 Ronnie Brown
2012 Chris Hunkler
2013 Ronnie Brown
2014 Chris Hunkler
2015 Chris Hunkler
2016 Jim Brown

In the mid-1930s, a foursome of "regulars" on the golf course were (from left) Dr. Robert W. "Red" Robertson, I.N. "Strick" Strickland, Horace Owen, and Hecht Lackey.

Norman Hely sits in his familiar spot as Don Hartline loads his bag on the blue cart.

Norman Hely was joined on No. 1 tee by Gresham Hougland (left), Bob Hougland, and Wilson Gunn.

The minutes from the Board of Governors' meetings prior to 1942 no longer exist, but from 1944 to 1948, the club champions' names were listed in the September minutes. The club tournaments were played on Labor Day weekend for decades.

Charles Mechamer won the trophy in 1944. Buck Burnett finished second. The champion in 1945 was Dr. Harry Wolfe, who just happened to have a hole-in-one on No. 5 to insure his victory.

In 1946 it was Bill List who took the title, with Bobby Stewart losing by one stroke. Pete Smith was the 1947 champion, defeating James Rieke by a narrow margin. James Stewart won in 1948, finishing ahead of Dixie Dunn.

Bill List

Golf was at the center of club life from the beginning; consequently, the 9-hole course was more crowded, with enthusiastic players of all skill levels with each passing year. Numerous publications verify that the sport was gaining in popularity all over Paducah and in other towns in Western Kentucky.

In a meeting of the governors in 1956, Tom Marshall reacted to the crowded conditions when he made the motion that "Ladies not be permitted to tee off between 10 a.m. and 4 p.m. on Saturdays, Sundays, and holidays." Golf Committee Chairman Tom Whittemore, Sr., said he was hopeful of getting some cooperation from the ladies without passing this rule, and the motion was withdrawn, Bunks Dallam recorded in the minutes. Whittemore's wife, Josie, and son Tommy were golfers, so he had a vested interest in accomplishing this task.

Vic Speck

Vic Speck won his first Men's Club Championship in 1960. He won at least four titles and possibly more. Speck won again in 1963, 1969, and 1970 and was a contender in many other championships.

Around 1952, this group of friends (left) paused before a round of golf. From left are Lawrence Dallam, Irv Bright, Pete Smith, and Vic Speck, a foursome of young men who represented what golf at the club was all about. Bright became President of the club and Speck was the Golf Committee Chairman many times. They were all champions on and off the course. Speck and Bright are pictured (below) in 1977 with Pete Smith and Henry Dallam.

"Gene Hipp Country Club Spring Champ" the headline read on July 4, 1966. "The new Spring Handicap Champion really puts a lot of 'Hipp' into his golf swing," the sports writer noted.

"Hipp polished off George Sullivan 2 and 1 in the championship match Sunday in claiming his first match play crown at the Country Club. Sullivan was busy, meanwhile, at the other end of the bracket setting charges to Jan Blanton, Frank Young, Sam Livingston, and City Open Champion Vic Speck."

Hipp received eight strokes. His win over Sullivan climaxed a trek through the 29-player championship flight, including victories over Jack Bailey, Jr., Dubber Young, Joe Sanders, and Dr. Clyde Peel.

David Paxton won the 1974 Club Championship at the old club defeating Henry Dallam while Paxton was a student. "I still consider it my best win," he said.

George Sullivan, who started collecting trophies in 1950, was the Men's Club Champion in 1975 and 1978. In 1978 he beat two outstanding players, Vic Speck and Bob Robinson, he proudly remembers. That was the final club championship played at the 9-hole course. The following year, he came in second to Tommy Thomas, who has the honor of winning the first championship played on the Robert Trent Jones course.

CARTING OFF THE HARDWARE — Gene Hipp "carts off" the silver championship trophy of the Paducah Country Club's Spring Handicap Tournament after defeating George Sullivan in Sunday's finals. Other flight winners are, left to right: Tommy Whittemore (first), Bones Underwood (second), and Bill Usher (third).

George Sullivan and Governor Julian Carroll in 1979 at the club.

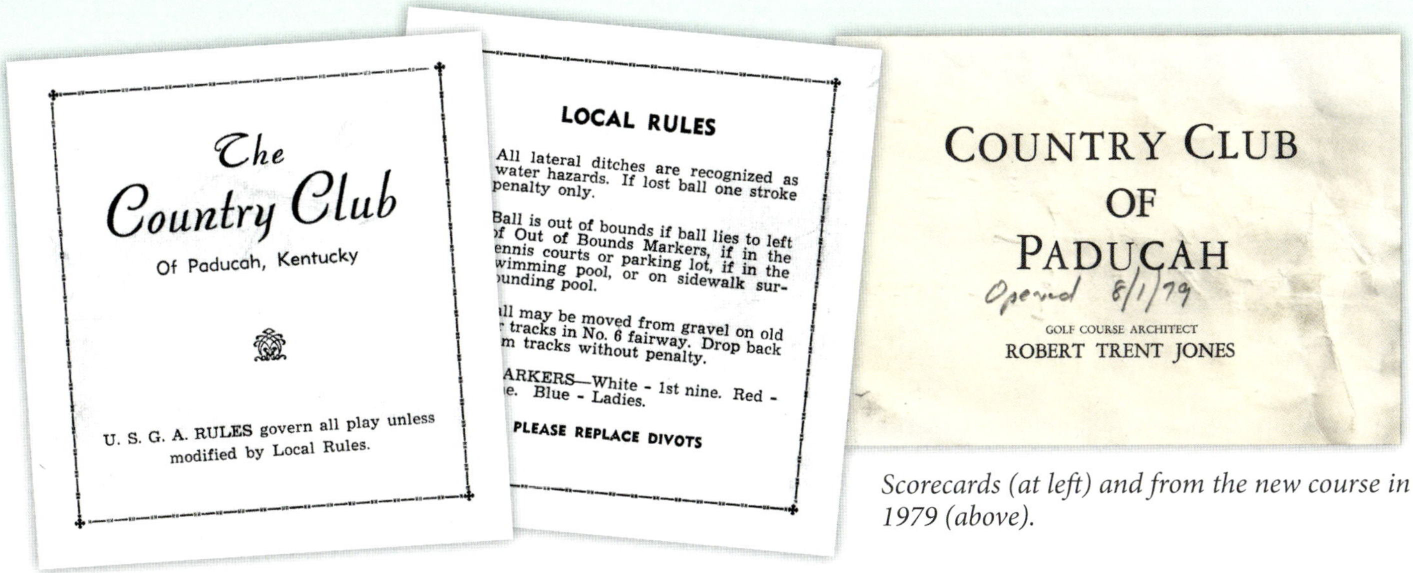
The Country Club
Of Paducah, Kentucky

U. S. G. A. RULES govern all play unless modified by Local Rules.

LOCAL RULES

All lateral ditches are recognized as water hazards. If lost ball one stroke penalty only.

Ball is out of bounds if ball lies to left of Out of Bounds Markers, if in the tennis courts or parking lot, if in the swimming pool, or on sidewalk surrounding pool.

Ball may be moved from gravel on old tracks in No. 6 fairway. Drop back from tracks without penalty.

MARKERS—White - 1st nine. Red - ...e. Blue - Ladies.

PLEASE REPLACE DIVOTS

COUNTRY CLUB
OF
PADUCAH
Opened 8/1/79
GOLF COURSE ARCHITECT
ROBERT TRENT JONES

Scorecards (at left) and from the new course in 1979 (above).

The Governor's Cup drew a host of celebrities and members to the club in 1979 to honor Gov. Julian Carroll. Jerry Page shakes his hand while Jim Flynn watches. In the background are Perry Driver, Sam Livingston, Joe B. Hall, and Royce Gregory.

Frank Paxton presents an award to Royce Gregory; Pat Kerr is in the foreground.

Dr. Henry Dallam, George Sullivan, Bill Reed, and Jim Flynn are ready to win.

Royce Gregory, Dr. Hilary Hunt, University of Kentucky Football Coach Fran Curci, and Charles Earhart.

Connie Trogolo is carried to the tee by Joe Rinella while Gene Fisher and Pat Cvengros have fun watching.

A group of long-time friends enjoy the moment in 2005 (from left) Frank Paxton, Jim Marvin, Jack Pedley, Ed Hough, Irv Bright, Jerry Page, and Henry Dallam.

Others who probably were club champions include Henry Dallam around 1957, Lawrence Dallam and Dr. Glenn Noss in the 1960s, Tommy Whittemore, Sr., in the 1950s, Don McClure in the late 1950s, and Jim Musgove in the late 1960s and early 1970s.

According to Tommy Whittemore, Jr., golf photos were displayed on the walls of Moody's Grocery Store, located near 32nd and Central Avenue near the old club. These champions and other country club golfers no doubt found their place on the store's walls.

Past President Ed Hough shared many memories for the history. "We had men's golf on Thursdays. Lots of men owned their own small businesses back then, plus others came and we had big crowds. We would have about 40 men play on Men's Day and the women would have even more for Ladies' Day."

The popular Governor's Cup was held when Hough was president in 1979. "Julian (Carroll) was running for governor that year so he was there, of course, but I don't remember him playing. I won with an 81 playing with Dwain Lowery. Frank Paxton gave me the Cup because he organized that event. Joe B. Hall was there and Fran Curci (University of Kentucky Wildcat head coaches). The next year, Dwain won it," Hough noted. (Lowry passed away in December of 2016.)

Golf on the Robert Trent Jones Course

In 1979, golfers teed it up for the first Men's Club Championship at the new course. Tommy Thomas has the honor of being the first winner, and Jason Seiner won the coveted title in 2016.

In between those two wins are the years when Jim Brown dominated the tournament. In 2015, he won his 23rd Club Championship at the Country Club of Paducah, a record that may never be broken.

Brown is the most decorated amateur golfer who has ever been a club member. Brown grew up at Rolling Hills Country Club and became a member of the Country Club of Paducah in 1980. He won the Kentucky State Amateur three times 1977, 1981, and 1982. Among an extensive list of local victories are nine Irvin Cobb Championships.

His lowest round at the Robert Trent Jones course from the current blue tees (they were white back then) was 63 and may still stand as the record low. "It was in the member-guest one year when I was playing with my dad and brother and brother-in-law," Jim said. "The lowest I had from the back tees was a 65."

"My most memorable round was nine holes I played with Russ Cochran many years ago and I shot a 29 with him on the back side!" It was July of 1988 when Brown was playing with Cochran, Buzz Peel, and Tim Lambert that he carded the seven birdies and two pars, quite an accomplishment!

Jimmy Brown with the Irvin Cobb Championship trophy in 1974.

"Another memorable finish was one year in the club championship when I birdied the last four holes to beat Mike Shelbourne," he recalled.

He also remembers a weak finish in a tournament. "It was in the State Amateur in 1994, I think. I was asked by a reporter before the tournament started, if I thought I had a home course advantage. My response was that I felt the pressure of playing locally basically negated the home course advantage, making it a wash. I then went on to say that I did believe that the home course advantage would work to my benefit—if I had a three-shot lead with four to go that I felt I could win the tournament.

Well, the golf gods didn't like that. I walked off 15 the last day with a three-shot lead and proceeded to finish bogey, bogey, par, par and eventually lost on the first hole of a playoff to a birdie."

Tommy Thomas has played more rounds of golf at the Country Club of Paducah than any other member since his family joined in 1957, an unofficial observation by his fellow golfers. It is not unusual for him to play 27 or 36 holes on a single day nearly 60 years later.

Thomas has won the senior division in many local tournaments and seven Senior Club Championships, despite the fact that he was not allowed to compete in the 1990s because he once qualified for a PGA Senior Tour event and was deemed a tour "professional" during those years. His lowest round at the club is 64, one of the lowest amateur scores from the regular tees.

The first time the Men's Senior Championship was played at the new course was the summer of 1980, when Hal Brown won. Starting in 1981, Jerry Shepherd took four titles; Jim Flynn, Ronnie Brown, Jim Brown, and Chris Hunkler have won three times, while Vic Speck, Jim Marvin, and Tommy Whittemore, Jr., are two-time senior winners. Vito Canonico, Bill Metzger, and Bob Garey have each won one championship trophy.

Tommy Thomas, first champ on new course.

In 1981, the board voted to allow a qualifying round for the Kentucky State Amateur to be held at the "Blandville-West" course in June. The greens committee chairman was Joe Rinella. Dave York was chairman of the golf committee.

Tommy Thomas waits his turn on No. 4, 2016

Russ Cochran, the club's claim to PGA Tour fame, pictured with Gloria and Harry Livingston early in his career.

THE PALM BEACH POST REAL NEWS STARTS HERE

SPORTS

After winning just once on the PGA Tour, Russ Cochran has won five Champions Tour events — including one major, the 2011 Senior British Open. ANDREW REDINGTON / GETTY IMAGES

Russ Cochran joined the club with his family in 1983. He is the only member to ever be a PGA Tour winner in the club's history.

Cochran turned pro in 1979 and received his PGA Tour card in 1982 after playing on the University of Kentucky golf team. He won the 1991 Centel Western Open near Chicago over Greg Norman coming down the stretch, which jump-started his career of seven wins.

He enjoyed many years of success before joining the ranks of the over-50 crowd on the Champions Tour in 2009. Although he has suffered several injuries in his career, Cochran has won three times, including the 2011 Senior British Open.

In 1992 he was awarded a lifetime honorary membership by the Country Club of Paducah. He and his wife, Jackie, have four children, Ryan, Reed, Case, and Kelly. Jackie and Kelly are tennis enthusiasts, while the sons follow in their father's footsteps as golfers.

Case Cochran won the Men's Club Championship in 2005 and Ryan won in 2009.

Today, members are always delighted to see Russ, wish him well, and hear stories that he shares when he is in Paducah.

News from Board Minutes and Newsletters

When the clubhouse opened in 1984, it only enhanced life on the golf links. The "die-hards" had been playing since 1978 or 1979 and utilizing the trailer for food and beverages.

The business of golf resumed. Head Professional Bill Bone became Director of Golf in April. *(See full story on Bone in Golf Pro chapter.)* Eighty new lockers for men and 56 for women became available at a charge of $60 per year.

Above: Inside the trailer, which was used as a temporary clubhouse in the early eighties, were golfers happy to be on the new course—from left, Tommy Thomas, Harry Livingston, Mike Mazzone, Dick Brown, Jim Brown, Ray Carlson, Oscar Gamble, John Dallam, and Pro Bill Bone.

Right: Playing in the Member-Guest in 1982 was the team of David York, Ted Fiorita, Ron Greenlee, and Phil Hayden.

Do you remember the Men's Golf Association? Hardly anyone does, but talk about forming one is ongoing. The Board of Directors composed of Rip Pugh, Charles Woods, John Williams, Burton Banks, Connie Trogolo, Louis Kirchoff, Bill Usher, David York, and President Doug Edwards addressed a few issues with the MGA in 1985.

According to Bill Usher, the MGA was dissolved because there were no articles of incorporation, by-laws, or report on the use of funds.

The 1985 Paducah Community College (PCC) fund-raising tournament and dinner was approved for October.

This was a very popular team event with celebrities such as UK basketball player, Sam Bowie, and PGA Pro Larry Gilbert "auctioned off" the night before the tournament to raise money for the school. Most teams bought a celebrity to enhance their chance of winning or having a memorable day on the links.

For many years, Paducah Community College hosted a fund-raiser at the club. Clockwise from right: Members of a 1986 team were (from left) Jack Wilson, Norman Greenberg, a UK star, Ed Hough, and Dr. Merle Fowler. Teams in 1993 included Jim Bowling, Ken Schuppert, Henry Mueller, John Harris, Wayne Shelton, and Harry Livingston; Russ Wagner, Dr. Riley Love, Pat Habacker, Mike Love, and Ted Fiorita with a UK celebrity; in 1996, Reza Danesh, Louis Michelson, Marilyn Metzger, Ted Fiorita, Terry Chandler, and Leo Green; UK guest with Dave Denton, Frank Shelton, Mike Wyatt, and Dick Walker.

Returning to the chronological history in the board minutes, the 1986 Kentucky Men's State Amateur was held at the club in June with Steve Flesch winning over Mike Shelbourne by a single shot. He turned pro soon afterwards and became a familiar name on the PGA Tour.

Burton Banks was winner of the First Annual (was it the last?) "Flat Belly Open" played from "the long tees."

In 1987, the scramble team composed of President Connie Trogolo, Golf Pro Bill Crabtree, Superintendent Roger Schmitt, and Club Manager Joe Connor won the Kentucky qualifier and advanced to the John Deere National Championships played at PGA National in Palm Beach Gardens, Florida.

Jim Brown won the club championship with Mike Shelbourne second and Vito Canonico third. Bob Garey won the first flight and Charles Metzger took the second flight. Ted Fiorita was declared the Handicap Tournament Champion.

Vic Speck edged out Mike Love in the Fall Match Play Championship on November 12, 1987. Mike and his father, Clyde, both had holes-in-one on No. 12 that year.

In 1988, Dan Dickerson had a hole-in-one on No. 14 and Steve Solomon had an eagle on No. 13, according to Bill Crabtree.

The American Cancer Society Division II team composed of Russ Wagner, Tim Jones, Ted Fiorita, and Fred Sanders placed 4th in the National Championship at Doral in Miami, another great showing for the club at a national event.

Russ Wagner, Ted Fiorita, Tim Jones, and Fred Sanders, sporting some spiffy shorts, in the 1988 ACS National Championship in Miami.

President Washburn charged the golf and tennis committees to meet with architects Coltharp and Kerr on a proposed golf and tennis facility beside No. 10 tee.

Dick Stacey and Bill Ragland reached the finals of the Fall Match Play Championship. A breakfast best ball event was played in November with the team of Lee Warren, Fred Nackley, Bill Usher, and Joe Rinella winning with a 128.

Once again, the club boasted a winning team in the John Deere Tournament—Banks, Crabtree, Nackley, and Schmitt. They traveled to Palm Springs, California, in November to compete and finished fourteenth. The board approved a request by the Kentucky PGA to hold its golf tournament at the club in 1989 and wrapped up another year in the club's history at the December meeting.

With all club sports planning many events and tournaments for the 1989 season, participation in golf and tennis was high.

Burton Banks was asked to look into the possible need of a starter or course marshal because of slow play due to walkers and non-member play.

Bill Usher, Kelly Cromwell, and Charles Metzger all recorded holes-in-one.

Jim Brown captured one of two spots Kentucky had for the U.S. Amateur Championship, his third one and an outstanding accomplishment. He missed moving into the match play by one stroke. Back at home, Brown went five extra holes in a play-off with Dick Stacey before winning the Men's Club Championship that summer.

Ed Hely "used his superior length off the tee to help him capture the 19-Man Shootout over Bob Wagner," the pro reported. Crabtree said "the longest running golf tournament in history as far as we can tell has finally come to a conclusion!"

The Spring Match Play began in May and concluded in November when Jim Brown downed Tommy Thomas in the Championship Flight finals. Mike Love defeated Oscar Gamble for First Flight honors.

The Men's Challenge Cup was retained by the Country Club, which remained undefeated for five years. Team members were Randy Lewis, Thomas and Brown, Rick Straub, Russ Wagner, Joe Semeraro, Jim Flynn, Ted Fiorita, Tommy Whittemore, Ed Hely, John Golliher, and Bill Metzger.

In the December 1989 newsletter, Pro Crabtree told the story of four golfers who made a two on the same hole on November 12. Charles Epstein, Vito Canonico, Charles Metzger, and Bruce McAbrey all made deuces on hole No. 14, "a very rare feat!"

Jerry Shepherd won the senior title with a 151. Gold tee winners were E.M. Bailey, Homer Austin, Jacques Moran, and Burton Haley. The 44 super seniors who participated were recognized at a senior-only banquet organized by Lee Warren with Doug Edwards as the emcee.

Scorecards, clockwise from above, 1990, 1984, and 2016.

Velma "Ozie" Bohle and Tommy Thomas took the Most Improved Golfers of the Year awards.

On the links in 1990, Mike Love won the 19-man marathon shootout, which took 6.5 hours to finish. Russ Wagner finished second and Rick Straub third in a hard-fought shootout.

Representing the club in the Kentucky Oldsmobile Scramble were Gene Hipp, Bruce McAbrey, Ray Carlson, and Pat Morello. Jim Marvin won the Senior Club Championship with a 150. Joe Rinella, Jack Hester, and Frank Paxton won their flights.

The annual Challenge Cup between the club, Rolling Hills, and Paxton Park was held for the first time at Westwood, the site of the old country club. Team members who edged out Westwood 26½ to 26 were Jim Brown, Steve DuPerrieu, Tommy Thomas, Tommy Whittemore, Vic Speck, Chip Cox, Jim Flynn, John Golliher, Hilary Hunt, David Pugh, and Bob Wagner.

Mitchell Spearman, a teaching partner of David Ledbetter, came to the club in 1990 to give private lessons on May 20. The computerized golf course irrigation system was installed, and John Barker had a hole-in-one on No. 12 on July 15.

Early in 1991, Bill Crabtree was leaving for another endeavor. Two months later, John Golliher announced that Larry Mullen was the new golf pro and Todd Trimble was later hired as an assistant.

The new golf shop was completed by the end of the year. President John D. Williams said that members think the length of grass on the course is too high, so he was going to mow it himself, one of his friends reported with a laugh.

In the Beat the Pro competition of 1991, Oscar Gamble, Roscoe Crane, Dr. Merle Fowler, and Tom Austin won. Pro Larry Mullen had an even par 72.

In August, Russ Cochran won his first PGA Tour Tournament, the Centel Western Open—club members were ecstatic!

Jim Brown won the club championship; Jim Marvin took the senior title. Joe Rinella, Vito Canonico, Bob Byars, and Bob Grimm finished one through four in the championship flight. Jack Hester, Bill Conyer, Lynn Habacker, and Olin Bryant won the first flight prizes; and Frank Paxton, Perry Driver, Andy Wood, and Ray Carlson took home second flight trophies.

Perry Driver cut a familiar figure on the golf course with his cigar and plaid slacks. Someone asked him what he shot one day and he said 112 and he won a lot of money. How could you win money shooting 112? "I had a good score!" Driver pointed out.

Members of the 1991 winning Paxton Cup team were the following: Jimmy Brown, Kelly Cromwell, Steve Martin, Chip Cox, Bill Metzger, George Sullivan, Greg Overstreet, David Hunt, Dan Dickerson, Dr. Bob Byars, Brad Adkins, Jim Flynn, Rick Straub, Jim Marvin, and Tommy Whittemore.

Also in the December newsletter, Todd Trimble took Mullen's position as the head golf professional. In March, Mark "Putter" Hahn was hired as a new assistant.

In 1992, a men's winter golf trip to the Bahamas was led by pro Todd Trimble. Larry Mullen was on board to help assist with golf programs and be available for teaching instruction to help with the overload on lessons.

Due to numerous complaints received by the board regarding the use of the golf course by non-members living in the Paducah area, a proposed amendment had its first reading in the spring of 1992. "Non-members who reside in any county, any part of which lies within 85 miles of the city of Paducah, may use the golf course as the guest of a member no more than three times in any calendar year."

President John D. Williams announced the tracking fee was $400, a reduction. He also said the new modern Fitness Center is coming! Gary Robertson and Steve DuPerrieu will supervise, according to the newsletter. A special thank you was extended to Jerry Shepherd for "all of his outstanding work on this project."

"When we combine this with our new golf shop, Kentucky Room, and tennis center, we can now say that our club is complete, unequaled in a wide area," Williams boasted.

During the summer of 1992, Tommy Thomas had a hole-in-one on No. 12, and Bud Glasser had one on No. 6. Thomas donated the clock located beside the driving range. Elliott Baskin donated the bell on No. 5 fairway, and Larry Jarvis contributed yardage markers for the course.

Mike Shelbourne won the club Spring Match Play Tournament with Mark Knecht finishing second after 22 holes of play. The Men's Member-Guest had a record of 108 members and guests, plus spouses, participating.

The team of Bob Jones, Tim Jones, Todd Sutherland, Chip Bohle and the pro won the State Oldsmobile Scramble and will compete in Orlando at Nationals.

Representatives from Robert Trent Jones were at the course on August 15, 1992, and will present a written report.

Jim Brown was the club champion. Vito Canonico won the Senior Club Championship. The men's winter trip was to San Destin Resort in Florida in 1993.

Jim Brown was crowned the first winner of the Mid-America Championship held at the Country Club of Paducah with five states represented.

John Golliher won the club match play tournament edging out Bill Metzger on the 19th hole, and Mark Knecht topped Brown in the club championship.

In 1993, President John Williams reported in his "President's Corner" of the newsletter that "John Harris was seen in Southeast Missouri borrowing sandbags for the weekend!" as he praised Harris' play in the men's member-guest.

In the "A.M. Briefing," a sports column in the *Paducah Sun* on January 30, 1993, a story ran about a pair of holes-in-one at the Country Club of Paducah. Russ Wagner watched Larry Jarvis card an ace on No. 6 from 170 yards with a 5-iron at the club.

"Wagner probably silenced some of Jarvis' bragging when he nailed the pin with one shot on No. 14 a few minutes later in the same group. Wagner used an 8 iron from 140 yards," the story said. Bob Garey and Tom Austin witnessed the fun all wrapped up on a freezing January day. "We were the only foursome on the course!" Jarvis laughed.

Jerry Shepherd won the Senior Club Championship, while the unflappable team Dick Stacey and Ted Fiorita took the Junior Division of the Men's Member-Member Tournament.

Gary Adkins was once runner-up to Jim Brown in the Club Championship.

Russ Cochran became a regular member. Fans for No. 4 green were purchased, and it was announced that the club would host the 1994 Kentucky State Amateur.

In 1994, Jim Brown won another club championship with Gary "Bear" Adkins finishing second. Sometimes second place winners are forgotten, but when a member is second to Jim Brown, it is a special achievement.

Also in 1994, Joe Rinella carded a hole-in-one; the team of Ray Carlson, Gene Hipp, Tommy Lambert, and Pat Morello won the gross division of the Oldsmobile Scramble; and Tommy Thomas won the Senior Club Championship. In the 1994 State Amateur, Brown lost to Dan Utley in a play-off on the Robert Trent Jones course.

According to Dick Stacey, he and Ted Fiorita won the Calcutta Tournament so many times the event came to a halt for awhile. The two won in 1994, 1995, and 1996, with dozens of "investors" attending the bidding parties before the competition kicked off.

Kevin Rhinehart was hired by Todd Trimble to be a new assistant professional. Casey Birney was already on board as first assistant and Jerry Barlett was also on staff.

In the September 1994 newsletter, a special tribute to a life ended too soon was printed. "In Memory of Tom Austin" cited what a wonderful golfer and club member Tom was. "He loved the Country Club of Paducah and lived on the 5th fairway. There were very few Friday or Saturday nights when Tom and his wife, Lynn, didn't spend time in the clubhouse with their friends," President Rick Straub wrote.

A scratch golfer who hailed from Mayfield where he grew up playing great golf, Tommy Austin's sudden passing was a shock to his golfing buddies who were waiting for him to come to the tee that morning. It was a sad day for all who enjoyed knowing Tom.

Summer was drifting away and signs of winter were showing as the golf season came to a close. Todd Trimble announced, "It's going to be a girl!" when he concluded the *November Golf News*. (Sydney is now Sydney Trimble Kelley, a senior on the 2017 Murray State golf team.)

In 1995, Wayne Whisman was the golf committee chairman and tennis player Hal Sullivan was the greens chairman. Jim Harris chaired the fitness/social committee; Burton Banks and John Harris, the house committee.

Steve Bright was the membership and pool chairman; Dr. Mark Owens, finance, and Ed Hely, tennis.

Superintendent Hantle urged golfers to consider "going spikeless." Pro Trimble instituted the Wednesday Men's Night event in the summer of 1996.

The Paducah Community College Celebrity Golf Tournament was once again held at the club.

Casey Birney, Tom Whittemore, Steve Wilson, and Dick and Kristie Wilson competed at the National Oldsmobile Scramble in Orlando after winning the state scramble in their division.

The BMW Net Better Ball of Two event was played with E.M. Bailey, Jr., and Hal Brown taking the trophy and the trip to Pinehurst!

Mark Knecht was the 1997 Men's Club Champion. Danny Reed, long-time assistant superintendent, was mentioned in Superintendent Hantle's golf course report.

The year 1999 brought many personnel changes at the club. Jason Cates, now a golf member, was added to the golf professional staff and Kevin Rhinehart took the head professional job with Rolling Hills after three and a half years at the club. During the summer, assistant Kevin Hurst took another position and Jason Stilley was named the new assistant, Trimble announced. Barry Kight was an assistant in 2000.

Turning to action on the links, John Eckstein and Ted Fiorita proved to be a formidable team in the net better ball event that kicked off the season. They fired a 61. Fiorita joined Dr. Charles Epstein, Pat Morello, and Bill Usher as the team won the Oldsmobile Scramble with a 60.

Bob Garey was the golf committee chairman and Frank Shelton the greens chair. Jim Brown was the club champion and Tommy Thomas won the senior title. Ed Hely won the 10-man shootout several times, not be outdone by Tommy Whittemore who made a habit of winning scrambles.

Pro Trimble announced the top five qualifiers for the club's 2001 Cup Match team—Jim Brown, Tom Whittemore, David Paxton, Gary Adkins, and David Hunt. The men's team won the cup in 1999, 2009, 2011, and 2012 and several years prior.

In 2001, Brown won the club championship again and Tommy Thomas took the Senior Championship over Vic Speck and Gary Adkins, one shot back.

In golf news from 2002, Pro Trimble extended special congratulations to Men's Club Champion Jim Brown. David Paxton finished second. (Brown has won 23 times as of 2016.)

Tommy Thomas repeated as the Senior Club Champion and Bob Grimm took the Super Senior title for those over 70.

Jason Stilley became the new head golf professional in 2003 as Todd Trimble left to establish The Golf Complex, a teaching facility in West Paducah that he co-owns with Barry Kight. (Stilley remained the pro until November of 2016.)

Winners of the 2002 Men's Member-Guest were Gary Zakutney and Darren Pollentier, who is now a member instead of a guest. Tommy Whittemore captured the Men's Spring/Fall Match play title and Ronnie Brown won the Senior Club Championship.

Will Cox accomplished something only a few have been able to do—he topped Jim Brown in the Men's Club Championship, but Brown finished a close second.

The next year, Pro Stilley announced the hiring of Brad Dunker as an assistant. Tommy Whittemore beat Scott Ware in a play-off for the 2004 Men's Senior Club Championship.

In 2005 when Case Cochran won the Men's Club Championship with a fine score of 139, Ric Webster was second, and William Hunt was third. Bill Bob Conyer claimed the Super Senior title.

The Kentucky PGA Championship was held at the club for the second time (first in 1989), with Kelly Maxwell

The golf shop and cart facility.

Dr. Jim Woods exhibits a finely tuned swing.

winning. Andy Kohl and Brad Guest were employed as assistants in 2005 under Stilley. Nathan Wolfe came on board as the first assistant in the golf pro shop in 2006 and in 2007 Cody Martin joined the golf staff.

The club hosted the Men's Ohio Valley Conference Championship in April, and the State Amateur Qualifier was held here in June with Paducah's own William Hunt qualifying.

The Hunt family continues a tradition of golfing excellence today. Dr. Hilary Hunt plays in a regular group at age 80-plus; (the late Mary Lou Hunt loved the game); Kenny Hunt continues to play with friends who grew up at the club—David Paxton, Jim Woods, Steve Bright, and others. Dr. Phil Hunt is the father of William and also a player. David Hunt and Kevin Hunt played as juniors.

Ric Webster won the 2007 Men's Club Championship with a 144 over Eric Straub. Bob Garey took the senior title. Mark Bryant recorded a hole-in-one on No. 2 that year.

The 2008 Men's State Amateur was hosted by the club for the third time in its history and for the first time since 1994. Over 150 golfers were in the field.

That year it was announced—"Donations from individuals, businesses, and proceeds from a Course Improvement Tournament will go towards the cost of the golf scoreboard, which will be constructed behind No. 18 green." Donations were made by Utilities Dynamics, John and Janet Colgan, Superior Care Home, Riley and Jill Love, Mike and Cindy Wyatt, Danny and Renee Allen, Jim and Brenda Brown, U.S. Bank, and Chambers Roofing.

The scoreboard was constructed through the efforts of members Gary Zakutney and Kevin Baer.

Pro Stilley won the club professional tournament at Valhalla in Louisville, and in board business, the board noted that subdivision restrictions state that a fence cannot be within 25 feet of the golf course boundary line.

Ric Webster won the club championship for the second year in a row, this time beating Ryan Cochran by six shots with a 36-hole score of 140. The Seniors was won by Jim Brown and the Super Seniors by Dr. Hilary Hunt. Dr. John Colgan was the golf chairman.

In golf news, 108 entries were received for the first Pepsi Amateur, hosted in 2009. Sammy Thompson tied for runner-up; Nick Thompson won the A Flight.

Ryan Cochran won the Men's Club Championship and Tommy Thomas took the Senior Club Championship title. Gary Zakutney was listed as handicap chairman in the 2009 Golf Handbook.

The first Witches and Warlocks Couples Tournament drew golfers from around the region and was a huge success, according to Pro Stilley. Sabrina Wheatley and Jerry Hale beat Chris and Vicki Hunkler in a four-hole play-off for this first title.

The 2010 summer season kicked off with a host of golf activities. The Junior Open Golf Tournament drew 65 players. The Golf Academy of America came on board as a major sponsor of the event for the following year thanks to member Chris Hunkler, who is the former President of the GAA.

Russ Cochran was named the PGA Champions Tour Rookie of the Year. Russ finished the season 17th on the money list and 10th in the Charles Schwab Cup points race. Russ won the Songdo Championship in South Korea over Fred Funk and then took the SAS Championship in North Carolina two weeks later.

Under "Golf News" in the newsletter, Mark Knecht was the winner of the Country Club of Paducah Amateur, with Tommy Thomas taking the senior title and Roberta Sentel the ladies title. This new tournament was open to non-members.

Jim Brown won the 2010 Club Championship "for the 103rd time," President Mike Wyatt joked in his column. Congratulations were extended.

The Men's Paxton Cup Match team lost a heartbreaker at Rolling Hills. Silos' team won by only a half a point over the club, 33 to 32.5 points.

In 2011 on the golf front, Russ Cochran visited the club and spoke to 200 golf enthusiasts at a cocktail reception hosted by Russ and his wife, Jackie. Cochran had just won the Senior British Open and members were anxious to hear about such an achievement.

Jason Stilley and J.R. Maxam won the Pro-Assistant Championship held at Persimmon Ridge.

Tommy Thomas and Bill Metzger took the Member-Member Tournament title, while the team of Pro Stilley, Leann Stilley, and members Stacia Smith and Kim Birch won the Dalhousie Cup.

Eric Straub and Emma Robinson, who are now Mr. and Mrs. Straub, were the winners of the Country Club of Paducah Amateur in their respective divisions.

Wally Bateman and his son, Reed, captured the Men's Member-Guest and Ben Brown took the Match Play Tournament title with President Wyatt referring to Bateman as "the Silver Fox who chipped in to win" in his newsletter column. Jim Brown won the Senior Club Championship over Chris Hunkler.

Ric Webster won the 2011 Men's Club Championship over Brent Gaines. The men captured the Paxton Cup.

The Ladies 9 and Dine, a new effort to have more ladies play golf, was held and Sunday couples golf was underway by 2012. Jason Stilley qualified for the PGA Championship, which will be played in California.

Sixty-three juniors played in the GAA Junior Classic. The 2012 Ladies Memorial Golf Tournament drew 124 players, the largest in its history. The Men's Member-Member had 22 teams in the field and the two-man event had a full field of 96 golfers.

The Country Club of Paducah Amateur had a field of 90 golfers with club members Jim Brown, Michael Byers, Jonathan McGregor, Brenda Rendleman, Tommy Thomas, Bob Garey, and Bill Metzger finishing in the top three in their various flights.

Don VanCleve enjoyed a big night on the golf course when he had a hole-in-one on Men's Night to take home $5,454! The pot had not been won since 2004.

Jim Brown added another jewel to his Club Champion crown, and Chris Hunkler won the senior title for the first time. The men brought home the Paxton Cup and the ladies won the Wooldridge Cup for the third year in a row.

Brown topped Jeff Holland in the finals of the Match Play Championship. James Eickholz and Tim Shiben took the Member-Member trophy.

It was 2013 when Jason Siener downed David Guess in the final match of the Men's Match Play Championship. Jim Brown won the club championship.

Ronnie Brown beat Chris Hunkler for the Men's Senior Club Championship in 2013 when he fired his third shot from 100 yards into No. 18 green—it went in for an eagle and a one-shot victory!

A bronze plaque was being designed to recognize the club's affiliation with Robert Trent Jones, golf course architect, and in other golf-related business, bids will be taken on repaving the cart paths.

In golf news, back-to-back holes in one were recorded on February 23, 2014, a remarkable happening on any golf course. Mark Edwards was the first in his group to tee off on No. 2. The 120-yard shot went in the hole!

Not to be outdone, his fellow competitor, Ronnie Brown teed off next in the group. Much to the dismay of Bob

The 2009 Winning Paxton Cup team members are (from left, standing, Bill Metzger, Brent Gaines, Michael Byers, Mike Sims, David Bailey, Jim Brown, John Colgan, Ryan Cochran; (from left, seated) David Paxton, Pro Jason Stilley, Bob Garey, Dan Weeks, and Justin McConnell.

The 2015 Cup Team with Assistant Professional Ryan Mitchell (left) and Professional Jason Stilley (right) are (from left, front) Jason Siener, Bill Metzger, Bob Garey, David Guess, Kevin Baer; (from left, back) Darryn Pollentier, Jason Goins, John Colgan, Ed Hely, Michael Byers, Mike Sims, Andrew Walker, and Burton Gregory.

Kenny Hunt, A&K Construction, hosts of the annual Sunrise Children's Services Golf Tournament, one of the largest charity events held at the club.

Kenny Hunt with Jamey Brown and Phil Justice, Director of Philanthropy for Sunrise.

Players in 2010 and 2012 include (clockwise from below): Mike Warnsman, Tony Reck, Rex Smith, Tom Greene; Wally and Jane Bateman, Tammy and Mike Zimmerman; Kurt Sutton; Jim Brown, George Long, Garry Shemwell, Bill Bryan; Craig Guess, Mark Chambers; Cory Samsil, Larry Stovesand, Jody Stivers, Jeff Holland.

Garey, Butch Bradley, and Kevin Baer, who had the pleasure of watching, it also went in the hole! This was Edwards' first hole-in-one and Brown's seventh. And that's why golfers "keep coming back" as the saying goes!

By September, golf members were congratulating the 2014 Club Champion Joey Mayo, who beat long-time contender Jim Brown. Mayo might be one of the youngest to ever win this title. (Mayo played on the golf team of Rhodes College.)

Joey Mayo, the 2014 Men's Club Champion, fired a 140 to win the trophy presented by Jason Stilley.

Brothers and winners Dan and Kim Homra.

Chris Hunkler took the Senior Club Champion title over Tommy Thomas. Ronnie Brown and Kevin Baer won the Member-Member Tournament title.

Vicki and Chris Hunkler won the Couples' Club Championship with a one-shot victory over Renee and Danny Allen. Ronnie Brown and Kevin Baer won the Men's Member-Member; Brown teamed with Kevin Baer to capture the Junior-Senior Tournament.

Baer also took top honors in the Top 24 Men's Tournament and was named "Player of the Year," with Bob Garey finishing second. All of the winners were invited to the First Annual Golf Awards Dinner on November 8, 2014. This special event was held for three years.

Dr. Kim Birch had a hole-in-one on March 29, 2015, on No. 14 and Harry Alvis aced No. 14 on September 22. Pat Gourieux had her first hole-in-one on October 14 on No. 14.

LPGA member Chelsea Phillips resigned as the assistant professional. In college, she had an outstanding record as an Ohio Valley Conference player before turning pro.

Chris Hunkler won the 2015 Men's Senior Club Championship with a 144 and Ed Hely was runner-up; Mike Mazzone topped his buddy Ed Wilson in a play-off for the win in the "A" Flight, while Larry Jarvis took the B Flight, and Hilary Hunt was the Super Senior winner.

Bob Garey teamed with his son-in-law Burton Gregory to capture the Junior-Senior Championship.

Kim Birch teamed with Tommy Thomas to take the Couples Championship title. Jim Brown topped the field in the Men's Club Championship, which is now played from the back tees at approximately 6800 yards.

The brothers Kim and Dan Homra were the Member-Member Champions; Kim also won the Top 24 Tournament. Burton Gregory was the Match Play winner; Jim Brown and David Bailey took the Team Match Play trophy. Chris Hunkler was named "Player of the Year" at the end-of-the-year awards dinner.

Jason Siener was the greens committee chairman. In June of 2016, the golf committee asked Mark Curtis to be the handicap "director" much like the job that Bob Ely did for many years. Golfers were urged to do a better job of turning in their scores, which will produce more accurate handicaps during competitions.

Ed Wilson, Mike Mazzone, Tommy Thomas, and Larry Jarvis in the bistro following play in the Senior Men's Club Championship 2015.

Top finishers Ed Hely (left) and Tom Garrett (right) with Chris Hunkler, winner of the 2015 Senior Club Championship.

Award winners at the 2015 end-of-the-year banquet are (from left) Greg Leneave, Kim Homra, Burton Gregory, Dan Homra, Tommy Thomas, Dr. Hilary Hunt, Chris Hunkler, David Bailey, and Jim Brown.

Jim Brown won the 2015 Club Championship. From left are Brown, Chris Hunkler, runner-up; Dr. John Colgan, Andrew Walker, Jason Goins, Steve Bright, and Greg Leneave, flight winners.

And the 2016 winners are…

The team of Bob Garey and Mark Edwards took the Memorial Day competition to kick off the 2016 golf season, and Lyn Smith and Jason Goins won the Junior-Senior Tournament. Bill Metzger took the Country Club of Paducah Amateur Senior Flight win; and Chris and Vicki Hunkler won the Couples' Club Championship.

The Men's Club Champion was Jason Siener, teeing it up from the back tees and overcoming some rough course conditions. This was Siener's first title.

Brad Walker won the 2016 Match Play Tournament. Kevin Baer and Jason Cates won the Team Match Play Tournament, and the team of Justin Halverson, Dr. Jim Zellmer, Rick Leeper, George Sirk, and Dr. Brandon Strenge won the Men's Year-End Scramble in a play-off.

Jim Brown won the Men's Senior Club Championship, shooting 69-71. Gary Adkins won the A Flight, Steve Bright the B, and Bobby Day the Super Senior title.

Kevin Baer won the "Player of the Year" award, which is based on the number of events played and finishes in those events.

What a summer of holes-in-one at the club! Chris Jordan had his first hole-in-one on No. 14 playing with Lyn Smith and Russ Hall. Mark Curtis aced No. 12 from 134 yards for his first hole-in-one. Tommy Thomas recorded his 8th ace, also on No. 12, and Bill Metzger aced No. 6.

Jason Siener

The tournament season drew to a close with the men's year-end scramble, a culmination of the regular Wednesday night competitions. Many golfers continued to play as the leaves changed and winter weather was anticipated, but winter entered with a yawn and the playing season was lengthened.

Life on the links ontinues to change, but the golfer's love for the game remains the same.

Bob Garey, Burton Gregory, and Bo Ryan with Mark Edwards.

Bill Metzger and Scott Ware lining up.

From left in the heat of competition are Jim Brown, Andrew Walker, and Jason Goins on No. 17 in 2016.

Mark Curtis chips.

Bob Day, 2016 Super Senior Golfer

Just another day at the course for Richard Trampe, Gary Adkins, Walter Taylor, and Bill Metzger.

Jason Siener, his wife Leigh Ann, sons Kip and Kase after his victory in the Club Championship.

Burton Gregory, Tommy Owens, Jonathan McGregor and Aaron Cobb in the 2016 Member-Guest.

Gary Zakutney and Bob Garey, happy Member-Member winners.

Since the first foursome teed off on the original course over 100 years ago, golf is still the cornerstone of activity at the Country Club of Paducah.

Ed Wilson, Mike Mazzone, Gary Rogers, Chris Hunkler in the Member-Member Tournament.

Club Anecdotes

People and their stories about golf at the club are what make its history interesting and oftentimes entertaining. Let's listen to some of the members in their own words.

♦ George Sullivan recounted a story he remembers vividly: "In 1957 or '58 after the old clubhouse burned down, I was tied for the lead or leading in a big tournament when I got to No. 6. A tree that was hanging over the fairway had been killed during the fire, but was still standing. There was a big gallery, and everyone was gathered around to watch us leaders. I hit a 3-iron on the bed of (railroad) tracks. The club flew out and went up in the tree and rattled around!" Sullivan laughed. "Everyone started yelling, 'The tree is falling!' Needless to say, I didn't win. Don McClure did."

♦ Tommy Thomas remembers playing golf in high school in the early '60s with George Crounse, Jr. "He was the fastest guy at Tilghman, a sprinter who ran the 100-yard-dash in 10.3 seconds. He liked to play golf and sometimes we'd carry 4-5 clubs and we would hit and say '1-2-3-Go!' and race to our balls!"

"One day on No. 7, George hit his ball in a tree beside the 8th green and we were looking for it and it was lodged in the tree. While we were there, we saw Mr. (Palmer) James take a swing off the nearby 8th tee. He took the club back in about three pieces and right at the top of the swing, he looked straight up at the sky and came back down and hit the ball. We laughed so hard, we fell on the ground and kept laughing!" Thomas said.

♦ Another humorous anecdote was shared by Bob Bell, who was born in 1924 and joined the club in 1947. "I lost a $50 bet to Woodrow Hook. Members were invited to see the progress that had been made out at the new club site back in the sixties. I bet Woody that after everyone saw it, they'd vote to make the move to the Holt Road location. I was wrong. It was voted down at that time and I paid him the money!" Bell laughed.

♦ Members recall hitting balls into the street if they hooked a shot on No. 2 along Pines Road because the course was very tight. Still, they have many good memories about the place.

♦ Barbara Backus Livingston, who lived with her family (Bill, Martha, Billy, and Nancy) across the street from the club in those days, said her father almost exclusively used the balls that were hit off No. 1 tee into their yard.

Bill Backus

(Bill Backus was an avid golfer on the 9-hole course and again at the new site; he played golf until he was past 90-years-old and quickly got over the move to the new venue on Blandville Road, an action that he opposed early on.)

♦ Around 1969, Dr. Glenn Noss, a lefty, and Tommy Thomas played sudden death in the Match Play Championship at the old club. Noss three-putted when he heard a dog barking on No. 1 and lost the tournament.

♦ "There was a little road out on the Blandville Road property that was used by the kids before the golf course was finished. They would play and swing on a rope over the lake and have a big time," Bill Usher reminisced.

♦ Tommy Whittemore, Jr., who was on the board for two terms in the 1990s, recalls that time when someone parked some old golf carts near the pool at the first club. "The brake went out on one and the clubs went into the pool!" he chuckled.

Tommy Whitemore, Jr.

♦ Jack Mike Wilson said Dr. "Red" Robertson was "quite a character" and very well liked. His son, Dr. Rob Robertson, said his father was not necessarily a good golfer, but loved to play the game.

Wilson also said that Norman Bronstein had a hole-in-one on No. 5 with a driver, so he never wanted to tell anyone that he had the ace! (Mike, Susan, Virgie and Jack Wilson lived on Central Avenue near the first club.)

♦ The ditch on No. 9 at the old club was the downfall of many a good lady golfer back in the day. Florence Paxton and Irene Keiler, who played together frequently as they grew older, did not let it get the best of them. "Miss Florence" would say her ball always got over the ditch, "Because we would put it in the cart and carry it over!"

Vic Speck and Tommy Thomas have shot their age how many time

Golfing Record???

GOLFING ODDITY—It's a rare thing indeed when a golfer scores a hole-in-one . . . and it's unheard of for two golfers, playing in the same sixsome, to score holes-in-one on the very same hole. Unbelievable as it may seem, it happened at Paducah Country Club Thursday. Ed Hannan (left) and Jerry Page were the surprised golfers on the 140-yard No. 5 hole. Hannan used an eight iron and Page converted with a seven iron. The two were playing with Irving Bright, Bill Reed, Bill Usher and Gene Hipp.

—(Staff Photo by Larry Teckenbrock)

♦ Vic Speck, Jr., grew up in a house adjacent to No. 3 green at the Country Club Lane site. He said when he was a kid he used to take his golf shot over the swimming pool on No. 4, much to the chagrin of some of the members.

"I remember December 7 when Japan bombed Pearl Harbor and I was living near the old club. When the war was over, we all got in the car, a 1941 Dodge, and drove downtown. People were whooping and hollering because the boys were coming home, August of 1945! Funny how things like that are etched in your mind," Speck said. Ed Hough said that right after World War II, the club members rallied and were in high spirits for a long time.

♦ Speck and Thomas recalled the day when Patty Berg did an exhibition when she was sponsored by Wilson Staff. "She played nine holes and was very personable in her hey-day. She gave a clinic behind 9 green at the old club, maybe in 1955 or on the opening day of the newly re-built club in 1956," Speck said. "She was impressive and a great talker," Thomas chimed in.

♦ Jerry Page tells about a very unusual happening on the old course:

"I had already played 18 holes with these guys, but we went back out for nine more. We were playing a sixsome. Before we teed off around dusk on No. 6 at the old club, we decided to play for a dollar a hole. One of the guys hit his shot and Eddie Hannan, who was the eternal optimist, said he thought mine went in. I said 'I haven't hit yet!'

"I then hit my shot and Eddie ran to the pin and yelled, 'They are both in!'" We stopped right there and went into the clubhouse and started ordering drinks!

Harry Bolser, a correspondent for the *Louisville Courier-Journal* from Paducah, happened to be there and called this story into the newspaper. Bill Bone sent it in to *Golf Digest* and they said it happens 4,000 times per year, believe it or not.

"I haven't had a hole-in-one since," Page laughed.

♦ According to Mike Wilson, when Mr. Ed Michael lived on Highland Church Road near the present club, he had gamecocks; on occasion when they would get loose, they would come over to No. 10 and surprise the golfers. Mr. Michael was known as "the mayor of downtown Paducah" when he ran his hardware store.

♦ Moving to more recent times, Usher said when the board decided to make the move to the present site, his job was to find out if people would buy condominiums in Paducah. "I thought, condos in Paducah? They are out of their minds! Within two days I had my answer and it was yes!" Meadow Links condos built along No. 13, 14, and 15 were the end result of this informal survey.

♦ There is hardly a golfer at the club who has not had the pleasure of meeting "Ginger." This loving golden retriever belongs to Ronnie and Tootsie Brown. Ginger rides in the golf cart, greeting golfers along the way, never interfering with anyone's concentration, unless you're a squirrel, of course!

Ginger Brown, course mascot.

George H. Goodman and Paducah's Golf Legacy

George H. Goodman's name was synonymous with golf in Western Kentucky for many years. In the July 1947, program for the Irvin Cobb Championships held at Paxton Park, he was asked to write an article on "Paducah's Golfing Background."

The forward states: "There's no one who can talk with more authority on golf in this section than Mr. Goodman. Not only a member of the Kentucky Golf Association Board of Directors, but also a crack golfer himself, Mr. Goodman was Paducah's 'Mr. Golf' for many years."

Goodman provides his own account of the birth of golf and country clubs in this area, stating that he thought Western Kentucky's and Paducah's first golf course was the 9-hole facility established in Wallace Park around 1905.

Goodman wrote about The Country Club of Paducah. He said the following men took the lead in bringing golf to the Purchase: Joseph L. Friedman, Louis M. Rieke, Charles F. Rieke, George C. Wallace, George Langstaff, Charles K. Wheeler, J.C. Utterback, Muscoe Burnett, J. Dennis Mocquot, and Dr. John Q. Taylor.

"Mr. Charles K. Wheeler was the first president of the club and continued his interest in it until his death in 1933. This group was supported by a surprisingly large membership. The attractive Pines Road property was purchased and the golf course, tennis courts, swimming pool, and club house developed into what is today, the center of social life of Paducah," Goodman said.

Goodman mentioned that the Country Club of Paducah (1929) took a leading part in developing the inter-city matches between clubs "that has resulted in much pleasure to players and a fine, neighborly spirit in this area." He referred to the golf courses in Mayfield, Metropolis, Fulton, and Princeton.

It wasn't until the late 1950s that the club captured the cherished cup for the first time. Members of that team were Jimmy Green, Jim Rieke, Tommy Whittemore, Pete Smith, Bill Backus, Jack Piers, Bill Smith, and Vic Speck, who competed in the singles matches. Smith and Smith were winners of the three-ball division. Vard Curtis, Bob Grimm, and Bill Bone played for Paxton Park.

Although it is not related to the history of the Country Club of Paducah, it is interesting to note the other clubs that sprang up around Paducah. According to Goodman's writings:

The third course in Paducah was the little Blue Bird Inn course (1924), a 9-hole layout south of Lone Oak; the fourth was architect Perry Maxwell's Lake View course with Bermuda grass greens (the first 9 holes opened in 1926), which eventually became the 18-hole Rolling Hills Country Club.

The fifth course was located at Noble Park, a 3,200-yard sand green course later changed to grass. It opened in 1927 and was open to the public. The next course established in 1940 was Paxton Park, the year Lake View Club closed. At that time, Goodman said that future development possibilities included a clubhouse, tennis courts, and a swimming pool, but today Paxton Park remains an 18-hole public golf course without tennis and swimming.

George Goodman won numerous championships at the Country Club of Paducah. George Sullivan still has many handsome sterling silver trophies that were presented to his grandfather as early as 1920.

Although Goodman was one of the earliest Country Club members, he played golf regularly at Paxton Park for many years. His family's home was located at the top of the hill (Goodman Hill) on the course perimeter where it stands today.

Engaged in his favorite pastime, Irvin Cobb, at right, is seated with his host, Will J. Gilbert, center, and George H. Goodman in this photo lent by Gilbert, retired Paducah druggist and longtime friend of Cobb. Mrs. Gilbert—the former "Bainie" Clark, lineal descendant of Paducah's founder, William Clark — is standing behind her husband.

Tommy Thomas remembers Mr. Goodman well. "I played at Paxton Park as a teenager before my parents joined the country club in 1957. That's where I would see Mr. Goodman."

"After I finished playing on several occasions, Mr. Goodman would say, 'Come on and play home with me.' We would play No. 1 and 2 (his house was on the side of the hill beside No. 2) and we'd stop there if he weren't playing well, but if he were playing well, we'd sometimes play 3, 4, and 5, and then he would walk home. When he played back then, he would walk and carry about five clubs in his hand. We probably did that 15-20 times in the late fifties," Thomas said.

George Sullivan has several stories to share about his grandfather. "My grandfather and Will Gilbert were very good friends. Will was a piano player and liked to gamble at the Elks. They played golf together as young men and took trips together. My grandfather started in the newspaper business as a paper boy for the *News Democrat* and eventually sold it to Mr. Paxton. He then got into the whiskey business, but when prohibition came along, he stopped, took the money he had made, and bought bank stock and hundreds of acres of land."

Mr. Goodman's daughter was Jane Goodman Sullivan. The Sullivans were a family of champions at the Country Club of Paducah. Lee Sullivan, Betty Sullivan Arterburn, Nancy Sullivan, and younger brother, Hal, were tennis stars for decades, shining city-wide and at the club, following in their mother's footsteps. (*See chapter on tennis.*) Their father, Harold, was a past president and golfer. Inheriting his grandfather's love of golf, George was a top junior golfer at the club and a past club champion.

Mr. Goodman and his family are among the generations of families who play an important role in the history of the club.

Ladies' Golf

Ladies' golf can be competitive and challenging, but also enjoyable. Most golfers who have played the game for years will say they would never voluntarily give up the game they love.

When ladies step on the course, chores are forgotten, obligations fly out the window, and the camaraderie they share with fellow golfers overtakes everything else for the next few hours. Ladies golf at the Country Club of Paducah is certainly no exception.

It has been said that the official birth of Ladies Day golf at the club was August 12, 1950, when Club President William F. Paxton called on Olivia Cave to organize the ladies for a weekly golf day to increase usage of the club.

Olivia and fellow golfer Libby Piers took Paxton's challenge seriously and proceeded to enthusiastically recruit a large number of players. Ironically, several years later some of the men at the club thought ladies' play needed to be restricted on the often crowded 9-hole course. The hours of play may have been restricted, but the golfers' spirits remained high.

Nineteen thirty-six is a more accurate date for the founding of golf for ladies at the Country Club of Paducah. A "Ladies Golf Club" was organized that year by a small group of interested players who arranged weekly games to be followed by luncheon at the Paducah Country Club, according to an article that ran in the local newspaper four years later. The story said the group had grown from eight or nine golfers to approximately 30 ladies.

"The luncheons are open to non-playing members of the Country Club, and out of these weekly affairs has evolved a Ladies' Day which continues through the winter months. Entertainment is informal, consisting of sewing, cards, badminton, ping pong, and any other games the members care to play," the story noted.

Ladies Day in 1938 ended with a photo on the club steps. Pictured on the front row are Dorothy Helson and Club Champion Frances Taylor, Mrs. Edwin J. Paxton, Miriam Weile, Jane Cave, and Helen Reed. Others pictured are Nell Jones, Sis Michael, Mary Jane Turner, Thelma Bailey, Ann Rust, Blanche Acree, Christine Speck, Helen Sights, Virginia Taylor, Eugenie Green, Nancy Kern, Terry Martin, Laura Carney, Lucille McMurry, Mabel Beven, and Edith Shelbourne. (The source did not provide all names.)

Ladies' Golf Club Members Are Shown At Formal Conclusion Of Season Tuesday

MEMBERS OF THE LADIES' Golf Club, Herbert Wallerstein, golf chairman, Robert J. Brown, professional, and R. V. Green, Country Club president, are shown after their weekly luncheon Tuesday during which tournament awards were presented. Reading from left to right the picture includes: First row, Mr. Waller-stein, Mrs. Edwin J. Paxton, president of the Ladies' Golf Club, Mr. Brown, Miss Betty Carney and Mr. Green; second row, Mrs. Edwin J. Paxton, Jr., runner-up; Mrs. Roy Shelbourne, Mrs. Louis List, Mrs. I. H. Strickland and Mrs. Parke Taylor, tournament winner; third row, Mrs. Loren Jones, Mrs. Leon Higdon, Miss Mary Jane Carney, Miss Sara Kathryn Fergerson, Mrs. Ed Cave, Mrs. Roscoe Reed and Mrs. Edwin B. Michael; at right, between third and fourth rows, Mrs. John Martin and Mrs. R. V. Green; fourth row, Mrs. Edward R. Miller, Mrs. Warren Sights, Mrs. Lanson Ditto, Mrs. Melvin Cornillaud, Mrs. James W. Kern, Mrs. William F. McMurry and Mrs. James Helson, Metropolis; top row, Mrs. Gayle Taylor.

Those attending were Golf Chairman Herbert Wallerstein; Club Pro R.J. Brown; Club President R.V. Green, and the following ladies: Miss Betty Carney, Mrs. Parke Taylor, Mrs. Loren Jones, Mrs. Ed Cave, Mrs. Roscoe Reed, Mrs. Edwin Michael, Mrs. John Martin, Mrs. R.V. Green, Mrs. Edward Miller, Mrs. Warren Sights, Mrs. Lanson Ditto, Mrs. Melvin Cornillaud, Mrs. William McMurry, Mrs. James Helson, and Mrs. Gayle Taylor.

A year earlier, Mrs. J.N. Bailey, Mrs. R.H. Rust, Mrs. J.B. Acree, Mrs. J.W. Kern, Mrs. Ramsey Martin, Mrs. C.J. Carney were also in a golf photo with many of those listed in the 1939 story. Mrs. Edwin J. Paxton, Sr., was president of the Ladies Golf Group in 1939.

Mrs. Parke Taylor's name was etched on many trophies in those days. Some of her competitors were Mrs. Paxton, Mrs. Reed, and Miss Mildred Watkins.

In other coverage in 1939, Marian Miley was pictured in her golf attire with several young gentlemen, including Ed Cave. Miss Betty Carney was the president in 1940. Mrs. MildredWatkins Washburn and Jane Shelbourne were in charge of ladies golf in 1943.

Like most activities around town, golf at club took a back seat during World War II. It was not until June of 1945 that Ladies' Day matches resumed on Tuesdays. "Any score turned in by noon will be eligible for the variety of prizes which are awarded weekly. Prizes are announced at the Ladies' Day luncheon which is served each Tuesday at the noon hour," one clipping noted. Mrs. S.R. Epperson and Mrs. E.B. Fergerson were hostesses that week. Mrs. H.E. Wolfe was in charge of ladies' activities at the club.

Thanks to the scrapbooks of Sara Kathryn Fergerson from the thirties and forties, many accounts of ladies' golf and accompanying social activities were verified.

Attending a Ladies' Golf Club luncheon at the club in 1939 were Mrs. E.C. Walter of Mayfield (grandmother of the late Dr. Frank Kolb), Mrs. Leon Higdon, Mrs. E.B. Michael, Mrs. R.V. Green, Miss Fergerson, Miss Mary Wheeler, Miss Bertha Wheeler, and a host of others.

Also, during the summer of 1939, club ladies met players from Mayfield and Fulton here and at their respective clubs. Mrs. Loren Jones was the winner of the handicap tournament, and Mrs. Parke Taylor and Mrs. Edwin J. Paxton, Jr., co-winners of the ringer tournament.

Ladies golf received extensive coverage in the newspaper almost every week. One such article informed the readers that Mrs. Leon Higdon and Miss Sara Kathryn Fergerson served as hostesses for a golf luncheon with non-golfers also invited.

Golf at the club continued to flourish.

Libby Piers was the Ladies Golf Chairman in 1950 and Marian Widener in 1951.

In 1956, the *Sun-Democrat* ran a photo of Mary Russell decked out in long bermudas and spectator-style golf shoes in front of the clubhouse on Country Club Drive. She was watching Vic Speck, Jr., tee off along with Jim Dunn, Tommy Whittemore, Sr., and Sam Livingston. Also pictured on No. 1 tee were Mrs. Burt Robbins, Mrs. Don McClure, Mrs. Earl Basham, and Mrs. Lee Russell.

Pat Sabel

Mirian Widener

In 1957, players from the club who entered the annual *Sun-Democrat* Women's City Championship, as it was called then, included Marian Widener, the winner in 1954 when the first tournament was held; Pat Sabel, Emma Bell, Nell Basham, Virgie Wilson, Betty Paxton, Jane Sullivan, Florence Paxton, Josie Whittemore, and Mary Martin.

Pat Sabel was crowned the City Medal Champion (*Sun-Democrat*) in 1960 with a three-day total of 260, according to a newspaper account. A photo with all winners and their silver awards included Country Club of Paducah members Wanda Mullinax, Jesse Gilbert, Florence Paxton, Mamie Kirchoff, Sue Haley, Alice Fisher, Mary Rose Greenberg, Virgie Wilson, Nell Florence, and Emma Bell.

Sabel played from the men's tees, mainly with her friend Carl Pfanstiel when they were young. By all accounts, no one at the club or in Paducah was a better woman player than Pat Sabel at that time.

In 1961, the Paducah Country Club flight winners and runners-up were: Marie McClure, Bobbie Underwood, Josie Whittemore, Virgie Wilson, Margaret Titsworth, Kitty Shadle, Sue Hely, Sue Haley, Mamie Kirchoff, Barbara Hough, Do Price, Jo Boeckman, Rebecca Anderson, Mary Rose Greenberg, Nell Basham, Jerry Tilley and Polly Helsley. Pro Eddie Verplanke was honored at the party.

The names of Nancy Fowler and Marilyn Whedon are mentioned as very good young players in the late 1950s and early '60s.

Country Club Ladies Close 1940 Golf Season

LADIES of the Paducah Country Club brought to a successful close Tuesday their 1940 golf program. Here they are pictured with R. J. Brown, club professional, who has developed golf interest among the ladies to a high degree. In the picture from left to right, bottom row: Brown, Mrs. Edwin J. Paxton, Miss Mildred Watkins, Miss Mary Jane Carney, Mrs. Dick Miller; second row: Mrs. E. W. Jackson, Mrs. Roy Shelbourne, Mrs. Roscoe Reed, Mrs. William Carson, Mrs. Leon Higdon; third row: Mrs. Loren Jones, Mrs. Parke Taylor, Mrs. Prewitt Lackey, Mrs. Gayle Taylor, Miss Sara Kathryn Fergerson; fourth row: Mrs. Melvin Cornillaud, Mrs. Eloise Richardson, Mrs. Ewing Dunn, Mrs. Joe Walker, Mrs. John Martin, Mrs. Vic Speck; back row: Mrs. Leo Keiler, Mrs. William Daley, Mrs. C. J. Carney and Mrs. Glenn B. Donoho.

Florence Paxton swings her way to victory.

WEDNESDAY, OCTOBER 18, 1967 SUN-DEMOCRAT, PADUCAH, KY.

COUNTRY CLUB WINNERS—Winners of the Paducah Country Club ladies' fall handicap golf tournament pose with prizes following the tournament Tuesday. From left to right are (back row) Mary Martin, second-flight runnerup; Pinky Dodson, third-flight handicap winner; Jeanette Watt, second-flight runnerup; Rose Sparr, third-flight runn up; (seated) Betty Pullekines, second-flig medalist; Sue Hely, first-flight medali Virgie Wilson, first-flight runnerup; Mary Renfro, third-flight medalist; Ora Brooks, third flight runnerup and Mamie Kirchhoff, second-flight handicap winner.

961 THE PADUCAH SUN-DEMOCRAT

CC TOURNAMENT WINNERS—These ladies won titles in club tournaments at the Paducah Country Club this season and were awarded special prizes at a party in their honor Tuesday. The winners include, front row, left to right: Marie McClure, Bobbie Underwood, Josie Whittemore, Virgie Wilson, Margaret Titsworth and Kitty Shadle. Second row: Sue Hely, Sue Haley, Mamie Kirchhoff and Barbara Hough. Back row: Do Price, Jo Boeckman, Rebecca Anderson, Mary Rose Greenberg, Nell Basham, Jerry Tilley and Polly Helsley. The ladies were awarded their gifts by club pro Eddie Verplanke, who also was honored at the party.

Mary Jane Harris began her long run of tournament titles both at the Country Club of Paducah and at other courses in the mid-1960s. (The last win for Mary Jane came in 2011 when she was presented the 9-hole flight trophy; she was past 90 years of age.) Josie Whittemore and Ginny Hougland appeared in one of many clippings with her as flight winners. In a 1967 photo, Harris was the opening day medalist with Sue Hely winning the first flight. Hely was also the fall handicap tournament medalist.

Other new faces in the crowd of golfers playing on Ladies Day at the club were Pinky Dodson, Jeanette Watt, Rose Sparr, Betty Pullekines, Mary Renfro, and Ora Brooks. In October of 1970, Judy Green, Helen Garrett, Myrna Chumley, Julia Dyer, Jean Penrod, and Lorri Dassing were among the winners in the fall tournament.

In a "battle of the girls named Sue," Sue Haley topped Sue Hely in the Spring Handicap Tournament. The *Sun-Democrat* said, "Mrs. Hely copped a silver prize for opening day medalist for the 36-hole event."

Joann Longton, known for her excellent short game, entered the champions' circle by the 1970s, winning the club championship in 1971 and 1975, 1982-83, and contending in the *Sun-Democrat*. Sylvia Davis, Gretchen Dallam, Maggie Igert, Dot Ely, Ann Bright and Frances Hougland won flight prizes in 1973.

Longton played golf at the club until she approached age 90.

Barbaranelle Paxton

1975

Country Club golf winners

Award winners during ladies' day play at the Paducah Country Club Tuesday are (front row from left) Ginny Hougland, third flight medalist; JoAnn Longton, first flight medalist; Carol Farrington, second flight medalist, and Donna Trogolo, fourth flight medalist. On the second row (from left) are Jessie Gilbert, second flight runnerup; Doris Gregory, fourth flight runnerup; Alice Fisher, first flight runnerup; Ann Bright, third flight runnerup, and Sue Fendley, most improved golfer. On the third row (from left) are Sylvia Danes, ringer; Judy Earhart, third flight handicap runnerup; Julia Dyer, third flight handicap runnerup, and Lori Dassing, first flight runnerup.

The American Cancer Society team playing at Doral: Denise Seltzer, Kristie Wilson, Vicki Fort, and Donna Trogolo.

Sue Fendley takes a practice swing.

Wanda Mullinax won her first of five club championship in 1987 with the last coming in 1997. She was competing against Alice Fisher, Donna Trogolo, Vicki Fort, and Joann Longton during the tournaments in the late eighties.

In 1989, the Ladies Golf Association hosted its first annual "Nips 'n Nibbles" Christmas party for lady golfers and their guests, now a tradition.

In 1988 and 1990, the team of Donna Trogolo, Denise Seltzer, Kristie Wilson, and Vicki Fort advanced to the National American Cancer Society Scramble held at Doral Country Club in Miami, Florida, finishing second in Division II in 1988 and sixth the next time. The foursome put Paducah on the map when they sang "You Can't Pooh-Pooh Paducah!" at the resort hotel.

In 1990, the sports season kicked off with Clara Weitlauf carding an eagle on No. 1—it was Friday the 13th, but a lucky day for Clara. Clara's lovely manner and smiling face were equaled by her love of golf and playing with friends.

A new bed of azaleas and dogwoods behind No. 12 green was established in memory of Gretchen Oelschlaeger Dallam by her garden club friends. The monument is still there and brings to mind a spirited, vivacious LGA member who enjoyed the game.

(All of the club champions who could be identified through newspaper clippings, plaques, and board minutes are listed in this chapter. Other tournament winners are occasionally mentioned, although the list is incomplete.)

A few of those from "modern" times include Monica Kim, who resided on No. 8 ladies' tee box for many years, and was a four-time champion starting in 1992.

Louella Archer and Assistant Pro Bryan Schumate.

On the links in 1994, Sue Fendley was still winning honors as she teamed with Willadean Myers and won the Member-Guest title. Newcomer Gen Tinkey won the Ladies Spring Golf Tournament in 1995 and in 1996. Margaret Caksackkar won her first of three club championship in 1998.

By 2003, Louella (Archer) Thomas captured her first of eight titles. Her 2013 win was over Lisa Kupper in a hard-fought tournament.

Dr. Kim Birch won the 2015 and 2016 club championships, but not without pressure from challengers Pam Baird, Pam Trimble, Vicki Hunkler, Louella Archer, Lisa Kupper, Joyce Vasseur, and Margaret Caksackkar.

Kim Birch and Tommy Thomas, 2015 winners, with Jason Stilley.

Kim Birch (left), club champion, and Pam Baird, runner-up.

Lady Aces

Many club members have recorded holes-in-one over the years, but Donna Trogolo's story of her aces is unique. Not only has she had five, but three of them occurred on the same day of the year—July 16.

"I had one in 1990 on No. 14 at the country club, and one on July 16 in 1997 on No. 8 at Paxton Park, and the third one was at the club in 2004 on July 16," Donna said.

It's amazing enough that they all happened on the same month and day, but they were seven years apart on the seventh month. "My other two were on June 3, 1989, on No. 12 at the country club, and on July 4, Hole No. 2, at the club. The last two dates add up to seven!"

Doris Gregory recorded a hole-in-one on Ladies Day, April 28, 1981, on No. 12. It was played from 125 yards, making it possible that the red tees were on the upper tee box. Barbara Grimes, Gloria Livingston, and Jane Jones witnessed the ace.

On April 18, 1989, Vicki Fort's Ladies Day group was ready to head to the clubhouse because it was raining. As they approached No. 14 tee, she urged them to just play one more hole—a wise choice on Fort's part since her shot took one bounce and went in the hole! The foursome was then forced to finish the round in the rain to make the ace "legal."

Virgie Wilson created some fireworks of her own when she had a hole-in-one on No. 14 on the 4th of July 1990. Now in her mid-90s, Virgie "preserved" the aces of many friends with her treasured needlepoint pieces.

During the 1992 summer season, Wanda Mullinax had a hole-in-one on No. 12, and Gretchen Dallam carded an ace on No. 6, while Margaret Rushing aced No. 6.

In 1994, Peggy Conyer made a hole-in-one on No. 2, and Pat Habacker had a one on No. 2 in 1996.

Clara Weitlauf had an ace on No. 12 in 2000; Margaret Rushing on No. 14 in 2003, Glenda Farmer on No. 2 in 2003; Pam Trimble on No. 14 in 2004; Mary Jane Park on No. 14 in 2006; Lisa Kupper on No. 14 in 2007; Louella Archer on No. 6 in 2012; and Cindy Wyatt on No. 12 in 2015, while playing with Anita Kerr.

More ladies have had holes-in-one on the course, but these were made on official Ladies' Days.

No. 13 looking back at the forward tee.

Presidents of the LGA From 1950-2017

1950	Libby Piers	1976	Lucinda Rudd
1951	Marian Widener	1977	Jean Penrod
1952	Lillian Lee	1978	Norma Moran
1953	Lucy Weil	1979	Pat Cvengros
1954	Katie Renick	1980	Myrna Chumley
1955	Sue Russell	1981	Phyllis Epstein
1956	Nell Basham	1982	Donna Trogolo
1957	Emma Bell	1983	Juanita Hester
1958	Lib Robbins	1984-85	Alice Fisher
1959	Marian Widener	1986-87	Pat Cvengros
1960	Emma Bell	1988-89	Norma Moran
1961	Nell Basham	1990	Vicki Fort
1962	Margaret Titsworth	1991	Margaret Caksackkar
1963	Virgie Wilson	1992	Sally Davis
1964	Mary Jane Harris	1993-94	Gretchen Dallam
1965	Sue Haley	1995-96	Wanda Mullinax
1966	Nell Koss	1997-98	Margaret Rushing
1967	Phoebe Hartline	1999-00	Maggie Bailey
1968	Ruby Myre	2001-02	Glenda Farmer
1969	Mary Martin	2003-06	Kristie Wilson
1970	Pinky Dotson	2007-08	Carolyn Mayo
1971	Willa Pedley	2009-10	Betty Lippert
1972	JoAnn Longton	2011-12	Lisa Kupper
1973	Sue Fendley	2013-14	Cindy Wyatt
1974	Helen Garrett	2015-16	Vicki Hunkler
1975	Judy Green	2017	Betty Lippert

The Ladies Club Champions From 1960-2016

(Names are listed as they were the years they won.)

1960	Nell Basham	1979	Mary Jane Alford	1998	Margaret Caksackkar
1961	Nell Basham	1980	Mary Jane Park	1999	Clara Weitlauf
1962	Nell Basham	1981	Mary Jane Park	2000	Renee Allen
1963	Margaret Titsworth	1982	JoAnn Longton	2001	Donna Trogolo
1964	Mary Jane Harris	1983	JoAnn Longton	2002	Margaret Caksackkar
1965	Mary Jane Harris	1984	Clara Weitlauf	2003	Louella Thomas
1966	Mary Jane Harris	1985	Alice Fisher	2004	Louella Thomas
1967	Sue Fendley	1986	Vicki Fort	2005	Margaret Caksackkar
1968	Mary Jane Harris	1987	Wanda Mullinax	2006	Louella Archer
1969	Mary Jane Harris	1988	Wanda Mullinax	2007	Louella Archer
1970	Mary Jane Harris	1989	Alice Fisher	2008	Roberta Sentell
1971	JoAnn Longton	1990	Wanda Mullinax	2009	Vicki Hunkler
1972	Mary Jane Alford	1991	Donna Trogolo	2010	Louella Archer
1973	Alice Fisher	1992	Monica Kim	2011	Louella Archer
1974	Alice Fisher	1993	Monica Kim	2012	Pam Trimble
1975	JoAnn Longton	1994	Monica Kim	2013	Louella Archer
1976	Mary Jane Alford	1995	Wanda Mullinax	2014	Louella Archer
1977	Mary Jane Alford	1996	Monica Kim	2015	Kim Birch
1978	Alice Fisher	1997	Wanda Mullinax	2016	Kim Birch

The Ladies Club Champions

Although many golf records at the club prior to the 1950s were destroyed, newspaper clippings do verify that one of the first club champions was Frances Hale Taylor in 1936, 1938 and 1939.

In 1939, Mrs. Taylor was presented her silver trophy by the club professional, Robert J. Brown, and the president, R.V. Green. Herbert L. Wallerstein was the golf chairman at the time. Mrs. Edwin J. Paxton, Jr., was the runner-up, and Mrs. Edwin J. Paxton, Sr., was the ladies group president, followed by Miss Betty Carney.

In the early days, the club champions received the Governors' Cup on Labor Day. In the fall of 1940, the newspaper ran a photo with the club professional, "who has developed golf interest among the ladies to a high degree," the story said.

The 1940 Ladies' Club Champion was Mildred Watkins (mother of Gary Gregory and Burton Washburn).

Miss Watkins defeated Mrs. Roscoe Reed in the finals of the 1940 Club Championship with a score of 38 on the 9-hole course. Mrs. Edwin J. Paxton and Mrs. Warren Sights tied for second with a 41. The handicap tournament was won by Mrs. Sights over Mrs. T.A. Paxton. Mrs. Florence Paxton was the champion in 1941 and possibly 1946-48; Mrs. Floyd Sperry in 1943.

Ladies Club Champions in the 1940s and 1950s were Lillian Lee in 1949 and 1951, 1954-55, 1957; Florence Mathis in 1950; Earline Crisp in 1952; Marian Widener in 1953, 1956, 1959; and Betty Paxton in 1958.

From 1964 to 1982, Mary Jane Harris prevailed as a tournament winner.

Also listed as Park and Alford, Harris captured twelve Country Club of Paducah Ladies Club Championships, more than any other golfer as of 2016. Only Louella Archer has gained on that number in recent years with her eight titles.

Those who played with or against Mary Jane testify that she was the best putter and the fiercest competitor at both club courses. She studied the game, practiced continuously, and preferred walking with umbrella in hand. One summer day in 1986, she made the turn after carding only nine putts on the front side. She was a remarkable competitor.

Below, one of the first club champions, Frances Hale Taylor, is presented a trophy by President R.V. Green (left) and Roy Shelbourne.

Club President Bill Paxton presents Earline Crisp the silver award for her 1952 Club Championship win; other ladies received flight prizes on Labor Day weekend.

Alice "Snookie" Fisher could have been the last champion on the old 9-hole course if that final tournament was held in 1978; otherwise, the last one was Mary Jane in 1979.

Roberta Sentel

In a 2002 club newsletter, Pro Todd Trimble congratulated his student, Roberta Sentel, a club member who resides in Illinois, for winning the Paducah Sun. Sentel also won the Illinois Women's Senior State Amateur.

"Our club has a very rich heritage of women's golf," he commented.

Top: The LGA gathered outside the pro shop in the late 1980s. Bottom: A group of past club champions (from left) are Mary Jane Park, Nell Basham, JoAnn Longton, Sue Fendley, Lillian Lee, Florence Paxton, Clara Weitlauf, and Alice Fisher.

Double Duty... Presidents and Champions

Eleven ladies at the club were both Club Champion and President of the Ladies Golf Association in their day. This information is based on the available written records from 1939 with a few years missing. They are as follows:

- Florence Paxton, president in 1939 and champion in 1941 and possibly 1946-48.
- Lillian Lee, president in 1952 and champion in 1949, 1950, 1951, 1954, 1955, and 1957.
- Marian Widener, president in 1951 and 1959 and champion in 1953, 1956, and 1959.
- Sue Fendley, president in 1973 and champion in 1967.
- Mary Jane Harris (Park), president in 1964 and champion in 1964-66, 1968-70, 1972, 1976-77, 1979-81.
- Joann Longton, president in 1975, and champion in 1971, 1975, 1982, and 1983.
- Donna Trogolo, president in 1982, and champion in 1991 and 2001.
- Alice Fisher, president in 1984-85, and champion in 1973-74, 1978, 1985, 1989.
- Vicki (Fort) Hunkler, president in 1990, 2015-16, and champion in 1986 and 2009.
- Margaret Caksackkar, president in 1991, and champion in 1998, 2002, 2005.
- Wanda Mullinax (Williams), president in 1995-96, and champion in 1987-88, 1990, 1995, 1997.

Top: Pat Cvengros and JoAnn Longton (left) pause on a John Deere in 2012 near No. 9 green.
Bottom: Pam Trimble putts on No. 18 in the club championship.

Country Club Ladies Have a Place in "The Sun"

Club members, and daughters of club members, who have won the Sun-Democrat Ladies Tournament, once known as the City Championship, and now called the Paducah Sun-Florence Paxton Memorial, are as follows (1954-2016):

1954	Marian Widener
1955	Lillian Lee
1960	Pat Sabel
1962	Pat Sabel
1964	Mary Jane Harris
1965	Mary Jane Harris
1967	Mary Jane Harris
1968	Wanda Mullinax
1969	Alice Fisher
1970	Mary Jane Harris
1972	Mary Jane Harris
1973	Mary Jane Harris
1978	Mary Jane Harris
1979	Alice Fisher
1985	Wanda Mullinax
1986	Mary Jane Park *(record 8 wins)*
1989	Vicki Fort
1994	Monica Kim
2002	Roberta Sentel
2013	Sydney Trimble
2014	Teri Doss
2015	Teri Doss
2016	Sydney Trimble Kelly

The Wooldridge Cup Matches

Country Club Ladies Win Eight Titles as of 2016

The first Wooldridge Cup Matches for the ladies were held in the fall of 2000 at the Country Club of Paducah. The matches were the brainchild of Country Club member Kristie Wilson and Rolling Hills member Nancy Ragland in an effort to promote camaraderie and a friendly competition among the local club lady golfers.

It was decided that the Country Club of Paducah, Rolling Hills, Silos, and Paxton Park would be represented by eight-person teams.

The naming of the competition has a history as well. "Pat Sabel Wooldridge was a wonderful individual and an accomplished athlete and competitor," Wilson said. "Pat was a loved and respected member of the local golf community."

After she passed away in January of 2000, Wilson suggested that the newly created Cup Matches bear Pat's name. It was unanimously accepted by those who participated in the inaugural event held later that year.

Wooldridge's daughter, Kathleen, and her sister, Ginger Usher, have attended closing ceremonies from time to time. Wooldridge is also the sister of Peggy Paxton.

The Country Club of Paducah team finished third that inaugural year with Kris Straub, Louella Archer, Mindy Whitworth, Maggie Bailey, Joann Longton, Gen Tinkey, Sue Fendley, Kristie Wilson, and Clara Weitlauf on the first team.

Wilson served as the team captain from 2000 to 2007. Carolyn Mayo was the 2008 captain and Margaret Caksackkar has worn the captain's hat since 2009. The captain is devoted to putting together the best team possible, promoting team spirit, even selecting the outfits.

Paxton Park and Rolling Hills have each won four times; Silos, once; and the Country Club eight in 2008 and 2010 through 2016.

The winning 2016 Cup Match players were Kim Birch, Pam Trimble, Lisa Kupper, Pam Baird, Vicki Hunkler, Margaret Cacksakkar, Leann Stilley, Joyce Vasseur, and Kristie Wilson. Donna Trogolo served as co-captain assisted by Anita Kerr and Cindy Wyatt.

"I feel like the matches have advanced women's golf in Paducah. The golfers from the clubs have come to know each other better and developed new friendships because of it. And that's what it's all about," Wilson concluded.

Right: Kristie Wilson (right), first Cup Team captain, with Pam Trimble.

Donna Trogolo and Margaret Caksackkar with the 2016 trophy. Members and alternates on the winning team were (from left, kneeling) Lisa Kupper, Donna Trogolo, Pam Trimble, Caksackkar, (from left, standing) Pro Jason Stilley, Leann Stilley, Pam Baird, Anita Kerr, Louella Archer, Joyce Vasseur, Kim Birch, Kristie Wilson, Vicki Hunkler, and Cindy Wyatt.

Below: Pam Baird lofts the 2015 Cup Match trophy in the club bar.

Winning at Paxton Park in 2014; celebrating at the club afterwards.

Margaret Caksackkar and Roberta Sentel in 2011.

The 2013 team on the deck.

Sporting the latest golf fashion in 2012 at the club.

The 2009 Ladies Cup Team members on their own course; Captain Carolyn Mayo with Kathleen W. Overlin, daughter of Pat Wooldridge.

Part of the team at Silo's Country Club.

Left: Around 1996, Peggy Paxton, Pat Cvengros, Barbara Hough, Kristie Wilson, and Clara Weitlauf.

Below: A few unnamed Wizard of Oz fans.

Front row, from left, Donna Trogolo, Betty Lippert, Cathy Trampe, Vicki Hunkler; middle row, from left, Wanda Williams, Pat Gourieux, Kim Birch; back row, from left, Cindy Wyatt, Louella Archer, Anita Kerr, and Margaret Caksackkar at the 2015 Witches Scramble on the pro shop steps.

The social side of golf at the Ladies' Member-Guest Tournaments. Clockwise from right: Ginger Usher, Mary Jane Park, and Jane Ann Nall; Guest Carol Robertson and Cindy Wyatt; Guest Terry Sorrell and Pat Gourieux at the beach-themed 2016 Member-Guest; Pat Habacker and Wanda Mullinax; Renee Allen and Cindy Wyatt; Pat Cvengros and Donna Russell.

Decked out in Christmas sweaters in 1994 are JoAnn Longton, Donna Kay Carlson, Donna Trogolo, and Gretchen Dallam.

Clara Weitlauf and Sue Fendley celebrate the season at another LGA holiday party.

Beverly Bradley and Pat Gourieux at a Christmas party in 2015.

Mary Lou Hunt was a fun-loving member of the LGA.

Donna Kay Carlson with Sara Chumbler at a luncheon after golf.

On their carts and ready to play are Mamie Kirchoff, Sylvia Davis, Mary Louise Conn, and Norma Sloan.

LGA members and friends outside the pro shop.

Virgie Wilson, JoAnn Longton, and Kris Straub work at the Calcutta.

Monica Kim (center, middle row) after one of her four club championship wins in the early 1990s.

Pat Wooldridge, Peggy Conyer, guest, and Mary Jane Park.

Doris Gregory, Gloria Livingston, Phyllis Epstein, Carol Farrington, Etta McAbrey, and Shirley Metzger.

Some of the golfers pictured are Velma "Ozie" Bohle, Margaret Caksackkar, Maggie Bailey, Lorene Rhear, and Mary Jane Park.

Left: Norma Moran, Lorene Rhear, Olivia Cave, Gloria Livingston, Doris Gregory.

Below left: Jessie Gilbert and Virgie Wilson.

Below right: Lady golfers in the pro shop when it was downstairs in the clubhouse.

The Memorial Golf Tournament

The Memorial, formerly called The Sue Haley Invitational, is a two-lady tournament that honors the memory of those Ladies Golf Association members who have passed away, including Sue Haley who was the tournament's namesake.

After Haley passed away, her husband, Dr. Burton Haley, donated funds for the construction of the rain shelter and restroom near No. 6 green and another behind No. 12. Juanita Hester, representing the LGA at the dedication ceremonies in 1982, commented, "We all loved Sue and will miss her. We are grateful she remembered us. We will think of her each time we pass these structures."

The "Sue Haley" as it was affectionately called, was her fellow golfers' way of ensuring that Sue's generosity and friendship would not be forgotten.

2015 winners Sydney and Pam Trimble.

The annual tournament was established that year and is hosted by the Country Club of Paducah's Ladies Golf Association in June. It attracts golfers from Western Kentucky, West Tennessee, Southern Illinois, and Southeast Missouri and draws a field of 46-52 teams.

Golfers take this golden opportunity to play the club's Robert Trent Jones course, which is considered by many the best in the region. Creative table decorations, a scrumptious luncheon, prizes, and tee gifts are all part of the attraction.

A 61 was shot by the Koch-Jarrett team in 2004, which is the lowest score current players remember. Three mother-daughter team have won: Vicki Vowell McLeary and Betty Vowell, Vicki and Mikki McLeary, and Pam and Sydney Trimble.

Dedication Ceremony for the Sue Haley shelter, June 8, 1982.

Winners of the Memorial Golf Tournament 1982-2016

Year	Winners	Year	Winners
1982	Virginia Davis–Nancy Nickel	2000	Vicki McLeary–Mikki McLeary
1983	Mary Jane Park–Lisa Bremer	2001	Vicki McLeary–Betty Vowell
1984	Faye Brundidge–Linda Brann	2002	Vicki McLeary–Mikki McLeary
1985	Faye Brundidge–Linda Brann	2003	Rained out
1986	Mary Bain–Mary Jane Park	2004	Shanti Koch–Lisa Jarrett
1987	Faye Brundidge–Linda Brann	2005	Vicki McLeary–Betty Vowell
1988	Vicki McLeary–Betty Vowell	2006	Brenda Rendleman–Pat Lewis
1989	Faye Brundidge–Linda Brann	2007	Jessica Castleman–Mary Lee Hendricks
1990	Vicki McLeary–Betty Vowell	2008	Jessica Castleman–Mary Lee Hendricks
1991	Mary Bain–Mary Jane Park	2009	Teresa Conyer–Melissa Tabor
1992	Faye Brundidge–Linda Brann	2010	Vicki McLeary–Mikki McLeary
1993	Mary Bain–Mary Jane Park	2011	Kim Birch–Sarah Haas
1994	Faye Brundidge–Linda Brann	2012	Mary Lee Cooper–Caroline Cash
1995	Vicki McLeary–Mikki McLeary	2013	Mary Lee Cooper–Emma Robinson
1996	Vicki McLeary–Mikki McLeary	2014	Cancelled due to course conditions
1997	Vicki McLeary–Mikki McLeary	2015	Pam Trimble–Sydney Trimble
1998	Vicki McLeary–Mikki McLeary	2016	Mindy Hargrove–Debbie Cooper
1999	Wanda Brown–Mary Bain		

History of Couples Golf

Couples golf was held on Friday evenings at the Country Club of Paducah and called "Twilight Golf" in the 1960s and probably earlier. When the club moved to the present site, couples continued to play in large numbers in the 1980s and 1990s.

"We had so much fun back then," said Wanda Mullinax. "Charles and I shared lots of memories with that group back in the day. We all looked forward to Friday nights."

Some of the couples who played at this course starting in the eighties were Joann and Bill Longton, Jack and Virgie Wilson, Pheobe and Don Hartline, Juanita and Jack Hester, Mary Lou and Hilary Hunt, Dave and Barbara Hutchison, Ed and Barbara Hough, Pat and Pat Cvengros, Doris and Royce Gregory, Jessie and Harold Gilbert, Gene and "Snookie" Fisher, Lynn and Pat Habacker, Clara and Jack Weitlauf, and Pat Wooldridge and Ken Schuppert.

Bob Wooldridge, Paul and Mary Martin.

Above: Gloria and Harry Livingston in the 1970s at the nine-hole course.

Doris Robertson and Harold Gilbert

Ed and Gerry Tilley

The Governor and His Lady was a fun tournament in 1979. Among the couples who played are (from left) Jean and John Penrod; Donna Kay and Ray Carlson; Ed and Mai Davis; and Dot and Bob Ely.

In the 1990s, some of the couples enjoying twilight golf according to the newsletters were Steve and Julie DuPerrieu, Tom and Lynn Austin, Irv and Jane Bright, Henry and Gretchen Dallam, John and Patti Freed, Kris and Rick Straub, Bill and Peggy Conyer, Donna Kay and Ray Carlson, Connie and Donna Trogolo, and Dick and Kristie Wilson.

The Kings and Queens Club Championship was established in 1983 with Gene and Alice Fisher winning the first crown. Discussion was going on about expanding the event to 72 holes over two weekends, Pro Bill Crabtree said in 1988.

The tournament was played through 1992 and then re-instituted in 2013 as the Couples' Club Championship. (If couples' tournaments were held at the first site, no records are available.)

Vicki Hunkler has seven Couples Club Championship wins, playing with Vito Canonico and later with her husband, Chris. Kim Birch and Tommy Thomas took the title in 2015. Other contenders in recent history have been Danny and Renee Allen, Ronnie Brown and Louella Archer, and Steve and Joyce Vasseur.

Couples Club Champions From 1983-2016

1983	Gene and Alice Fisher
1984	Andy and Monica Kim
1985	Vito Canonico and Vicki Russell
1986	Vito Canonico and Vicki Fort
1987	Rick and Kris Straub
1988	Vito Canonico and Vicki Fort
1989	Connie and Donna Trogolo
1990	Vito Canonico and Vicki Fort
1991	(not held)
1992	Roscoe Crane and Peggy Conyer David and Brook Bradford
1993-2012	(not held)
2013	Chris and Vicki Hunkler
2014	Chris and Vicki Hunkler
2015	Tommy Thomas and Kim Birch
2016	Chris and Vicki Hunkler

Clockwise from below: Kim Birch, Allen Behbehani, Louella Archer; Pat and Anita Kerr; Pam and Del Baird; Pam and Todd Trimble; Butch and Beverly Bradley; Betty and Aubrey Lippert.

Debby and Mark Curtis

David Guess, Cindy and Mike Wyatt

For the past few years, Sunday Couples Golf is played once a month with dinner following. Regulars in the 18-hole group are Bev and Butch Bradley, Pam and Del Baird, Pam and Todd Trimble, Ellen and Sam Wise, Pat and David Gourieux, Cathy and Richard Trampe, Betty and Aubrey Lippert, Tammy and Mike Zimmerman, Kristie and Dick Wilson, Debbie and Gary Rogers, Anita and Pat Kerr, Joyce and Steve Vasseur. Brenda and John Anderson, Robin and John Grubbs, and Debbie and Ben Taylor, and Barbara and Mike Livingston are the regular 9-hole pairs.

Steve and Joyce Vasseur spearheaded a Friday night 9-hole scramble "just for fun" in the summer of 2016, much like Twilight Golf in the seventies.

"The couples' events have always been about meeting friends and having fun," Wanda smiled.

Kim and Sue Homra, Renee and Danny Allen

Leann and Jason Stilley established the Witches and Warlocks Couples Invitational Golf Tournament in 2009. This scramble is held annually in October and draws 128 golfers from the region as well as Paducah and the club. It is known as a great weekend of golf on an excellent course with a dinner and dance following play on Saturday.

Witches and Warlocks Winners 2009-2016

2009 Jerry Hale & Sabrina Wheatley
2010 Daryl & Brenda Rendleman
2011 Bob Berry & Nikki Orazine
2012 Bob Berry & Nikki Orazine
2013 Brad & Jenny Clendenen
2014 Chris & Vicki Hunkler
2015 Chris & Vicki Hunkler
2016 Chris & Jennifer Hartlage

Chris and Vicki Hunkler

The Ladies Golf Association ...Promoting the Game

The Country Club of Paducah has hosted numerous ladies' events over the years in addition to the Paducah Sun, the Memorial, the Club Championship, and the Cup Matches. Tri-State tournaments, member-guests, the witches scrambles, and spring and fall tournaments are an integral part of the LGA schedule.

When the Turnberry Foundation began the Forward Tee Project in 2014, the LGA voted to donate $5,000 from monies raised toward the construction of six new tees. This entitled the LGA to one vote by a current president as a member of the foundation. The association also donated to the construction of the scoreboard near No. 18.

The Ladies Golf Association spearheaded a landscape enhancement of No. 1 and No. 10 tee boxes in 2012. The ornamental grasses and flowers were planted near the bench on No. 10, which was given in memory of Pat Wooldridge after she passed away in 2000.

For 60 years, the LGA enjoyed a membership of 40 or more ladies. In the last decade or so, the number of women playing golf throughout Paducah and the region has decreased significantly.

With this in mind and the desire to grow the game, the 2016 Ladies Golf Association established a cash award to be used toward the recipient's college expenses. A deserving high school senior golfer who attends McCracken County, Paducah Tilghman, or St. Mary High School is eligible.

The first winner for the 2016-17 school year was Ryan Lee who played for the Lady Mustangs of MCHS. The daughter of Caren and Chris Lee, Ryan shot the low score of 78 at the Regionals to lead the team to State. The scholarship committee chose Ryan based on an interview, outstanding contributions to her church, school, and the community, plus her essay on how golf will be a part of her life for years to come.

Funds raised at the annual LGA Memorial Golf Tournament will go toward this award in the future, according to the scholarship committee members, Cathy Trampe, Vicki Hunkler, and Tammy Zimmerman.

The history of ladies' golf at the club is filled with championships and defeats, birdies and bogeys, humor and frustrations, but friendships prevail and the game continues as it has for the past 80 years at the Country Club of Paducah.

Junior Golf

"Ability may get you to the top, but character will keep you there."
—John Wooden

Junior golf is a game of character building where kids learn to play by the rules, develop self-control, and respect their fellow players. Since the founding of the club, members have realized the importance of promoting junior golf. All of the club's professionals have encouraged boys and girls to play, attend camps and clinics, and compete with fellow golfers.

One of the earliest references to junior competition at the Country Club of Paducah was in the early 1950s, when George Sullivan was a youngster.

Sullivan still has the junior boys' golf trophies he won when he was the Boys' Club Champion in 1950 and 1952 and the handicap winner in 1951. Tommy Thomas has a trophy from 1958 when he was the club's junior winner, and Mike Livingston has his 1957 trophy. Little is mentioned about junior golf at the club prior to the 1950s. Clippings from the sports pages of the *Sun-Democrat* and from members' scrapbooks do provide some information from the sixties.

Weldon Grimsley's by-line appeared almost daily in the sports section of the *Sun-Democrat* in the 1960s, and many times he covered the club's golf news.

In the summer of 1964, for example, the Sports Editor wrote about the annual Pepsi-Cola Junior Golf Tournament with several of the Country Club of Paducah golfers in the field. Young Jan Blanton won the

Tommy Thomas heads to the Boys' State Tournament in 1961.

THE COURIER-JOURNAL, LOUISVILLE, KY.,

Staff Photo by Harry Bolser

SNEAD-MINDED . . . Tommy Thomas, 17-year-old Paducah Tilghman golfer, has patterned his complete game after a pretty fair golfer, Sam Snead. The Slammer's tactics must have been pretty good for Thomas was the second best scorer in the state regional tournaments last week with a 75. He'll play in the state high school meet Tuesday and Wednesday at Fort Knox.

Mike Livingston's trophy from the 1958 Table Tennis Championship. Mike won the Boys' Junior Golf Championship in 1957.

Junior golf winners at the club in 1964.

COUNTRY CLUB WINNERS—Prize winners in the annual Paducah Country Club Junior Golf Tournament were, from the left, front row, Linda Lowery, Nancy Backus, Susan Bichon and Ann Fowler; and, back row, John Harris, Dwain Lowry, Dave Lindroos, Hoy Widener, Jim Rieke and Charles Anderson. Prize winners not pictured are Jan Blanton, Charles Anderson, Bo Futrell and Buzz Peel.

JUNIOR GOLF—Junior golf again is going strong in West Kentucky this summer, especially at Rolling Hills and Paducah Country Club. Here are some of the youngsters at Paducah Country Club. Watching Barbara Smith lining up at putt are, from the left, seated, Tandy, Ginny and Peg Bichon, Jackie Brooks, Cindy Underwood, Jill Brooks and Cathy Weitlauf; and, standing, Jim Rieke, Tom Whittemore, "Bouchie" Bichon, Bill Ragland Jr., "Peanuts" Lowry, "Buzz" Peel, Jim and Scott Musgove, Bill Rieke, Mark Gunn, Ed Hannan Jr., and Bud Mullen.

event with a 145 and Stan Chase won the Boys' 16-17 age group with Marty Curtis also making a good showing.

Anne Fowler (Gwinn) won the Girls' 14-15 division with Roxie Thomas (Jarvis), Linda Lowry (Green); Nancy Backus (Roniger), and Cindy Tate (Ragland) finishing in the top 12.

In the Boys' 14-15 division, among the competitors were Richard Trampe, Jim Rieke, Jimmy Harris, Dubber Young, Edward Bichon, Marty Samuels, Hoy Widener, Hal Gilbert, Bill Ragland, Tommy Whittemore, Jr., and Sammy Wise.

John Harris, Bobby Wooldridge, Scottie Musgove, and Keith Crawford represented the club in the Boys' 12-13 age group with Harris firing a 178 for third place honors.

In additional coverage in the *Sun-Democrat* that summer, Blanton, Jim Rieke, John Harris, and Dwain Lowery placed in the Bob Guthrie Youth Association Golf Tournament—another nice showing for the Country Club junior players.

Jan Blanton's next trophy in 1964 came when he won the "Paducah Country Club Junior Golf Tournament" firing a 72 after playing the 9-hole course twice. This is the first mention of a Junior Club Championship winner since the 1950s.

Jim Harris was over-all runner-up. He was competing as a 15-year-old and won that division over Hoy Widner, Bo Bell, Dubber Young, Bob Koven, Tommy Whittemore, Burton Banks, and Hal Gilbert, in that order.

Jim Rieke won the Boys' 13-14 division and John Harris finished first in the 11-12-year-old group with Dwain "Peanuts" Lowry and Steve Musgove a close second and third, respectively.

The Boys' 10-and-under title went to Bo Futrell with Buzz Peel, Jimmy Musgove, Ed Hannan, David Paxton, and Bill Fowler finishing in that order after nine holes. Ann Fowler and Linda Lowry won the two girls' divisions.

In another newspaper story, the club's junior golfers were photographed on a hill with trophies in hand. Bill Conyer, Jimmy Musgove, Eddie Hannan, Edward Hely, Jill Brooks, Jenny Bichon, Scott Musgove, Peg Haley, Sarah Musgove, Tommy Whittemore, Jimmy Rieke, Cassie Curtis, and Jackie Brooks were the winners and runners-up. Rieke was the over-all winner, the caption says.

T. PADUCAH, KY. PAGE TWENTY-ONE—B

JUNIOR GOLF WINNERS—These are the winners of the various divisions of the Country Club Junior Golf Tournament Wednesday. The winners include, front row, left to right: Bill Conyer, runner-up in 11-12 year division; Jimmy Musgove, winner of 11-12 division; Eddie Hannan, winner of 10-and-under division, and Edward Hely, runner-up in 10-and-under division. Second row: Jill Brooks, winner of 13-14 division; Jenny Bichon, runner-up in 11-12 division; Scotty Musgove, winner of 13-14 division; Peg Haley, winner of 11-12 division, and Sarah Musgove, winner of 9-and-under division. Back row: Tommy Whittemore, runner-up in 15 and over division; Jim Rieke, overall champion; Cassie Curtis, winner of 15 and over division, and Jackie Brooks, runner-up in 15 and over division.

Adding to that list of promising young golfers were the names of Barbara Smith, Tandy, Ginny, and Peg Bichon, Cindy Underwood, Jill Brooks, Cathy Weitlauf, "Bouchie" Bichon, Bill Ragland, Jr., Bill Rieke, Mark Gunn, Ed Hannan, Jr., and Bud Mullen.

A year or two earlier, the newspaper ran another story entitled "Jan Blanton Captures Honors in Junior Golf."

Blanton fired a 77 and beat Sonny Bailey who shot 88 in the annual Paducah Country Club Junior Golf Tournament. Blanton was playing in the 15-and-over division.

Carol and Tommy Garrett in 1967.

Jimmy Harris won the Boys' 13-14 with an 89 and Bo Bell was runner-up. Anne Fowler and Nancy Backus tied with a 114 in the girls' competition with Miss Fowler winning in the play-off.

John Harris had a 45 and won the Boys' 11-12 trophy with Bob Wooldridge finishing second. Debbie Fendley and Cassie Curtis were first and second in girls' 11-12 with Karen Lund winning the girls' 10-and-under.

In the summer of 1971, Dr. Glenn Noss and Richard Noss took the father-son title in the club's junior competition shooting a 74 with the team of Tom and Tommy Garrett one stroke back. Jim and Jimmy Musgove finished third.

In the 13-and-under father-son division, Dr. Don Boucher and son Bobby were the winners.

Sarah Musgove won the girls' 13-14 over Carol Garrett; Paula Donner won the 11-12 title with Gail Cvengros second. Jane Pedley was the 10-and-under trophy winner over Suzanne Adams.

David Paxton took the boys' 13-14 over Edward Hely; Bobby Bohle was the 11-12 champion, and Mike Davis took the 10-and-under title over Bill Woods. Bill Woods and Beau Hammett received trophies and Hank Dallam was the winner of the boys' 15-17 division.

In 1978 at the old club, 74 junior golfers were signed up to play. Bill Bone was commended for developing the junior programs; he said that Sylvia Davis was his right-hand helper and he could not have had such success without her.

Chris Livingston won the Club Junior Championship in 1985.

In 1987, the names of H.B. Banks, Findley Ransler, Andy Whiting, Elizabeth Parsons, John Bell, Kerrie Allen, Matt Rottgering, Will Black, Aaron Rottgering, Brian Gilbert, Ward Jarvis, Rickey Rezek, Joe Bradley, Kyle Shelbourne, Charles Drew, Mike Wilson, Chris Bell, Alex Edwards, Jeff Bright, and Tina Whitelock were listed in the club bulletin as winners in age groups 5-15.

By 1988, Ward Jarvis was the dominant junior golfer at the club, but other standouts were developing into excellent players as well.

The '88 Junior Club Tournament winners were Rob Allen (8-year-old division); Chad Gamble (12-13); Carrie Speck and Sarah Chase (10 girls); and Jarvis (9-10) with the lowest score, a 57 on nine holes.

In another competition, Rob Allen won the 9-year-old division; Michael Sullivan the 7-8 division and Ward Jarvis the 10-11 category. Jarvis shot a career best 45 to win by 13 shots. Elizabeth Parsons and Caitlin Sullivan won their girls' divisions, a great showing for the club.

The Paducah Tilghman golf team won the High School Regionals and finished 6th at State. Mike Wilson, Chris Bell, Chris Livingston, Jeff Livingston, Alex Edwards, and

Scotty Musgove, Frank Young, and Tommy Garrett at one of the Calcuttas.

Tom Garrett watches his son, Tommy, make a great turn at the old course.

Boys who loved the game at an early age were (from left, front) John Bell, Ward Jarvis, Drew Allen, John Russell; (from left, back) Stevie DuPerrieu, Brian Gilbert, (Ward's father, Larry Jarvis), and Jamey Brown.

In 1990, Dr. Merle Fowler and grandson Fowler Black won the annual Father-Son Tournament, edging out Larry and Ward Jarvis and Mike and Kyle Shelbourne.

Winners in the 1990 Junior Club Championship were John Semeraro, John Presley, Brad Whisman, Elizabeth Parsons, Andy Whiting, and Ward Jarvis, who fired an 83, his personal best. It was Jarvis' third club championship win in a row.

Ward Jarvis defeated Burton Gregory in a sudden-death playoff to capture the 1991 Boys' Club Championship. Carrie Speck took the girls' title with Elizabeth Parsons in second place. Andy Whiting was the 9-hole winner with John Elliott runner-up; John Semeraro was the best of the 4-hole boys and Reed Jarvis finished second.

Todd Sutherland were on that team. Bell won a number of tournaments in the area as a high school player and finished second at the State High School Tournament.

The 1989 Junior Club Championship was held with Jarvis victorious. Winners in other age groups were Matt Rottgering, Steve DuPerrieu, Ward Jarvis (medalist in all age groups), Rob Allen and John Semeraro, respectively. Elizabeth Parsons won the girls 4-hole group.

A junior boys' scramble was also held that summer with three teams tying for first with a 42 on the front nine: Jarvis, Allen, Miller Grumley, B. Hancock; and DuPerrieu, Joe Bradley, Brett Duwe, and H.B. Banks; and the team of Rottgering, Will Cox, Paul Stovesand, Don Presley, and Jimmy Gwinn.

Teams composed of Burton Gregory, Brad Whisman, Jeremy Case, Fowler Black and Kyle Shelbourne; and Brian Gilbert, Brett Golightly, Andy Whiting, and Ricky Rezek finished fourth and fifth. (Burton Gregory has continued to win in club competition as recently as 2016.)

The First Annual Junior Golf Invitational was held in 1989 with 85 golfers participating. Nationally known Buddy Demling was on hand entertaining the golfers with his famous trick shot exhibition. Chris Bell, son of Bo and Carol Bell, won the 16-18-year-old division with an even-par round of 72 from the blue tees.

The 1992 Junior Club Championship was once again won by Jarvis, his fourth title. Watch out, Jimmy Brown! Ryan Cochran was first in the boys 8-9 age group; Bret Jones in the 10-11; and Andy Whiting in the 12-14.

Did you know Barry Kight played junior golf before moving up in the ranks to PGA Professional? He was the 1993 Junior Club Champion in the boys 15-16 division ahead of Steve DuPerrieu.

Other winners were Brad Whisman, Alex Metzger, and Reed Cochran in their respective age groups. The "Little Juniors" (ages 6-7) competed in a separate division. Reed Cochran was the winner and Chris Miller was runner-up.

Erin Bradford was the girls' champion; Jackie Wagner finished second in the age 8-11 group.

Ward Jarvis (left) and Alex Metzger (right) show the swings that pivoted them to junior golf success.

Parent-Child Tournament winners were Mike and Joey Whitaker, Bob and Andy Whiting, Ed Hough and Reid Boland; Steve and Daniel Miller. Burton and H.B. Banks, Larry and Reed Jarvis, Dave and Ryan Bradford, and Hal and Brian Gilbert all carded second place finishes in their divisions.

In 1994, Todd Trimble announced that the club reached a total of 80 participants in the four junior programs.

Jarvis won the Junior Club Championship again in 1995 with Reed Cochran finishing first in the 8-10 Division ahead of Reese Bright; Ryan Cochran first in the 11-12 age group ahead of Daniel Miller. Brandon Mullen was second to Jarvis in the 13-17 division. Others juniors who excelled in those days were John Bell and Burton Gregory.

Lindsey Golliher was the winner of the girls' 8-10 age group and Katie Shelbourne was runner-up.

In 1997, David and Jamie Paxton and Bill and Alex Metzger took top honors in the parent-child tournament.

In 2007, two country club golfers were pictured in *Sports Illustrated*'s "Faces in the Crowd" column, Case Cochran and Mason Jacobs. Cochran won the state tournament playing for St. Mary High School and Jacobs took the Illinois championship for Massac County, both for the second consecutive time. He was also the Men's Club Champion in 2005.

The 2007 Junior Club Tournament was won by the following club kids: Sammy Thompson, boys 13-15; Matthew Zakutney, boys 10-12; Vincent Shiben, boys 7-9; Sydney Edwards, girls 13 and over; and Zoe Edwards, girls 5-7.

In 2009, Kurt Averill, the coach of the St. Mary High School Boys Golf Team captured the First Region title in Murray with sons of club members on the team—Sammy Thompson, Nicholas Thompson, Matthew Zakutney, Joey Mayo, John Edwards, and Wes Averill.

Two years later the St. Mary High School's golf team won the Class A State Championshipwith team members Nick Thompson, Mathew Zakutney, John Edwards, Joey Mayo, Wes Averill, Seth Powell, Owen Workman, and Hunter Dickens.

Club "kids" who fared well in the 2011 Junior Classic, hosted by the club, included Charli Doss, Teri Doss, Mayo, and Trimble.

River Stilley, the 10-year-old son of Leann and Jason Stilley, is making great strides with his golf game. He placed third in his age division and won the chipping division in his pursuit of the 2012 Drive, Chip, and Putt competition.

In 2015, Rocco Zakutney and Stilley were on the Paducah All-Star PGA Junior League team that won the Kentucky PGA Junior League Championship. Zakutney is a student at St. Mary, while Stilley attends Lone Oak. They were also 2016 All-Stars.

Alex and Gray Edwards, Nicole and Sloane Edwards, Jason and Kip Siener, Jason and Charli Siener, Dave and Nicolas Hoffman, Tom and Caroline Gruber, Andrew Walker and Walker McNeil, and Chris and Whitson McNeil won "gold" in the 2015 Parent-Child Golf Tournament.

Sydney Trimble was born when her father, Todd, was the golf professional at the club. She has a long list of wins to her credit both as a Heath High School golfer and as a Murray State scholarship player. She has already won the Paducah Sun-Florence Paxton Memorial Tournament twice (2013 and 2016).

Teri Doss, daughter of Greg and Lori Doss, won the 2014 Region I High School Golf Championship as a Paducah Tilghman stand-out. She also won the 2014 and 2015 Paducah Sun before graduating and playing for Mississippi State University.

Clayton Turnbo, son of Dr. J. Kyle and Nikole Turnbow, played on the Kentucky PGA Junior Tour during the summer of 2016. Turnbo was a member of the McCracken County High School team coached by Nick Mills.

Matthew Zakutney, Nick Thompson, and Joey Mayo.

Assistant Professional Chelsea Harris with Teri Doss.

Sydney Trimble wins the Junior Classic in 2011 in the 16-18 age group.

Club "Kids" Advance to College Golf

Outstanding junior golfers who played at the club in recent years and went on to play for college teams after high school are as follows:

Case Cochran	Texas A&M
Charli Doss	Murray State University
Eric Straub	Missouri State University
Hunter Ford	Murray State University
Jason Straub	University of Kentucky
Joey Mayo	Rhodes College
Laura Clemmons	University of Kentucky
Mason Jacobs	University of Illinois
Mathew Zakutney	Murray State University
Peter Zellmer	Methodist College
Ryan Cochran	University of Florida
Sydney Trimble	Murray State University
Teri Doss	Mississippi State
Will Cox	Murray State University
William Hunt	Murray State University

Hunter Ford

In 2011, Pee Wee golfers honing their skills at an early age are, from left, Spencer Cates, Gage Dugan, River Stilley, Caden Kern, Brody Miller, and Cole Haynes.

Below: Participants in the PGA Junior League in 2015 are Rocco Zakutney and William O'Neill.

Junior golfers at the club in 2015.

Young men and women who called the club their "home course" are still playing golf today in other parts of the country and in Paducah, proving that junior golf is one of the club's greatest investments.

Let's take a look at what life at the club was like during the Verplanke-Curtis according to a past employee, Paul Jett, Sr.

Paul Jett Remembers...

"I started as a caddy at the country club during the summer of 1954 when I was eleven-years-old. The clubhouse had burned to the ground and the club was operated from a couple of railroad box cars. On weekends we would have 40 to 50 boys show up to caddy and usually all of us got a job. The fee was $1.00 per nine holes and the usual tip was 50 cents.

Mr. Gresham Hougland and a few others were really kind and they gave you $3.00 for 18 holes. One time when caddying for Mr. Hougland, I marked his ball on the green with my dime. Being just a kid I was too embarrassed to ask for my dime back and he took my dime to his grave. One of the perks for caddying on the weekend, both Saturday and Sunday, the club let us play on Monday from 8:00 until noon.

In 1957, the club had a new clubhouse and I went to work in the pro shop for Mr. Ed Verplanke as caddy master. About that time electric carts started being used and there was not near as much need for caddies. Mr. Verplanke was more of a club manager than golf pro. Every day he wore his white shirt and tie to work.

About 1962, Mr. Vard Curtis came to work as the pro and he was great. We got a new supply of equipment and clothing to sell. At that time the popular shirt was the Munsingwear shirt with its embroidered penguin logo. The retail price of Spaulding golf balls went from $1.00 to $1.10 per ball and I thought they would never sell. Wilson Staff clubs were very popular and Ping putters started appearing.

James "Mitch" Mitchell was one of the great waiters at the country club because he knew how to host and take care of his customers. I get a smile every time I think about one of the things I saw Mitch do while he was working. On Monday the club was closed except for the 19th Hole and the pro shop. Drinks and snacks were available but no cooked food.

Late one Monday afternoon the president of the club, Mr. Bill Carson, came in for a late afternoon drink. Mitch decided he would have a drink with the club president so he got a can of his favorite, Budweiser, held it under the bar counter, put a towel over the top of the can and opened it. He held the can under the counter and poured it into his cup and proceeded to have his drink with the club president.

On New Year's Eve I would assist with parking cars for the big party. It was 1959 and my transportation was a '51 Chevy. When I got to work I parked the Chevy at the front door of the club. The parking lot was full and a late arrival was Mr. Bob Hougland. I explained to Mr. Hougland that the lot was full but if he would pull to the front I would move my Chevy. I backed out and then jumped out to help the Houglands and their guest out of their Cadillac. Mr. Hougland gave me $20, a lot in 1959, and I took that and the other tips I had gotten that night and bought me a corduroy suit.

Working at the Country Club of Paducah was a great experience because of the many wonderful members, some of whom I still enjoy and cherish their friendship."

(Jett graduated from Murray State and worked for a pharmaceutical company out of Columbia, SC, until he and his wife, Becky, retired in Southern Pines, SC, to be near Paul, Jr. and his family.

Paul Jett, Jr., has achieved a tremendous amount of success as a greens superintendent. He was the South Carolina High School Golf Champion and went to Clemson University on a scholarship where he obtained an agronomy degree. His first job was as an assistant superintendent at Pinehurst. He then became the superintendent at the Washington Club, Duke University's home course. In the mid-90s as a superintendent, he oversaw the rebuilding of Pinehurst No. 2 for the 1999 and 2004 United States Open Championships. Jett is also an excellent golfer.)

The Bill Bone Chapter...The Longest in the Club's History of Golf Pros

When Vard Curtis resigned as the "pro" in 1963, a well-known young golfer named Bill Bone pursued the opening at the club. Bone, a 1953 graduate of Paducah Tilghman High School, grew up honing his skills at Paxton Park. He had won numerous tournaments and the respect of the local golf community.

Eddie Verplanke and Curtis worked diligently to recruit their friend and fellow competitor, who was working in Metropolis after a one-year stint at the Cairo Country Club. Their influence paid off and Bone was hired that spring. Little did any of them know that this was the beginning of a 21-year career at the Country Club of Paducah.

"Bill was a fine player and worked very hard. He put in a lot of hours at the club. He was especially nice to young players and helped us with our games. Bill, Hilary Hunt, Hal Brown, and I used to travel around the area on Mondays when Bill had a day off and play at least 36 holes at different courses. We had lots of fun," Tommy Thomas recalled.

Bo Bell was a junior player when Bone was the pro at the old club. "He is a first class nice man. He put up with a lot from us when all us kids used to play," he chuckled.

Bone was not a PGA member like many of today's PGA club pros are, but he was professional in every way. He was an "old school" club pro who devoted almost every waking hour to his job. Sixty hours a week was typical for Bone. He taught lessons, sold merchandise, coordinated course play, handled the golf carts, ran tournaments, and maintained relationships with members that are intact to this day. The length of his service to the club is a testament to the man's dedication, abilities, and character...but all good things come to an end.

Bill Bone

On May 13, 1984, *Paducah Sun* sports writer Larry Schmidt reported: "Time for a new beginning...Bone decides to end 21-year-reign as golf pro at local country club."

"I think I could have finished my years here," Bone said in the story. "But, I really think this is a good time for me to move on. We have a new course and clubhouse. Maybe the club needs new blood, new ideas." And the rest is history.

Let's listen to some interesting information and stories Bill Bone shared for this history.

From the Memory Book of Bill Bone

"I was at the club for a long time and have lots of memories," Bill Bone reminisced.

Gresham Hougland used to come in the shop and buy three Spalding Dot golf balls every week. I began to wonder how many golf balls does that man need? I happened to be back in the locker room one day when he was taking a shower. His locker door was open and all those golf balls were stacked in there. He was just doing it to support me. I thought the world of him. He was super!

Back then three balls were probably $2.50. I remember selling Po-Do balls. Members paid half fare to use their own carts.

The club spent a lot of money building sand traps back in those days because the greens committee wanted it done. Greens committee chairmen were in for a couple of years and each one had ideas about how things should be done, and then the guy coming in behind him would hate sand traps, for example, and would have them covered up. When Jim Brown was in he loved fast greens and some of the members wanted them slower.

Harry Livingston was good about recruiting people to work at the club. He was always bringing someone in. Take Bill Newcomb for instance.

Newcomb was the best one from the old days. He knew food. He had the best bean soup and cornbread you could ever put in your mouth.

We had Carol Mann at the club one time. I saw her hit 5-6 practice balls, and I thought I'm glad I don't have to play her. She was about 6'3 or 6'4" and came to the club for a clinic. Vince Genovese, the pro at Paxton Park, used to arrange those things like the one with Patty Berg.

"No-Bogey-Yogi" came once. He said he could take any female golfer and beat any two of the best amateurs in the city, so Vince lined me and Tommy Whittemore up to play him. Brooks Starr's sister was his partner and we beat them to death. The greens were unbelievable bumpy. He got on in three on the first hole and had a 25-foot putt—he said "No Bogey Yogi" and knocked it in, and he did it all day long.

Norma Moran, Jesse Hugg, and Sylvia Davis with Golf Professional Bill Bone.

I loved junior golf—at one time there were 85 or more juniors. Sylvia Davis was my right hand and helped run the program. What a doll she was! Junior golf was very important to me.

At the old club, I had a net at the bottom of the hill and I scheduled 15 minute sessions with each child. When it first started it was really popular and busy and it was worth it. I saw some good results—Kenny Hunt eventually won the club championship and is an example. He and Phil and David and Kevin all played and I guess still do. The Musgove boys were good in the '60s and so were Bo Bell, Bill Ragland, and "Dubber" Young. We had lots of good junior golfers.

Carol Garrett was another one of my juniors. Hers is the swing I remember as the smoothest of the girls.

One of the hardest things I had to do at the club was keep non-members and non-members' kids from sneaking onto the golf course, especially the kids. When I was their age, I would have probably tried to do the same thing!

Lee Anderson owned six golf carts when I first started. I bought those six and added four more. I had close to 100 when we moved out here and when I left the club. I owned them until the fall of 1982 when Doug Edwards (club president) approached me about a slightly different arrangement, which suited me to death. He wanted the club to own the carts and the pro shop and he wanted me to run the operation and the club would provide all the help.

I was compensated a good salary to do it, but the problem was it worked well in the winter months, but when March rolled around and we got busier I started asking Doug for some help. I had one employee with me in the pro shop and we were cleaning the carts and picking up the balls and doing everything that needed to be done.

Doug said times were pretty tight and to wait. Then we got really busy in April and I asked him again because it really wasn't the arrangement we had. I could tell it wasn't going to happen.

I told him if I didn't have help by May 15, I was leaving, but he didn't think I would. I also told George Sullivan that I had 85 junior golfers out here at the new club and that I was leaving soon and they needed to find someone to take over golf. He also didn't believe me.

May 15 came. I washed all the carts, picked up the range balls, and about 11:30 p.m. I walked my keys up to the manager's office and laid them on his desk. I didn't look back.

Bill Bone was 49 then and had been at the club for 21 years when he left on May 31, 1984. Today Bill is a retired real estate broker in Paducah. You might still find him occasionally hitting balls at Paxton Park.

Jon DePriest

Jon DePriest, the assistant golf professional at the Memphis Country Club, was hired for Bone's position in the spring of 1984.

In a *Sun-Democrat* newspaper story, Assistant Sports Editor Larry Schmidt introduced the 25-year-old pro with the headline "DePriest sees long range security with his position at Country Club."

Doug Edwards spearheaded a search for Bone's replacement, the story read. Edwards knew about the young PGA member because his son was a member of the Memphis Country Club.

DePriest and his wife, Terri, and son, Andrew, make up Paducah's newest golf family, Schmidt wrote. DePriest was here from 1984-86 and was a PGA member. He resides in Edwardsville, Illinois.

Roger Schmitt and Jon DePriest

Jon DePriest in the downstairs golf shop with Doris Gregory and Clara Weitlauf.

Bill Crabtree surrounded by lady golfers Donna Trogolo, Norma Moran, and Oliva Cave at a luncheon.

Bill Crabtree

Bill Crabtree, PGA, was hired by Club Manager Joe Connor, in 1986. Hailing from Santa Claus, Indiana, Crabtree was the golf professional until February of 1991.

A contact in Indiana at Christmas Lake Golf Club said that Crabtree now lives in China and teaches golf to promising young players.

Larry Mullen

Larry Mullen was hired by the club in 1991 when President Burton Banks urged him to take the position. He agreed to a one-year contract.

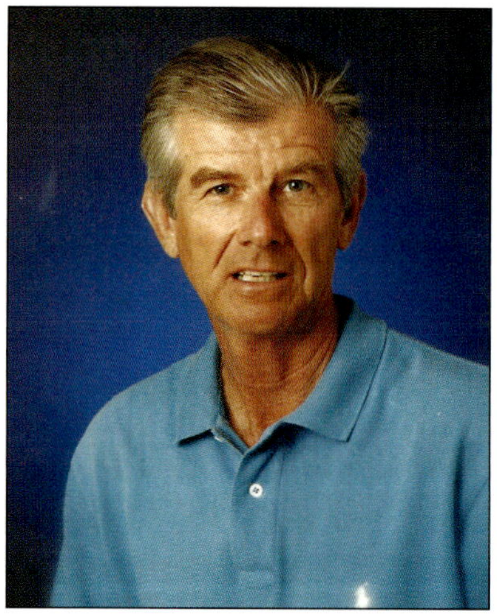

Larry Mullen

Mullen was an NCAA All-American as a senior on the Murray State University golf team in 1967 and then turned pro.

His career as the professional at Hollywood and Edgewood Country Clubs in New Jersey totaled 22 years. While in New Jersey, he won the Horton Smith Award and was New Jersey Golf Professional of the Year. He also was elected president of the New Jersey PGA.

Mullen is a life-time member of the PGA of America and once was elected to its National Board of Directors. He won four PGA Senior Championships in Kentucky and was inducted into the Murray State Sports Hall of Fame in 1991.

Like Bill Bone, Mullen grew up playing on the Paxton Park links where his brother, Kayo, ran the operation, and now his nephew, Danny, is the professional. Larry and his wife, Jeannie, reside near the club.

During his brief stint at the club, Mullen recruited Todd Trimble from Oak Ridge, Tennessee, to be his assistant in 1991.

Todd Trimble

Todd Trimble graduated from Morehead State University in 1988 and became a PGA member in 1992. He served on the Kentucky PGA Board of Directors for two years.

Todd Trimble

Trimble succeeded Larry Mullen and served as the club's head professional until March of 2003 when he resigned to pursue full-time teaching and establish The Golf Complex in West Paducah with business partner Barry Kight.

He has been named the Kentucky PGA Section's Teacher of the Year four times, 2006, 2008, 2009, and 2013. Trimble has many outstanding players on his roster of students, but probably the most well-known is Emma Talley, winner of the U.S. Amateur and NCAA Women's Championship.

Todd and his wife, Pam, have one daughter, Sydney Trimble Kelly.

Jason Stilley

Jason Stilley became first assistant under Todd Trimble in 1999. When Trimble left in 2003, he moved into the head pro position where he remained until November of 2016.

Stilley was a member of the Southern Illinois University golf team, graduating in 1995, and was the assistant golf professional at Crab Orchard Golf Course before coming to Paducah.

Stilley won the Kentucky Section PGA Assistants Championship and was named the 2000 Kentucky PGA Assistant of the Year. In 2002, he became a member of the PGA of America. He is a three-time National Club Professional Championship Qualifier and won the Kentucky PGA Section Championship at Valhalla Golf Club in 2008.

He and his wife, Leann, are the parents of River Stilley.

Jason Stilley

Chad Martin

On March 1, 2017, the Country Club of Paducah welcomed Chad Martin from Rock Hill, South Carolina, as the new head professional. With 16 years of experience in the private country club industry under his belt, Martin was the head professional at Spring Valley Country Club and then Rock Hill Country Club.

Chad Martin and son

He started his career in golf at Effingham (Illinois) Country Club in 2000 as an assistant pro. An Illinois native, Martin became a PGA member in 2007. He served as a director and secretary in the Carolinas Section.

He and his wife, Sara, an Illinois native, have two sons, Parker and Grayson.

The golf professionals at the Country Club of Paducah are there to assist the members in all areas of the game six days a week, year after year. As Sam Snead said, "When experts run into trouble, they seek the advice of another professional. When you run into faults, do likewise."

Courses and Superintendents

When spring shifts into summer, the club's focus is on the golf course and those who maintain it. Since 1913, the club is indebted to the men who have had this responsibility.

The Early History

For the first 25 years, the employees who worked on the 9-hole golf course were overseen by a designated member of the Board of Governors who worked closely with them. The first available record of a "superintendent" or head groundskeeper for the Country Club of Paducah was in 1943 when Ben Bolte was hired to be in charge of the maintenance of the 9-hole course at a salary of $22.50 per week.

Vic Speck said he remembers Mr. Bolte in the late 1940s and early 1950s. "When I was in junior high around 1950, we'd play football on the 3rd fairway and he would run us off," he laughed.

Before Mr. Bolte was hired in 1943, Palmer James, who was a member of the Board of Governors and president of the club, was active in supervising the maintenance of the golf course, according to the board minutes. C.J. Carney also played a role in course maintenance; he was commended for taking care of the course and grounds, and for building the caddy house and four bridges across the ditch around that time.

"Palmer James obtained dirt to be used for top dressing greens," Board Secretary Bunks Dallam indicated in his meticulous minutes. James suggested using fertilizer and the board authorized him to do it on October 4, 1943.

In 1947, the minutes noted that Ralph McRight, who assumed the role of "manager" several different times, was going to work from June through August and would supervise the groundskeeper and caddy master.

The annual report issued for 1954-55 mentioned a greenskeeper and four helpers working at the club. By all indications, Mr. Bolte was still the hands-on worker in charge of course maintenance.

In 1958, James "Jim" Davidson was hired to be in charge of the golf course. His son, Jay Davidson, was promoted to "groundskeeper" in August of 1966 and followed his father as superintendent.

(Homer Thompson, Bill Reed, and Steve Reed worked on the course in the late 1960s. The minutes say that Louis Slusmeyer was asked to consult the club about fertilizing and the greens in the late sixties.)

Jay Davidson's son, Rick, said he worked at the club as a kid. Rick remembers caddying for Tommy Whittemore, Sr., "He was the nicest man. I learned rules and etiquette and how to play from him."

The Davidsons managed the nine-hole golf course for many years.

"The upstairs at the clubhouse was supposed to be haunted," Davidson reminisced. "My dad was also the night watchman. We'd sit downstairs, just the two of us sometimes, and you could hear something upstairs like there was a bunch of glass shattering. We'd run upstairs and there would be nothing. If you were upstairs, you could hear the same sounds coming from downstairs. It was really scary to me at the time."

The Davidson families lived in the house on the front of the property from 1966 to around 1976. The house, which was also occupied by a few other employees over the years, was eventually moved from that site to 34th Street where it stands today.

The Course on Country Club Lane

The "old" course, as it is referred to now, was built on a relatively small piece of property on Country Club Lane, but it served the members well for forty-plus years.

Yes, there was talk about too many people on the course, and more talk about having to play the same holes twice. Once in awhile, a golf ball bounced along the street; the pool and clubhouse occasionally took a hit from an errant shot, but those who played on the course still share good memories about it.

The following is a hole by hole description as remembered by Tommy Thomas:

(Note: Yardages are approximate. All holes had the same greens, but different tees, which offered some variety when playing 18 holes.)

No. 1—Par 4, 275-280 yards, you teed off up by the parking lot and went in the valley and back up. There were two big trees on either side of the green and you tried to drive between those two trees. If you hit a really good drive on hard ground, you could roll it onto the green.

No. 2—Par 5, about 500 yards long, it ran all along Pines Road. The fairway was a hog back. It had a big tree about 220 yards out in the middle of the fairway and you had to go around that tree. Usually your drive would go down in the rough on the right.

No. 3—Par 4, about 350 yards long. The tee was at the corner of 36th Street and Pines Road with a creek about 50 yards short of the green running across. You would hit your drive short of the creek and pitch up onto the green. The green was elevated and severely tilted from back to front.

No. 4—Par 5, 485 yards long. It ran along Central Avenue with out of bounds left designated by a creek. It was severely slanted right to left. The green was at Country Club Drive and Central Avenue.

No. 5—Par 3, 150 yards from front tee and 165 from the back. You teed off behind the 4th green at the corner of Country Club Lane and Central. You would go up the hill and the green was between the tennis courts to the left and swimming pool to the right.

No. 6—Par 4 on the front side and par 5 on the back. On the front tee, you could hit your drive over the creek, a slight dog-leg left and it played about 375 yards. A good drive would go over the creek with an 8 iron to the green. From the back tee, you would choose a club according to how hard the ground was and lay up in front of the creek, which was fronted by the remains of the trolley tracks. If you were close to the mound where the tracks were laid you would be in pretty good shape to go for the green, which was about a 200-yard shot in on the par 5.

No. 7—Par 4, about 400 yards from the back tee and 370 from the front. It was a straight hole. A ground depression that was likely the remains of an old creek bed was about where an average tee shot would land.

No. 8—Par 3, from the back tee about 200 yards and the front tee was about 175-185 yards long.

No. 9—Par 4, 365 yards up hill, it came back to the clubhouse across the creek and up a hill and the green set right in front of the back patio of the clubhouse. The front tee was shorter. You could drive the green from the front tee when the ground was really hard.

Superintendents and the Robert Trent Jones Course

As the club prepared to exit the 9-hole course and look toward its future on Blandville Road, Howard Gardner was hired as early as 1977 to work at the new site. Gardner was eventually the first superintendent at the Robert Trent Jones course.

Superintendent Howard Gardner

According to Tim Gardner, who worked with his father, he liked being the "grow in" superintendent. Howard Gardner was the superintendent when the club officially opened it in August of 1979.

Before the course was finished, Bill Usher, the greens committee chairman, walked the property many times. He studied it all from the location of trees to the placement of bunkers. "I had talked to the architect's people on numerous occasions. Jim Musgove and I knew that course backwards and forwards."

Mark Curtis captured the golf course when it first opened in 1979. Clockwise from above: No. 12, No. 2, No. 14.

"No. 15 was supposed to be a dogleg left, but it was changed to a dogleg right. Robert Trent Jones had a small lake in front of No. 4, but we decided it would just be too difficult for the majority of the members, so we changed that, but everything else pretty much went according to the plan," Usher said.

When the new Robert Trent Jones golf course opened for play, golfers started their rounds on what is now No. 18 tee box. This was changed in 1980 or 1981.

In December of 1981, Howard Gardner left the course that he "grew in" and went to work at Houston Hills Country Club in Knoxville, Tennessee. Assistant Ray Huff became the acting superintendent, with Tim Gardner remaining on the crew.

The club turned to the Golf Course Superintendents of America Association to find a new superintendent. The greens committee narrowed the list to 12 from the 83 applications received. At the February 2, 1982, meeting, the board selected Roger Schmitt.

In 1983, the superintendent reported that two long-time employees, Tim Gardner and Mark Taylor, were leaving his staff. Gardner accepted a position as superintendent at the Murray Country Club; Taylor went with the State of Kentucky.

In 1990, the course suffered drastically due to the loss of the main deep well among other issues, Schmitt said. He resigned in 1991 after many productive years as the superintendent.

Vic Speck and Burton Banks were on a search committee to find a new superintendent. Speck said, "We narrowed it to 10 and decided on Mark Spire, an assistant at the Country Club in Brookline, Massachusetts. He was pretty good, but he wasn't familiar with our climate, bent grass greens, etc."

"During a tournament, or right before it, he cut the greens to roll about 14 and the next morning they were dead. He didn't think to ask any other area superintendents. They were fast and brown—cooked," Speck recalls.

A special called meeting was held on June 14, 1993, to allow the board to hear concerns from members involving the golf course. Discussions centered around mowing heights, condition of bunkers, and outings. After a culmination of issues, Mark Spire resigned. He was superintendent from 1991-93.

President John D. Williams and Greens Chairman John Golliher announced that Larry Hantle would be the new golf course superintendent in the fall of 1993.

Hantle came to the club from Newburgh, Indiana, where he had been the superintendent at Rolling Hills Country Club since 1978. Hantle has a bachelor's degree in ornamental horticulture and a Turfgrass Management Degree from the University of Illinois in Urbana. He and his wife, Judy or Julie, moved to Paducah with their three children.

When the club celebrated the Millennium in 2000, Superintendent Hantle reflected in the club newsletter on the last 100 years of golf courses:

"From actual horse drawn mowers and real push mowers, the industry has progressed to hydraulic power units, mechanized sand rakes and radio controlled irrigation systems. With all of the latest gadgets, turf managers today feel like they are on the cutting edge. Actually though, the turf still grows in the same psychological manner that it did 100 years ago," he said in the newsletter.

"Our greens are better today because of a new growing medium and hardier bent grass seed.... As the new century approaches and unfolds, I am pleased with the progress that has been made here."

"As the new year, new century, and new millennium begin, life on the golf course remains the same. Y2K is not something the turf and trees care about...We will be looking for better ways and ideas to improve the course...1999 was a good year for the golf course. Being ever the optimist, we expect 2000 to be even better."

Course maintenance continued as usual for several years with scattered reports in the minutes and newsletters about progressions and set-backs. In 2002, Hantle reported that the summer was the third hottest on record. In 2006, the superintendent and Sanders Nursery were working on a plan for the rebuilding of No. 4 green, according to Oscar Gamble, greens chairman. Gamble mentioned the need to rebuild greens since the existing ones are about 30 years old. In September 2006, a microburst blew through the course at No. 2, 3, and 4 tee toppling 60 trees. The front nine was closed for about a week during cleanup.

Then came the ice storm of 2009, one of the most monumental events to ever affect the golf course.

The ice storm ripped through Paducah with a vengeance in late January, severely damaged the operation of the Country Club of Paducah as well as the rest of the area. The golf course was closed until further notice. "The course is very dangerous with all of the limbs hanging from the damaged trees," Pro Jason Stilley wrote to the members.

Larry Hantle said, "The debris amount is massive... many thanks go to Jason Cates who helped with the cleanup around the clubhouse by providing us with a chipper and trucks to haul the material away."

"Mother Nature delivered a knock-out punch!" he said.

Much discussion took place for weeks regarding the golf course cleanup after the ice storm, including the possibility of reimbursement by FEMA. The estimated cost was $260,000.

Not only was the golf course covered in debris, limbs, and uprooted trees, but the phone system was inoperable; food and beverage had to offer a "general store" take-out menu; and electrical issues were a problem. Members came to the course and volunteered labor to pick up debris and do whatever they could to lighten the load on the maintenance crew. The "raking party" took place on March 21, 2009.

Mother Nature strikes the course in September of 2006 uprooting trees and scattering debris across the property. The windstorm did major damage to the course and tennis facility.

Brian Lasko and Kristie Wilson (left) are among those club members who came out in force on March 21, 2009. Chris McNeil and his son, Walker McNeil (below), also helped with the golf course clean-up. Photos courtesy of Mark Curtis.

It was March before the front nine holes were opened. The board agreed not to replace damaged trees that year and created a master plan in 2010. By November, the course clean-up was complete.

At the June 2011 meeting of the board, Hantle reported that the greens committee decided to have a first and second cut to enhance the course appearance.

He added that the USGA Director and Agronomist Bob Brame said if our greens were well maintained, there would be no time frame for replacement or major reconstruction.

Jim Brown, member of the greens committee in 2012, mentioned the pros and cons of transitioning to one of the new Bermuda strains for the greens. Today that remains a topic of discussion.

In other golf business, the need for bunker work on No. 15 was a top concern. The board voted to change it from a sand to a grass bunker.

Manager Straley presented a report about the expected life cycle of various items on the golf course, and from all indications the USGA agrees that the club is past due on the longevity of the greens, bunker sand, asphalt cart paths, practice range tees, and other items.

In other golf business, a committee composed of David Bailey, Jim Brown, Gary Adkins, Kurt Averill, Richard Trampe, Todd Trimble, Chris Hunkler, and Larry Hantle worked diligently on *"The Golf Course Maintenance Standards for the Country Club of Paducah."* The final Standards include a mission statement, objectives, and a vision statement for the course and golf operations.

"The Vision of the Country Club of Paducah is to produce the best conditioned golf course in the State of Kentucky and to be annually ranked in the top 10… as defined by the Golf Digest parameters (shot values, resistance to scoring, design variety, memorability, aesthetics, conditioning, and ambience).

The golf course will be maintained year-round within the financial resources, club assets and equipment to provide an exceptional golf experience to all members of the club."

Standards for greens, Zoysia tees, collars, fairways, roughs, bunkers, flower beds, cart paths, ditches, and course set-up are laid out in detail. The board approved the standards at the October 2012 meeting.

In January of 2014, Superintendent Hantle noted that the green committee's "Improve the Environment" program was a great success with tree removal around greens and tees and sodding of those areas with shade tolerant Zoysia or Bermuda. The most noticeable to golfers was the take down of trees on the left of No. 1 rough. The renewal of the landscaping behind No. 12 green restores that area to the original concept with dogwoods and azaleas.

When summer came after a winter of freezing weather, the fairways were deemed "lost" and the board voted to replace them with Zoysia grass. (*See related comments by Jamey Brown in President's Chapter.*)

The Fairway Project to strip dead turf and begin sprigging and then sodding began on June 19, 2014, according to greens chairman Kurt Averill. By July 19, the last piece of sod was in place. The superintendent and his crew were commended for their hard work during this difficult

The replacement of Zoysia grass on the fairways of No. 13 and No. 1 (below).

time and the members thanked for their patience throughout the summer.

In Superintendent Hantle's "Golf Course News" in 2015, he explained the Audubon Cooperative Sanctuary Program, a guide to environmental stewardship on the golf course. The program consists of six segment—environmental planning, wildlife and habitat management, chemical use reduction and safety, water conservation, water quality management, and outreach and education.

Hantle enrolled the club in the program in the late 1990s and this year appointed assistant Scott Foreman to handle it. One of the first jobs was constructing six new birdhouses for the course. "We are considering participating in the Monarch butterfly program and Operation Pollinator that helps with bee populations," Hantle said.

Larry Lear, a dedicated head mechanic who had worked in golf course maintenance since 1978, retired. Other news on the golf course included a cart path installation across No. 11 fairway to accommodate golfers who live on the adjoining property.

Larry Hantle received a distinguished honor when he was named the Winfrey P. Bunton II Kentucky Turfgrass "Man of the Year" at the Kentucky Turfgrass Conference in October of 2015.

Hantle is past president of the Kentucky Turfgrass Council and the Tri-State Golf Course Superintendents Association.

In 2016, the following items made the news in golf operations:

Superintendent Larry Hantle announced his plan to retire at the end of 2018 after 24 years at the club.

Shannon Watson came on board as the assistant superintendent in 2016. He was at Crab Orchard Golf Club in Illinois for 15 years. Watson has a turf degree from Southern Illinois University and experience with Zoysia tees and fairways and bent/poa greens. Watson was an assistant here in 2000-2001 and is transitioning into the superintendent's job.

Shannon Watson

Scott Wisneski, a stabilizing force on the grounds crew who has been with the club for 20 years, was commended by Tim Straley.

The year 2016 was an eventful one for the golf course itself. The beautiful Zoysia fairways were "the talk of the town," but mid-summer temperatures hit all-time highs and the bent grass greens felt the blow. Extreme heat and huge amounts of rain hampered many events, outings, and tournaments. The board of directors and greens committee resumed discussions on how to deal with the bent grass in the ever-changing climate in Western Kentucky.

Despite ice storms, high winds, and other elements bestowed by Mother Nature during the past 37 years, the Robert Trent Jones course remains the best place around to play the game.

No one is better qualified to describe and reflect upon the Country Club of Paducah's golf course than the veteran superintendent, Larry Hantle.

The Robert Trent Jones Course in the words of Larry Hantle

Moving out of town to an 18-hole course designed by the premier architect of the time, Robert Trent Jones, Sr., was an enormous step in club history. Penn cross bent grass greens were quite the change from the old Bermuda greens and Tifway 419 fairways were like velvet compared to common, and all were watered by an automatic irrigation system. The first real challenge came after the cold winter of '83 and '84. The brutal weather took its toll on Bermuda grass across the mid-south. As per the standard of the day, the grounds staff fertilized, sprigged from surviving turf, and seeded the fairways the best they could and waited as the fairway turf slowly recovered. By year's end the recovery was nearly complete.

In the late 1980s, the limitation of not irrigating the rough became an issue as the turf was not up to standards of the greens, tees, and fairways. The remedy came with an updated and expanded triple row computerized irrigation system that allowed for better turf in the rough. Shortly thereafter, the club decided to move the golf shop into its own building. This caused the old, small practice green to be abandoned and the current practice green to be built by the staff.

Periodically, the club had Roger Rulewich (head designer for Robert Trent Jones) visit and offer suggestions for improvements to the course. The first large scale additions occurred in '94-'95. Tees were added on No. 2, 8, 13, 16, and 18. Additionally, new tee complexes on No. 4 and 14 were built and the practice tee underwent wholesale changes expanding and lengthening it. At the same time, the challenge to the course was enhanced by adding fairway bunkers on No. 3, 4, 15, and 17 (which had been removed in previous years). The norm for tee care was to cover the Bermuda with straw for the winter. The club decided to look ahead and as a final part of the project, had the all the tees laser graded and sodded with Meyer Zoysia which allowed year-round play.

In 1996 another update was undertaken. This time the bunkers were the main focus. They were cleaned out, shaped for visibility, sodded around with Zoysia, had new drainage installed, and filled with fresh, white sand. The course had several in play ditches in the rough and pipe was added to them on No. 1, 10, 11, 16, 17 and then sodded. Lastly, the railroad tie retaining wall that had fallen into the pond on No. 12 was replaced with a stone wall from the tee to the green. Earlier in the year, a new pumping station for the irrigation system was added to add reliability to course care.

Starting in the late 1990s and continuing into the new century, the winter weather toyed with the survival of the Bermuda fairways in some areas. In 2001 after some areas had died for the third time, the club was willing to try Zoysia in these areas. Patches on No. 1, 3, 7, 11, and 18 were sodded in late summer. The small fairway on the 14th had Zoysia introduced into the Bermuda as a test to see which turf would take over. The patches solved the winterkill problem in those areas but the harsh winters would not return for over a decade.

The stone retaining wall on No. 12 provided the impetus for the club to install them on all the remaining ponds. Although the design has changed some, the look continues to enhance the course. They were installed in 2003 (No. 14), 2006 (No. 5), 2008 (No. 16), and 2013 (No. 1 and 2). The bunker renovation was also such a success that they outlasted their normal longevity. The club began another renovation of the bunkers in 2014 using a technique known as the Better Billy Bunker system. To date seven bunkers are completed as the project continues.

The greens have remained mostly intact except for No. 4. After several years of struggling to maintain good turf coverage, the club had the green moved slightly and rebuilt to modern standards in 2006. The staff has

Golf Course Superintendent Larry Hantle

employed many strategies over the years from Hydro-Ject to Drill N Fill to Dri-Ject to Deep Tine along with light and frequent topdressing to keep the greens in top condition. The irrigation system around the greens was redesigned in '98 to afford better coverage and the sprinklers were updated then and again in 2013.

The 419 Bermuda fairways were always envious to nearby facilities because of their fine texture. The winter of 2013-14 though hit them as hard as the one 30 years earlier. By the middle of May, it was apparent that over half of the turf was dead. With the Zoysia patches surviving without incident, the club decided to make the switch in all the fairways and embarked upon a summer long program of removing the Bermuda and replacing it with either sod or sprigs of Meyer Zoysia. It was a complicated program that tried to return the course to playability as fast as possible. Tees were set to play each hole as a par 3 for about 5 weeks as the sod rooted and sprigs grew. The course returned to full playability in less than three months. That same spring under the direction of Roger Rulewich and Drew Rodgers, the club added six short tees on No. 3, 7, 9, 10, 15, and 17.

The largest change in the course over its 38-year history is probably trees. In the mid '90's, new trees were planted to give separation to some holes like 5 and 6 and 8 and 9. By the early 2000s, it was becoming apparent that in some areas of the course, shade from large trees was causing damage to the turf.

Two natural events jump started the tree removal program. The first was in September 2006 just as No. 4 green was being rebuilt. A microburst blew through the course at No. 2, 3, and 4 tee toppling 60 trees. The front 9 was closed for about a week during cleanup.

The second event was a 100-year ice storm that covered western Kentucky in late January, 2009. This devastating event closed the front 9 for 6 weeks and the back 9 for another 4. The final tally from the storm was that over 1300 trees were climbed and had broken limbs removed by arborists. However, the most telling statistic was that 472 trees were not able to be saved and were cut down.

That event led to the creation of an "Improve the Environment" program that targets specific trees that are adversely effecting turf growth and golf playability.

A golf course is not a static entity. It is ever changing. Effects of trees, maintenance practices, and golfers are being evaluated at universities and on courses. New management techniques for turf are constantly being developed.

When Robert Trent Jones was selected to design the course, the club signaled to the golfing world that it was ready to be at the forefront of the industry and it continues to be there today.

The Country Club of Paducah golf course is proudly listed (1979) on the Robert Trent Jones Society website among some of the most elite courses in the world. The club is also included on Jones' list of remodels (1994). Jones' 70-year career as a golf course architect began in the 1930s. More than three dozen of his designs, such as Spyglass Hill, Hazeltine, and Firestone, have played host to national or international championships.

Tennis

The willowy young lady in white strolled out onto the porch, squinted at the glaring sun, and reached for her hat. Youngsters, sensing the freedom that only summertime extended to them, scurried off to enjoy games with their friends.

It was going to be another carefree day filled with lemonade, green apples, and perhaps even a Coca-Cola. If she hurried, she might catch the trolley and be at the club before lunch.

Wearing the lightest white cotton skirt and polo shirt, the girl donned the hat and grabbed her wooden racquet. The tennis courts beckoned. Let the games begin!

Tennis at the Country Club of Paducah began on two courts at the original site, possibly as early as the 1930s. The courts, which were probably clay, were located at the south end of the parking lot near Country Club Lane and protected by a chain link fence.

The earliest reference to tennis appeared in the 1944 Board of Governors' minutes when Club President Palmer James stated that he thought one of the tennis courts should be put in playable condition, which would necessitate the purchase of wire netting, a new tennis net, and other minor repairs.

Irving Bright was authorized to spend up to $100 in making these improvements, a motion that carried unanimously. From this entry in the board minutes, one can derive that the two courts must have been old by 1944, since they were already in a declining state of repair.

In 1947, the Board of Governors authorized $200 to resurface one tennis court, but by the next year members said the tennis courts still needed improvements. On December 10, 1949, a discussion was held by the board regarding repairing the tennis courts and backdrops, and obtaining a price for bleachers. In 1952, an estimate of $1,500 to install "first class" lighting on one court was discussed.

By the 1950s, club members and their children were keeping the courts full most of the time.

The Sullivan family ruled the courts in those days. Jane and Harold Sullivan were the parents of five children, Lee, Nancy, Betty, George, and Hal, all excellent tennis players. George became a golfer like his father, Harold, and his grandfather, George Goodman, while his mother played both sports.

A trophy inscription says that Betty Sullivan won the 1955 Junior Mixed Tournament, probably with her brother, Lee, while her mother was winning the adult division mixed doubles title.

Betty Sullivan and Lee Sullivan with Jack Kramer racquets in 1960. They won dozens of tennis titles at the club and around Paducah for many years.

The Paducah Country Club's Annual Mixed Doubles Tournament was held in 1955 with these participants: (from left, front) Wynn Watson, Robbie Robertson, Pat Fabry, Betty Sullivan, Lee Sullivan; (from left, back) Eleanor Crounse, Jane Sullivan, Jimmy Dunn, Jack Keiler, George Sullivan, Melvin Cornillaud, and Johnny Russell.

Jack Keiler was the member in charge of tennis for several years. During a board meeting on April 12, 1954, Keiler mentioned tennis professional Mary Hardwick's upcoming visit and gave details about the upcoming Tennis Exhibition Matches.

John Powless was hired to run the club's tennis program in May of 1958. A 1957 graduate of Murray State University where he starred on the tennis and basketball teams, Powless was the Ohio Valley Conference singles and doubles champion all three seasons he played.

Prior to that 1958 board meeting when Powless was hired, there is no record of a tennis manager or tennis professional at the club, although Preston Shoup remembers taking lessons on the Rubico clay courts from Paducah's Johnny King around 1957.

Powless was an imposing figure at 6 feet 5 inches. A native of Illinois, he played in the U.S. National Tennis Championships six times between 1955 and 1964. He was also the six-time captain and coach of the U.S. Junior Davis Cup team.

The Country Club of Paducah was very fortunate to hire Powless when he was in Paducah to coach a year at Tilghman. In 1959, he became an assistant basketball coach at Florida State University; a year later he helped coach the University of Cincinnati when they won two NCAA titles.

By 1963, Powless was at the University of Wisconsin as an assistant under John Erickson, and was also the head tennis coach. After five years as the head basketball coach, Powless returned to tennis as the owner of his own tennis center in Madison. He added the 1999 U.S. Senior Open singles title to his long resume while playing on the international senior circuit.

In 2016, John was ranked as the world's No. 1 singles player for 80-and-over—quite a feather in the cap of the club that hired him when he was just beginning an illustrious career.

Lee Sullivan was one of Powless' top students and remained friends with the pro for years after he left the club.

John Powless, the club's first tennis pro.

Mrs. Muscoe Martin agreed to be the tennis chairman in 1963. Two years later, Arch Kleet was chairman of the tennis committee. In 1968, when board member Jack Kerr was in charge of tennis, he reported a need to repair the tennis courts and backstops.

Steve Bright made the headlines in 1970 as a 9th grader when he upset Joe Powell in the Paducah Country Club Tennis Tournament, according to the *Sun-Democrat.* "Fourteen-year-old Bright rallied after a rain delay Saturday to win the men's singles title," the story said.

Steve Bright shows the form that made him a winner in 1974 at the club.

The unseeded Bright upset three seeded players including No. 1 seed Fred Paxton, No. 3 seed Powell, and No. 4 seed Trigg Render. Powell had ousted No. 2 seed Bill Conyer, Jr., in the semi-finals.

In the club's men's doubles division, Conyer and Render squared off against Paxton and Powell in the semifinals, while Conyer and Render downed Bright and Bill Usher first and then Hal Sullivan and David Reed. Paxton-Powell beat the Buzz Peel-Calder Ezzell team earlier.

In the women's doubles tournament, Polly Usher and Jane Bright defeated Peggy Paxton and Pat Bradley before beating Barbara Lackey and Barbaranelle Shelton in the finals to take the crown.

In another tournament, Sullivan and Peel defeated Jimmy Paxton and Ric Ladt to win the 19-and-under doubles. Render won the singles and Ezzell was runner-up.

Conyer and Bright were stars on the Paducah Tilghman High School team during the days when Murray's Mel Purcell was a high school player. Country club tennis players were stand-outs not just on the club courts—they were ranked by the Paducah Parks and Recreation Department on the city-wide ladder.

Richard Roberts was ranked No. 5 in the men's division; Bill Conyer was No. 6, Trigg Render, No. 8, Steve Bright, No. 9, Alan Nagel, No. 12, Tom Russell, No. 15. In the 19-and-under juniors, Conyer was ranked No. 1.

In the summer of 1972, Conyer won all four events in the annual Country Club Tennis Tournament, taking the boys' and men's singles and doubles titles. Render was his doubles partners in both divisions. They beat Bright and Reed in the men's doubles and John Dallam and Sullivan in the boys' 18-and-under doubles.

Other boys' division winners were John Dallam over Brad Renfro in the 14-and-under singles; Conyer over Bright in the 18-and-under as well as the men's division; Renfro and Dallam over David Rudd and Bobby Bohle in boys' doubles.

The Ladies Doubles title went to Mimi Wiley and Usher over Sis Newsome and Lackey. Sarah Abell won the girls' 10-and-under singles over Mary Taylor; Nancy Paxton was the 14-and-under champion over Julie Bright. Paxton teamed with Renee Peel to win the doubles over Bright and Paula Cvengros.

Jerry Page, who was once tennis committee chairman, said the courts lacked the lighting and surface that players would have preferred. At some point in the 1960s, the courts were changed from clay to asphalt.

Paul Rowton ran the tennis program at the club longer than any other professional as of 2016. He was hired in 1970 and left in 1983, according to the board minutes.

He instituted the Western Kentucky Doubles Championships, which the club hosted for a few years, taught numerous junior members how to play, and inspired his adult players as well.

In a *Sun-Democrat* sports story that published around 1973, junior girls from the club who competed in the Doubles Championships were Nancy Paxton and Renee Peel. Junior boys who won matches were John Dallam, Steve Bright, and Russell Shelton.

The club courts on Country Club Lane were the site of many tournaments and special events. One of the most memorable was when comedian Bill Cosby came to town and played a challenge match in the '70s with Edna Hipp, Polly Usher, and Rowton. Those who saw the match say that Cosby did not like losing.

Lee Sullivan practices his serve on Country Club Lane.

Junior winners of tennis and golf in 1971 were (front) Mike Davis, Bobby Bohle; (middle) Nancy Paxton, Lynn Bradley, Paula Cvengros, Kathy Davis; (back) Phil Hunt, Lee Powell, David Paxton, Mark Davis.

Hal Sullivan hits a forehand volley with his wooden racket around 1975.

In 1974, Fred Paxton and Jim Renfro asked the board to consider increasing the number of tennis courts, the minutes reflected. At a later meeting, the motion to increase the number was tabled perhaps in anticipation of a move to Blandville Road where new courts would be built.

"Fred Paxton was always a staunch supporter of the club's tennis program," past President John D. Williams said. "When we needed help, he was there, and he was a heck of a tennis player."

A year or so later in a meeting of the board, Dr. Don Boucher moved that the club build four more new tennis courts at the new property with certain facilities on the new site.

Bill Dyer was the tennis chairman in the fall of 1976. The following year, Henry Dallam advised that Leslie Feast has repaired the backstops at the old tennis courts.

Nancy Paxton had the best girls' tennis record and was first on the ladder. She won the 13-and-over singles and teamed with Bradley for the No. 1 doubles ranking. Lee Powell was first on the boys' ladder and Mark Davis had the best boys' tennis record. All others won their age groups in singles or doubles. Kyle Katterjohn was listed as the tennis instructor who presented the awards.

In the summer of 1980, the board switched its focus from golf to tennis when the committee composed of Polly Usher, Kayla Page, and Tom Russell appeared at the meeting, along with board member George Sullivan. They presented their ideas for building the new tennis courts.

When the ideas were accepted, the board went into contract with the Louisville Paving Company to construct six Laykold, all weather service tennis courts at a cost that could not exceed $100,000.

In July of 1980, bids for six courts and lighting was discussed by the board. The cost without lights was $100,000. On October 26, 1980, the six new courts were christened. By the time the November newsletter was published, the courts were up and running. Pro Rowton echoed the feelings of all of the tennis members when he said, "We can all be proud of a dream come true."

Denny and Dianna Lane won the first tournament on the new courts with Jim Harris and Judy Green coming in second. There was mention of playing under lights

The year was 1978. Players just finishing a social game are (from left) Lana Sirk, Rainey Apperson, Jane Bright, Libby Piers, Edie Hardy, and (kneeling) Polly Usher and Mimi Wiley.

Left: Players on the new courts at the present site around 1980 were (from left, front) Judy Milford, Sue Borders, Phyllis Russell, Mai Davis, Sheri Duwe, and Carol Wilson; (from left, back) Jennifer Gay, Connie Culbertson, Dabney Haugh, Jackie Curtis, unknown, and Peggy Conyer.

Below: Cynthia Pfanstiel talks to Beth Garey.

during the 1981 season. A trailer was used as a temporary "clubhouse" until the new facility opened in 1984.

When Hal Sullivan moved back to Paducah, he continued the family tradition of tennis excellence both as a player and as a board member. He worked diligently to secure the indoor tennis facility.

When Paul Rowton resigned in March of 1983, the board went with the Washington Tennis Service to provide the club with professionals. The first was Mark Craig who probably spent two summers as the pro before Craig Garrison came.

Garrison was the pro from October 1, 1984-September 30, 1985, when talk was going on about a "bubble" to cover the tennis courts.

Tennis in the late seventies and early eighties at the "new" facility was played outdoors as it was world-wide. Wooden racquets had been replaced by aluminum and titanium and many players, dressed predominantly in white, focused on singles rather than doubles in those days.

Club tournaments were bracketed and players were seeded. Lady players were placed in A, B, and C divisions for regular season competition. Rowton recognized top players—Edna Hipp, who remained at No. 1 for many years; Polly Usher, Barbara Livingston, Vicki Russell, Peggy Conyer, Jane Bright, Mai Davis, Sue Kerr, Lorene Clark, Shelbye Hall, Brenda Anderson, Sue Kerr, Judy Green, and Lucinda Rudd when play began on the new courts.

Three sessions were played each year—spring, summer, and fall. Two players could move up or down into different divisions depending on their wins, Peggy Conyer recalled. Peggy was known for her well-placed lobs and endurance on the courts.

The trend for the ladies to play more doubles in leagues came when the USTA system came to the forefront in the mid-1980s. According to Ellen Wise, "We were starting to compete in the USTA doubles tournaments as a team and we didn't like the idea of competing against each other."

Men competing at the "A" level in the early 1980s included Ken Cooper, John Wise, Edwin Albritton, Hal Sullivan, Lee Powell, Denny Lane, Steve Bright, and Dr. Tom Clark. Records of junior players are scarce, but Chris Livingston took home a trophy in the Boys' 14-17 Singles in 1984.

(Records of all tennis champions at the club could not be found. Some of the names mentioned are based on what members recall or what newspaper clippings and board minutes indicate.)

When Louie Kirchoff was tennis chairman, he announced the acceptance of the Ladies Tennis League's proposal to construct a 16x16 shelter at a cost of about $3,500 on the west side of the courts.

Kirchoff mentioned that another year was left on the contract with the Washington Tennis Service, therefore, Craig Garrison received a nod of approval to continue as pro, but by 1986 when Connie Trogolo was president of the club, Garrison resigned to take another position in Florida. The pro was commended by the board for undertaking the operation of the facilities and the physical plant, and for completing them all before he left.

Tennis committee chairman Dell Washburn interviewed Brian Martin from the WTS; the board hired Martin to be the "Director of Tennis," a new title which is still used today.

The club's summer newsletter mentioned that opening weekend was a huge success on the tennis courts with Jim Hank and Edwin Albritton winning the First Flight; Ted Fiorita and Frank Nagel, Second Flight; Bob Whiting and Ron Wright, Third Flight; and Jerry Martin and Harold Clark, the Fourth Flight.

Ladies Winners were the teams of Pat Bradley and Peggy Conyer; Sherri Duwe and Marzie Miller; and Mary Ann Wright and Roseann Whiting. A moonlight mixer was held with so many players participating that in the future play will be limited to the first 40, Tennis Director Martin said.

YORK JONES HOWE HIPP CONYER WISE

DUWE GREEN DAVIS LANE

Transition to team tennis

Country Club ladies surprised themselves and Volvo field

The team of Ellen Wise, Edna Hipp, Elaine Howe, Melodie Jones, Diana Lane, Sheri Duwe, Peggy Conyer, Judy Green, Shirley York, and Mai Davis thrilled club members when they captured the National USTA Volvo Tennis League National Championship, defeating teams from 17 regions in the 3.0 division.

Men's Tennis Association officers were Ron Wright, president; Lynn Foster, treasurer; Clark Anderson and Mike McDowell, assistants.

The Ladies Tennis Association chairman, Julia Roberts, alerted members that the final day to sign up for summer league was coming soon, which confirms that league play had started by 1986.

In October, board discussions focused on the tennis bubble. The tennis bubble completed project was estimated to cost $110,000; $31,000 had been collected from members, according to Dell Washburn. About $13,000 more was pledged for 1987.

Washburn said that a bubble made for another customer could be purchased for $81,000 with an estimated maintenance and labor cost of $15,000 a year, a proposal that received the board's approval.

The bubble was delivered in November, according to the board minutes. In tennis news in 1987, the debt for the bubble was estimated at $90,000.

Among the night league winners mentioned in the December newsletter were Tina Pennick and Rhonda Edwards; Ruth Williams and Jane Kolb; Susan Jones and Debbie Paxton; and day league winners Rose Ann Fiorita and Debbie Paxton; Theresa Owens and Terri Holland; Edna Hipp and Shirley York; Catherine Vest and Ellen Wise; Marzie Miller and Sissy Wilson.

JoAnne Russell was scheduled for a tennis exhibition in May. The Volvo tennis program reached 95 participants, up 23 from 1987.

The Country Club of Paducah

Blandville at Holt - P.O. Box 9585 - Paducah, Kentucky 42002-9585

OCTOBER 1987

CONGRATULATIONS!
1987 NATIONAL CHAMPS

Pictured above are the 3.0 champions: (starting first row lower left) Peggy Conyer, Ellen Wise, Edna Hipp, Elaine Howe, Diana Lane. (Second row) Coach Brian J. Martin, Shirley York, Melodie Jones, Sheri Duwe, Judy Green, and Mai Davis.

We are so proud of our champs! In June, this group won the state Championship in the USTA Volvo tennis League. In July they became the Regional Champs and representatives of the southern region by defeating 9 state championship teams at Mobile, Alabama. Upon return, Brian put them through intense training in preparation for the Nationals. From September 17 through September 20, this group played at Seabrook Island and came back victorious out of a field of 17 regions! A big **congratulations!**

(P.S. Heard around the club, **"We are so tired of tennis, I think some of us might take a week off!"**)

Thanks to the women's tennis league and The Country Club of Paducah for your support. It made us work harder and be proud to represent the club at Nationals.

In the history of women's Volvo League tennis at the Country Club of Paducah, the crowning achievement came in 1987 with a national doubles title.

In June of 1987, the Country Club of Paducah's Ladies Tennis Association 3.0 team advanced in Volvo competition after taking the state title and then winning the Southern Regional Championship in Mobile, Alabama.

Coach Martin put them through intense training in preparation for the Volvo National Championships, which were scheduled for Seabrook Island in September. Members were thrilled at the prospect of having a national championship team!

The *Paducah Sun* account of the victory said that the Conyer-Davis team finished off a 6-2, 6-7, 6-4 match for the third and decisive match win against San Francisco. Melodie Jones won a 6-2, 6-2 match playing No. 1 singles, while the Green-Davis team won its doubles match 6-2, 3-6, 6-2 to ensure the victory. Wise and York lost 5-7,1-6 in the last doubles match, but the Country Club of Paducah cinched the 4-1 victory.

Paducah was 17-0 during the different tournament steps. "Considering this team was only conceived five months ago, they did far better than expected," Coach Martin said.

The Country Club of Paducah had never won a national team title in any sport until this group did.

Ann Webb and Catherine Vest won in singles and the teams of Hipp-York, Lane-Green, and Overstreet-Wise won in doubles. Barbara Livingston was also on the team.

The 3.0 team that captured the State Tournament title was composed of Debbie Paxton, Barbara Hartley, Brenda Williams, Peggy Smith, Ann Nagel, Rose Ann Fiorita, Susan Jones, Diana Kelley, and Shirley Bowland. The team advanced to the regionals in Little Rock, Arkansas.

The Senior 3.0 team finished third at the National Championships in Tuscon, Arizona. Playing for the club were Phyllis Curtis, Sue Kerr, Brenda Williams, Shirley Higdon, Polly Fowler, Judy Shepherd, Dot Warren, and Reva Harper.

Tennis in 1988

Hal Gilbert, tennis committee chairman in 1988, reported that Tenni-Trac Sports Surfaces submitted a proposal for court work. Jeff Maren was a new assistant pro.

The Country Club of Paducah's Ladies 2.5 Volvo Team won the state championship in 1988 with Rose Ann Fiorita and Susan Jones serving as captains. Other members of the team were Brenda Williams, Shirley Bowland, Ann Nagel, Debbie Paxton, Peggy Smith, Barbara Hartley, and Diana Kelly.

According to Pro Brian Martin's report in the club newsletter, the club sent four teams to "Southerns" in three years with 12 wins and five losses, the best club record in the State of Kentucky. Thirty-five club members have attended the "Southerns" one time and seven who have been at least twice, Martin reported.

Back home in men's league competition, the players recognized were Denny Lane, Ted Fiorita, Jim Hank, Gary Robertson, Bob Haugh, J.T. Bowland, Lars Blythe, Clark Anderson, and Pat Powell.

In the Ford Motor Mixed Doubles Championship, Catherine and David Vest were winners and Ron and Mary Ann Wright were second place finishers.

One-hundred and forty kids signed up for tennis that summer.

The 1988 Hard Court Singles Club Champions announced by Brian Martin were as follows: John Wise, first; Jim Hank, second; Melodie Jones, first; and Catherine Vest, second. In the Second Flight, the winners and runners-up were Ted Fiorita and Lee Powell; Shawn Lindblad and Rose Ann Whiting. Third flight honors went to Gary Robertson, Ron Wright; Rhonda Edwards, Mary Ann Wright.

The hardcourt doubles winners and runners-up were Hipp and Green; York and Overstreet; Vest and Whiting; Bradley and Wright; Wilson and Fiorita; Lindblad and Paxton.

Junior tennis players commended in the newsletter were Mark Parsons, Christy Clymer, Allison Sirk, Matthew Anderson, John Bell, Chad Gamble, Katie Garey, Josh Paxton, Christa Clymer, Blann Hancock, Jay Kolb, David Black, Tate Myers, Jamie Gibbs, Kate Metzger, and Audrey Gay. Brian Martin was excited about the junior tennis prospects at the club.

Diana Lane and Rhonda Edwards won the "A" division of women's tennis night league and Lee Powell and Ed Hely took the men's "A" division title, Brian Martin noted. JoAnne Russell, the top female players for many years on the ladies' pro circuit, was at the club for a clinic and exhibition.

The 3.0 team coached by Pro Brian Martin are (from left, standing) Debbie Paxton, Barbara Hartley, Brenda Williams, Peggy Smith, Ann Nagel; (from left, front) Rose Ann Fiorita, Susan Jones, Diana Kelly, and Shirley Bowland.

Practive makes perfect...Polly Usher and Mai Davis (right).

On the road again...Betty Higdon (left) and Phyllis Curtis.

Ready for a match...Phyllis Curtis and Betty Higdon (right).

A new men's tennis board was elected with Steve Wilson, president; Clark Anderson and David Vest, vice-presidents; J.T. Bowland, secretary; and John Elliott, treasurer.

In Ladies League in the open division, Polly Usher won the A-1 title; Sissy Wilson and Rose Ann Whiting tied in A-2; Debbie Paxton won A-3; Ginny Young, Rose Ann Fiorita, and Brenda Williams, tied A-4; Barbara Hartley (B-1); Shirley Bowland (B-2); Susan Gillespie (B-3) and Dee Dee Long (B-4).

Winter night league winners were Tina Penick and Rhonda Edwards, Ruth Williams and Jane Kolb, and Susan Jones and Debbie Paxton. Winter day league winners were Fiorita-Paxton, Theresa Owens and Terri Holland, Hipp and York; Vest and Wise; Miller and Sissy Wilson.

John Wise was the Singles Club Champion on hard and clay courts. Edna Hipp and Shirley York were the Doubles Club Champions on both surfaces, and the most improved awards went to Ron Wright, David Vest, Shirley Higdon, and Debbie Fallon.

The men's 4.5 USTA team members were John Wise, Ken Cooper, Joe Semeraro, David Paxton, Hal Sullivan, Ted Case, Dr. Jeff Case, Frank Nagel, and Dr. Brazzell.

Tennis in 1989

The Parent-Child Tournament, part of the club championships, was won by the mother-daughter team of Brenda and Andrea Beth Proctor. The mother-son winners were Roxie and Reed Jarvis and E.J. and Nathan Roberts, and the father-son winners were Steve and Pat DuPerrieu, Jeff and Jeremy Case and the Ransler duo. Bob and Katie Garey won the father-daughter division.

The Challenge Ladder listed Ann Webb as No. 1 and Edna Hipp as No. 2. Others mentioned were Catherine Vest, Kay Arterburn, Judy Green, Marzie Miller, Mary Sue Withrow, Jane Gamble, Debbie Fallon, and Karen Semeraro.

The Men's and Women's Clay Court Singles Championships were won by Ann Webb and Frank Nagel. Women's runner-up was Edna Hipp and men's runner-up went to Ted Fiorita. Hal Sullivan and John Dallam were the Men's Clay Court Doubles champions. Runners-up were John Anderson and Lynn Foster.

The Junior Club Champions were Andrea Beth Proctor, Gretchen Case, Reed Jarvis, Allison Smith, Melissa McCracken, Josh Paxton, Jamie Gibbs, and Rob Gould in their respective age groups.

The junior "superstars" as they were referred to in the club newsletter included the following: Joanna Dickerson, Andrea Proctor, Nathan Roberts, Caitlin Sullivan, Deanna Wise, Rob Gould, Matt Anderson, Tom Russell, Clay Cecil, Jimmy Gwinn, Jamie Gibbs, Miller Grumley, Blann Hancock, Tara Wise, Allison Smith, Beth Wise, Whitney Myrick, Jason Albritton, Sarah Wallace, Chris Dallam, and Fowler Black.

They were honored at a banquet on September 7, 1989, for excellence in tennis, putt-putt golf, and swimming.

Jeff Case won the 4.0 singles at the 1989 Men's State Tennis Tournament with Joe Semeraro taking the 3.5 title. Ted Fiorita and Frank Nagel placed first in 4.0 doubles, a fine showing for the Country Club of Paducah.

Diana Lane and Ken Cooper downed Rhonda Edwards and John Wise in the Mixed Doubles Club Championship on hard court. Clay court winners were Brenda and Bob Proctor. In singles, Catherine Vest topped Marzie Miller with Edwin Albritton topping Ken Cooper.

Also in 1989, the Women's 4.0 Volvo team from the club were runners-up at state and went to the Southern Championship finishing third in the nine-state Southern region. Four-hundred 4.0 Volvo teams participated. Representing the club were No. 1 singles, Ann Webb; No. 2 singles, Barbara Livingston and Catherine Vest; No. 1 doubles, Edna Hipp and Shirley York; No. 2 doubles, Judy Green and Diana Lane; and No. 3 doubles, Ellen Wise and Joyce Overstreet (co-captains).

The Country Club of Paducah had the best record in the State of Kentucky and one of the best in the Southern Region in Volvo competition for the past three years. The records show the club teams winning two state titles, one Southern title, and one national title in 1987. In 1988, they won one state title, two state runners-up titles; and one 8th place at Southerns where in 1989, they had three state runners-ups and one third place. Hats off to the Country Club of Paducah women tennis players who competed!

On their home courts, players who won the 1989 Hard Court Singles Club Championships were Catherine Vest and Edwin Albritton. Doubles champs were Edna Hipp and Shirley York and John Wise and Ken Cooper. Mixed Doubles Club Champions were Diana Lane and Ken Cooper. Hal Sullivan and Edna Hipp won the second flight. The Clay Court champions were Brenda and Bob Proctor. The Clay Court Singles Titles went to Ann Webb and Frank Nagel.

Junior Tennis Champions were Andrea Proctor, Gretchen Case, Reed Jarvis, Allison Smith, Melissa McCracken, Josh Paxton, Jamie Gibbs, and Rob Gould, all finishing first in their divisions.

In tennis happenings for September of 1989, committee chair and board member Hal Gilbert reported that a long-range committee comprised of Burton Banks and Dan Dickerson (and Gilbert) was meeting with architects and forming a building committee regarding a new tennis center.

Mario Dorado, the assistant tennis pro, left and moved to French Lick, Indiana.

Tennis in 1990

In the spring of 1990, the new tennis center plans were finalized by Mike McDowell, project architect with Peck, Flannery, Gream, and Warren and placed with contractors for bids with B.H. Green and Son receiving the nod to start building. On November 25, the grand opening of the new center was held at its present location.

Summer league tennis winners in their divisions were Joyce Overstreet, Kay Arterburn, E.J. Roberts, Robin Woods, Karen Semaranro, and Vicki Woods.

Hal Sullivan and Edna Hipp won the hard court mixed doubles tournament with David and Helen Shepard coming in second. Jane Gamble and Kay Arterburn won the Calcutta.

The team of Clark Anderson, John Anderson, J.T. Bowland, George Bowland, Dave Hartley, and Ken Higdon were state runners-up in the Senior Men's 3.5 Volvo Championship.

Lance Outhouse was another new assistant tennis professional.

Hal Sullivan and Edna Hipp topped the field in the 1990 Mixed Doubles Club Championship and Larry Heflin and Denny Lane won the men's clay court doubles title. Jane Gamble and Rose Ann Whiting topped the field in the ladies' competition on clay.

Ellen Wise won the Open Tennis League with Lucinda Rudd runner-up.

Moving into 1991, the club held a tennis invitational (KTA-USTA Open) with the following club members winning: Judy Green-Ellen Wise, Joyce Overstreet-Kim Ford, Frank Nagel, Kay Arterburn, and Denny Lane.

On the hard courts, the Singles Club Champions were Hal Sullivan and Dawn Van Wyck. David Shepherd and Edwin Albritton won the men's doubles and the Judy Green-Ellen Wise team won the women's title.

Matt and Clark Anderson won the Parent-Child Tennis Championship, while Judy Shepherd and Shirley Bowland took the Women's 2.5 Clay Court title. The Ford-Green

The Tennis and Fitness Center

team won the 3.5 division. Adam Paxton and Emily Gay were named "Most Improved" junior players.

John Wise, David Vest, and Lynn Foster were undefeated in state competition.

One-hundred and thirty-three tennis players signed up for USTA league play in 1991.

The three state runners-up teams were captained by Robin Woods, E.J. Roberts, and Clark Anderson and John Anderson. Members of the 2.5 women's team were Mary Edwards, Dee Dee Long, Vicki Case, Joanie Walden, Connie Johnson, Ann Nagel, Sandy Garrett, Susan Gillespie, Pat Habacker and Vicki Woods.

Players joining Roberts on the 3.0 team were Debbie Fallon, Brenda Williams, Denise Gilbert, Dot Warren, Shirley Bowland, Mary Sue Withrow, Phyllis Russell, June Keiler, and Judy Shepherd. J.T. Bowland, George Boland, Dave Hartley, and Ken Higdon were on the men's senior team with Anderson and Anderson.

In the open division of the Hard-Court Championships, John Wise repeated as the winner and Shawn Lindblad took the women's title.

A new assistant tennis pro, Mike Argabright, began his duties in 1992, and in other tennis news, Dr. Bryce Young was scheduled to conduct a performance clinic in April at the Country Club of Paducah.

The 1992 tennis program included boasted the largest number of participants in the program's history—300. Over 250 juniors were playing at the club.

The board approved the installation of two more light poles for the lower hard courts at a cost of $12,000 for the spring.

Pro Fred Schwan reported that the team of David Vest and John Anderson won the Men's 3.5 Doubles Round Robin and also finished third at state. E.J. Roberts and Debbie Fallon won the women's 3.5 and Judy Green and Joyce Overstsreet won the 4.0 division. John Anderson III was the singles round robin winner in the 3.5 division. Junior winners were Audrey Gay and Allison Howe.

Robby Robertson won the Joe Creason Tennis Tournament in Louisville in the 16-and-under category.

In other tennis news, the youngest junior players given awards at the end-of-the-year banquet included Hunter Ford, Ben Vest, Logan Gay, Adam Paxton, Chris Massey, Jamie Brown, Martin Rains, Peter Wulff, and Josh Paxton. Girls who were recognized included Allison Albritton, Maggie Johnson, Katie Shelbourne, Amanda Brown, Jessica Ogden, Joanna Paxton, Katherine Clark, Amy Martin, Allison Howe.

Robby Robertson, son of Tina and Gary Robertson, was the Boys' Singles Champion for the KHSAA State High School Championships.

The tennis club champions on hard courts were Ellen Wise and Kim Ford. Pat DuPerrieu was the junior champion. Lauren Gilbert and Allison Howe reached the finals of the 14-and-under girls doubles in the Kentucky Indoor

The 4.0 team in 1991 gathered in Louisville. They are (from left) Joyce Overstreet, Ellen Wise, Edna Hipp, Lucinda Rudd, (back) Barbara Livingston and Judy Green. Kim Ford was absent from the photo.

In 1992, tennis friends are Lucina Rudd, Julie Brigance, Greta Drury, Brenda Anderson; (back) Polly Fowler, Brenda McKnight, Cindy Tolar, and Kathy Jones.

Mary McKeown (left) and Becky Hanrahan, 3.5 players, in "The Bubble."

The Ladies Volvo Teams dressed for success. In July of 1995, the 3.0 team won the Southern Sectional in Mobile, AL. Decked out in the much talked about outfits are (from left) Judy Shepherd, Brenda Williams, Sue Kerr, Dot Warren, Phyllis Curtis, Shirley Higdon, Polly Fowler, Pro Fred Schwan, and Reva Harper. Shirley was the fashion coordinator for the group.

Left: The Senior 3.0 team traveled to Tucson in 1995 and placed third in the National Championship.

Championship played in Elizabethtown.

The new fitness center opened on October 26, 1992, below the tennis center. (It was revamped and modernized at the same location in 2014.)

On the tennis courts: George and Reid Boland won the parent-child event with Todd Crawford winning most of the Junior Club Championship titles. Rob Gould topped the 14-and-under bracket.

Leslie Bassi and Ann Edwards took the Women's (2.5-3.0) Round Robin event with Carol Wilson and Barb Hartley and Mai Davis and Polly Fowler winning 3.0 doubles.

The year 1995 was another active one on the tennis courts. The club hosted a Senior District USTA/KTA event with 327 tennis players competing.

According to the newsletter, *"The country club had its first state championship team since 1988. The Senior 3.0 team members were Brenda Williams, Sue Kerr, Shirley Higdon, Judy Shepherd, Reva Harper, Dot Warren, and Captain Phyllis Curtis with Fred Schwan coaching the ladies.*

The team went on to win the Southern Regionals and advanced to the semi-finals of the nationals in Tucson. That team included Shirley Higdon, Brenda Williams, Phyllis Curtis (captain), Polly Fowler, Judy Shepherd, Sue Kerr, Reva Harper, and Dot Warren.

"The USTA Senior ladies have put Kentucky on the map as far as representation at the national finals. We are very proud of this accomplishment and recognize this as the Wimbledon of amateur recreational tennis competition," said Tennis Chairman Hal Sullivan.

The 3.0 team placed third at the national tournament.

Taylor Rains won the 12-and-under singles club championship; Clay Pfanstiel and Amy Martin, the 14-and-under; Martin Rains, the 16-and-under.

In November of 1995, the board approved a plan to build an indoor tennis facility. This brought about a signed

Steve Massad, Shirley Higdon, and Brenda Williams.

petition. A search committee reviewed over 40 applications for a head tennis professional before hiring Kevin Hamilton. When Brian Martin left, the two tennis associations were discontinued.

Lee Ann Massey, daughter of Sandy and David Massey, an avid tennis player, was recognized in the newsletter for winning a special award for girls' scholastic achievement.

In May of '96, a new tennis professional was hired—Steve Massad, a former Murray State University tennis team member, who came to the club from Dayton, Ohio. Massad was a Texas native where he was ranked No. 1 in singles in the 25 age bracket in 1988.

The club had a group of junior tennis players who traveled and competed. Chad Bassi, Adam and Reed Batement, Liz Conyer, Adam and Todd Crawford, Lindsey Erickson, Craig and Drew Fairhurst, Rob Gould, Melissa Harper, Charles Key, Joanna Paxton, Clay Pfanstiel, and Edward Zellmer represented the club in fine fashion.

A "Farewell Bubble" social was held on April 12, 1996. The board minutes said the bubble has been sold and is scheduled to be taken down soon. The four-court "indoor" tennis facility will be finished in 1997, President Ed Hely said.

The men's 5.0 team won the state tournament along with the ladies 4.0 senior team. Members of the 5.0 team were Hal Sullivan, Larry Heflin, Robby Robertson, Shannon Mungle, Ben Harwood, Greg Koch, and Kevin Merritt. Ellen Wise, Joyce Overstreet, and Judy Green were part of the ladies' team.

Tennis Pro Massad also congratulated the men's team consisting of Mark Edwards, Rob Webb, Larry Stovesand, Ron Wright, Sam Wise, Bill Massey, Bob Whiting, and Mike Perry for finishing second in state competition.

Over 100 club "kids" participated in the Junior Clay Court Tournament with Adam Paxton, Todd Crawford, Adam Crawford, Rob Gould, Amy Martin, Liz Conyer, Caitlyn Cecil, and Lindsay Golliher taking home the trophies.

By the end of the year, President Hely said the new tennis building was finished with grand openings scheduled for January 1997. Board member Hal Sullivan spearheaded the project.

"Sullivan was the driving force behind the planning and ultimate construction of the indoor tennis facility as well as the many improvements that have been made to the tennis facility and the overall tennis program," Manager Lopez said.

The Dee Dee Long Memorial Award was won by Robin Woods, who was recognized by the Kentucky Tennis Association for her outstanding work.

Jeff Maren was named the new assistant tennis pro in 1998. Rob Gould and Adam Crawford finished second in the high school state tournament, and Edna Hipp captained the 4.0 ladies team of Kay Arterburn, Julie DuPerrieu, Kim Ford, Jane Gamble, Joy Lentz, Brenda Proctor, and Joanie Walden.

Playing for Captain Jerry Martin in the men's 4.0 were Henry Cary, Dan Clark, Brian Geveden, Carl Johnson, Lee Powell, and Alan Mills.

Golfers know that Kim Homra is an excellent golfer, but how about Homra's tennis prowess? He took a 3.0 singles title in an Adult Sanctioned Tournament for players around the area, and hosted by the club. Lisa Lillevig (3.0) and Terri Lundberg (3.5) also took first place in singles.

Junior "stars" on the clay courts included Amanda Maddox, Kara Long, Caitlyn Cecil, Amy Martin, Ellen Cary, Hank Dallam, Vic Mazzone, Thomas Grumley, Edward Zellmer, and Monte Schell. Pro Massad congratulated Anne Wallace and Meredith Durbin for outstanding travel team play.

Rob Gould and Adam Crawford made it to the finals of the State High School Boy's Doubles. They captured the championship in 2000.

The 3.5 team played in the Kentucky State Seniors' Tennis Tournament (USTA) in Louisville in 2000. From left are Becky Hanrahan, Phyllis Curtis, Connie Perry, Betty Higdon, Sue Kerr, Shirley Green, Judy Shepherd; (from left, front) Shirley Higdon, Sue Henry, and Brenda Williams.

Players with their coaches are (from left) Brenda Anderson, Peggy Conyer, Mai Davis, Lucinda Rudd, Cindy Tolar, Greta Drury, Steve Massad, Pat Bradley, Jeff Maren, and Sissy Wilson.

Early in 2000, the Senior 7.5 Combo USTA State Champions were from the Country Club of Paducah. Sue Henry, Betty Higdon, Connie Perry, Edna Hipp, Elaine Howe, Brenda Anderson, Lucinda Rudd, Joyce Overstreet, Kay Arterburn, and Judy Green made up the team.

The 5.5 team or the highest ranking lady players at the club in those days were Lisa Lellevig, Mindy Paxton, Lynn Wagner, and Carol Hank.

Jeff Maren was promoted to Director of Tennis from Head Tennis Professional. Chris Dallas joined the staff; he had been Director of Tennis at Rolling Hills Country Club after serving as a tennis instructor at the Westside Athletic Club in Nashville where he played on the David Lipscomb University college team.

In March of 2002, Maren played in the National 35-and-over Hardcourts, Indoors, and Clay Court Championships, while Dallas played in the National 30-and-over Hardcourt Championships. The two were ranked in the Top 10 in Kentucky Singles and Doubles and the Top 20 in the Southern United States.

Liz Conyer ready to return a volley.

State rankings were achieved by some of our members—Will Gillespie ranked No. 2 in boys' 14 doubles and Todd Crawford No. 2 in boys' 18 age group.

Terin Roof, Liz Conyer, Todd Crawford, and Hank Dallam won regional high school tennis titles. St. Mary's tennis team finished second in the region with club "kids" Lindsay Erickson, Anne Wallace, Mary Beth Bray, Emily Woods, and Joanne Paxton leading the team.

Liz Conyer was a singles finalist in the State High School Tournament in 2002 and 2003.

Clay Court Championship winners included Will Gillespie, Vic Mazzone, and Laura Bredniak. Ellen Wise and Doris Glaz qualified for the National USTA League Championships with their respective teams.

"Super Circuit Adult Champs" named in the newsletter were Gary Little-Robb Webb, 3.0 doubles; Webb, 3.0 singles; Doris Glaz, mixed 4.0 doubles; Connie Perry, 3.5 singles; and Vicki Woods-Robin Woods, 4.0 doubles.

Doris Glaz and Bev Ezzell were members of the Western Kentucky team that won the National 4.0 League Championships in Arizona. Ellen Wise played in the Senior National 4.0 Championships.

Amanda Bedniak was on the State High School Girls' Doubles winning team. In 2004, Max Pittard qualified for the prestigious Bullfrog Junior Circuit tennis event in Mississippi.

Kevin Kerns was named the new Director of Tennis in 2005. Kerns was the most "decorated" tennis professional who has been employed by the club in modern times. The

Robin Grubbs

Sophie Hollowell

Dave Massey

statistics and biographical information furnished by Steve Tennis online lists numerous matches in which Kerns played prior to coming to the club. Kerns played on the Junior Davis Cup team in 1978 and was on the pro tour for five years.

He was competitive in the professional ranks, especially in the early 1980s, playing in the 1981 Cincinnati Masters, singles and doubles hardcourt, and in the 1981 U.S. Open men's doubles on grass. He and his partner won one set off of Peter Fleming and John McEnroe losing 6-7, 7-6, 6-3 in the U.S. Open.

Kerns also played in Tampa with Ron Hightower as his doubles partner and in Mexico City and San Juan, Puerto Rico, with partner John Hayes, on clay and hard courts. He came to Paducah after six years as Director of Tennis at Dolthan Country Club in Alabama.

At its next meeting, the board of directors expressed concern over a large tear in the tennis bubble due to inclement weather.

The tennis structure was discussed again when two substantial insurance claims were filed. The future of the indoor structure did not look good. Pro Kerns had verbal quotes for a metal structure over the four indoor courts at a cost of approximately $650,000.

In 2006, Max Pittard and Charlie Pittard advanced to the finals of the State Boys' Doubles Championships.

Jane and Oscar Gamble, Jane Bateman, and Steve Tilley assisted in renovating the tennis shop.

Juniors who qualified for the state competition in singles were Charlie Pittard, Brian Bredniak, Mark Kaltenbach, Paige Harrison, and Mary Catherine Zellmer. In doubles, the qualifiers were Michael Love, Conrad Love, Alex Johnson, Grace Pittard, and Meredith Durbin.

The USTA Junior Team went on to win the state championship defeating Louisville by one point to take the title. Members of the team were Kelly Cochran, Carson Love, Abby Gillespie, Grace Pittard, Charlie Pittard, Zach Pittman, Conrad Love, Bobby Kaltenbach, Paige Harrison, and Brian Bredniak. Kay Pinkley coached the team.

At the end of the year, Kevin Kerns congratulated the winners of the tennis Calcutta: Crystal Bailey and Robby Robertson, Holly Locken and Steve Schiff; Kristi Schaaf and Joe Harpole, and Connie and Carl Johnson.

Tennis Chairman Dr. Rosemary Shiben and Pro Kerns received a preliminary quote of $500,000 to build a metal structure using existing footer for the indoor tennis building. They are members of a committee to organize a USTA Country Club League.

Vincent Shiben, who is ranked in the top five juniors in the state, won the Bowling Green 10-and-under Championship.

The ladies 4.5 division of USTA Tennis is for players who compete at a high level of play—Jamie O'Hara and Rosemary Shiben, represented the club at state in this division. (O'Hara later joined the tennis staff at the club.)

The 4.0 team was composed of Staci Averill, Abby Lafont, Mindy Paxton, Lyn Kerns, Joanie Walden, Sue Homra, Kim Cates, Vickie Pittard, Cindy Erickson, Joy Lentz, Brenda Proctor, Kay Pinkley, and Jil Baker.

Joanie Walden won the 2007 Ladies League at the 4.0 level. Leslie Bassi was the 3.5 winner, and Carolyn Allen took the 3.0 title. Allen and Mitzi Fugate won the Super Circuit rated tournament (3.0) at the club. Pro Kerns recognized Mindy Paxton and Vickie Pittard for their 4.0 league victories.

Dr. Rosemary Shiben and Andrew Coiner were heading the tennis committee in 2008. President Oscar Gamble wrote about the damaged tennis bubble in the December newsletter. He said the severe damage to the exterior panels of the tennis facility was caused by the high winds on September 14.

Country Club junior players holding down the No. 1 spot on their school teams are Charlie Pittard, Tilghman,

Dr. Peter Locken, Rob Proctor, Ron Wright, and Phil Higdon.

Brian Bredniak, Lone Oak, Conrad Love, St. Mary's, Grace Pittard, Tilghman, and Paige Harrison, St. Mary's.

Turning to tennis in 2010, a new awning was erected on the two hard courts with new awnings for the clay courts in the works, according to Dr. Shiben. Because seven tennis courts were in dire need of repair, the board approved a $75,000 repair project.

Club member Crystal Bailey was recognized by the Kentucky division of the USTA with an Educational Merit Award for her tireless work with junior team tennis at the club. The Pittard family was named "Family of the Year" in Kentucky for their outstanding involvement and promotions of tennis.

Bailey, who is the league coordinator for the Paducah Tennis Association, announced that the 100th birthday of the Kentucky Lawn Tennis Association, now USTA Kentucky, will be celebrated throughout the year. "Wood and White" was the theme for a mixed held at the club to commemorate the birthday.

Jane Gamble became the State United States Tennis Association president.

In other tennis news Carl and Jil Baker were congratulated for winning the Calcutta for the second time.

Vincent Shiben won the Kentucky State Championship in his age group, while Lillie Coiner won the Sportsmanship Award at the USTA Junior Team Tennis Championship.

Vincent and Sophia Shiben, Grace Cappock, Devin Starnes, and Brock Sigler turned in great finishes at a sanctioned junior tennis tournament, representing the Country Club of Paducah.

Kevin Kerns was named a state coach for the 2010 Southern Junior Cup, which represents the best kids in the south.

The men's teams have not received quite the amount of recognition that the ladies have, but these two teams who won at State deserve a special "hats off, the pro said. The 3.5 team members were Adam Chustz, Tim Farmer, Jeff Taylor, Ed Hely, Jeff Golightly, Steve Durham, Brent Gaines, Guthrie Allen, Pete Locken, Bill Conkwright, and John Colgan.

The 3.0 winning team members were Pete Locken, Bill Conkwright, John Colgan, Ron Wright, Guthrie Allen, John Grubbs, Nick Paxton, Kevin Baer, Cameron Taleban, and Brad Williams.

The 2011 Junior Tennis Open standouts were Sophia and Vincent Shiben. She was first in the girls' 12 division and he was runner-up in the boys' 14.

Gary Little, a 10-year employee as the tennis shop clerk, was thanked for his service to the tennis operation after he announced his departure.

Tennis committee chairman Brent Gaines announced the hiring of a familiar face in Paducah tennis, Chris Dallas, to fill the void when Pro Kerns was out of town. Christina Haynes came on board as a new full-time employee at the shop.

Vincent Shiben and Sophia Shiben qualified for the Southern Closed Championships in Cary, North Carolina, while the 4.5 team, captained by Staci Averill, went to the USTA League State Championships, along with the

Vincent and Sophia Shiben, talented siblings playing for McCracken County High School.

Kristi Schaff and Carolyn Allen on Ladies Doubles Day 2014.

Sue Homra (left) anxiously awaits the serve coming to her partner Connie Perry.

Mindy Paxton, one of the club's best.

Mindy Paxton, Vickie Pittard, Rosemary Shiben, Staci Averill.

3.0, 3.5, and 4.0 club teams. Playing with Averill were Rosemary Shiben, Kim Cates, Doris Glaz, Mindy Paxton, Vickie Pittard, Lauren McAtee, and Laura Witte.

Mother Nature 2013 struck the club property once again. A storm damaged the canopy at the front entrance on May 30, and also damaged fencing around the tennis courts and the bubble.

Cardio tennis with Chris Dallas provided members with a high-energy workout every Friday morning. Adult clinics with Jamie O'Hara kept the courts buzzing as did the Member-Member and Member-Guest Doubles Calcutta. The tennis committee talked about the possibility of converting the clay courts to hard courts, according to chairman Jeff Holland.

Chris Dallas became the tennis professional on February 1, 2014.

Leslie Bassi and Debe Sullivan were the 55-and-over 4.0 tennis champions in the 2013 USTA Southern League tournament. They advanced to the 2014 Nationals played in April of 2014 in Arizona, where they placed fourth in the 8.0 division.

At the Ladies Tennis Mixer, Brenda Williams offered touching remarks about long-time tennis player and friend, Shirley Higdon, who passed away.

Tennis director Dallas said the ball is rolling on the fitness center upgrades with new flooring, strength training and cardio equipment, and other cosmetic updates nearing completion.

Congratulations went out to Sophia Shiben who added another jewel to her trophy case when she won the Girls' 14 Racquet Club Junior Championships in Memphis, Tennessee. Sophia also took the USTA Level 3 tournament in Little Rock, Arkansas, this summer. She was invited to train at the Evert Tennis Academy in Boca Raton, Florida in 2015.

Chris Dallas commended Jennifer Gaines, the USTA Kentucky Captain of the Month, for her dedication to USTA tennis and the game as a whole. Others club members serving as captains of the USTA teams are Darla Sims and Karen Petter.

The success of junior players continues with these club "kids" winning top honors in the region and at state during the high school tennis season: Ben Knight, Madelyn Chambers, Taylor Sprouse, Sophia Shiben, Vincent Shiben, and Allie Farmer. Vincent was the 2015 Region I Boys' Singles Champion.

2016

The First Annual French Open "Spectaculaire" Mixed Doubles Championships were held with Adam Chustz and Carol Gillespie taking the gold flight. Cindy and Jonathan Erickson won the silver flight, and Jeff and Kelly Halverson took the bronze.

Dallas congratulated these high school tennis stars: Taylor Sprouse, Sophia Shiben, Logan McKinney, Vincent Shiben, Zach Althouse, Allie Farmer, and Isabella McKinney, all playing for McCracken County High School.

Sophia Shiben won the Girls' 16-and-under Singles Championship as a 14-year-old as well as the Ryan Holder Kentucky State Closed, the *Paducah Sun*, and the Kentucky State Clay Court Closed tournaments.

Hats off to Leslie Bassi, Betty Higdon, and Tanya Spaulding who are part of the USTA State Championship 7.5 Combo Team.

At the conclusion of 2016 tennis, new club champions were crowned for the first time in many years.

Pro Chris Dallas offered congratulations to Elliot Treece, the 2016 Country Club of Paducah Men's Singles Champion and Amy Anderson, the Ladies Singles Club Champion.

Elliot defeated Conrad Love in the finals, 6-2, 6-2. Elliot and Conrad defeated Sam Wright and Adam Chustz in the semi-finals.

Amy Gregory Anderson shows the style that puts her in the winner's circle. Perhaps she inherited her tennis prowess from mom, Ellen Wise, who has plenty of wins of her own.

In men's doubles, the champions were Carl Baker and Conrad Love over Adam Chustz and Tim Farmer.

"Amy defeated Cindy Erickson in the finals in a very well-played match. To make Amy's feat even more impressive, she and Farideh Reck teamed up to win the 2016 Ladies Doubles Club Championship. Amy and Farideh won the 'robin' event by going undefeated," Dallas concluded.

Pickleball, a hot new trend on the courts, is now in Paducah. Nancy Sutton and Mary Ann Wright are helping Chris Dallas promote the club's pickleball play. "If this craze is going to sweep the nation, it needs to be cutting a path straight through the Country Club of Paducah!" Dallas said.

On the court with 2016 Club President Adam Chustz.

Professionals Serving Tennis For Nearly 50 Years

1958	John Powless
1970-1983	Paul Rowton
1983	Mark Craig (Washington Tennis Service)
1984-1986	Craig Garrison (WTS)
1986-1990	Brian Martin (WTS)
	Mario Dorado (assistant)
1990-1994	Fred Schwan (WTS)
	Kevin Merrit, Tom Whiten, Lance Outhouse, Mike Argabright (assistants)
1995-1996	Kevin Hamilton
1996-2000	Steve Massad
	Ben Harwood, Jeff Maren (assistants)
2000-2005	Jeff Maren
	Chris Dallas (assistant, 2001-2003)
2005-2013	Kevin Kerns
	Jamie O'Hara (assistant, 2013)
	Chris Dallas (assistant, 2013-2014)
2014-present	Chris Dallas
	Jamie O'Hara (assistant)

Sophia Shiben

Tennis professional Chris Dallas joins Isabella McKinney and Allie Farmer (right) at a Sunday clinic.

From the days of clay courts, wooden racquets, and one-handed backhands to those of indoor courts, cardio workouts, and power tennis, the Country Club of Paducah's tennis program has evolved.

Managers and Staff

It is late morning on a beautiful mid-summer day at the Country Club of Paducah. Relaxing on the patio, you see the 18th green of the region's premier golf course. Children's voices float up from the pool. Golfers round the clubhouse and break for a beverage. Tennis players meander over from the courts.

During lunch served by the friendly, familiar staff, you replay the morning's matches with your friends. Others in the bar and dining rooms are enjoying a similar experience.

Comfortable surroundings, conversation with friends, good food, and excellent service provide the atmosphere that keep members returning for more. That "experience" is a team effort created by the club manager, dozens of staff members, and an expert chef, all working for you, the members.

The Managers

Seventy-five years ago, when the first mention of a manager appeared in written records, he was called that—The Manager. Through the years, however, the person who ran the day to day operations was referred to by a variety of titles—Food and Beverage Manager, Directors of Food and Beverage, Clubhouse Managers, and more importantly, the General Manager.

Employment records before modern times are incomplete, but those listed here are documented in office records, board minutes, club newsletters, or in the memory banks of current staff and club members.

Let's begin in 1942 with Ralph McRight. He performed a variety of jobs and was employed for several different stints, usually working from June to October. He left the job and returned from 1947 to 1949. McRight supervised the groundskeeper, took care of concessions, gave golf lessons, advised the club presidents, and did anything else the board asked him to do, but he did not want a full-time position.

The club did hire a hostess to supervise the help and assist members in giving parties in 1942, but the governors thought all areas of the club needed management on a daily basis. In 1948 with McRight still working part-time, Club President Palmer James said the Board of Governors was experimenting with the idea of a full-time club manager. The board thought it was "an absolute necessity."

Coach McRight acquired the advisorship position in 1949 when Morgan Boggs was hired and the board wanted McRight to stay on in some capacity. They gave the coach a membership and paid him $100 per year. He was a trusted and beloved friend to club presidents, boards of directors, and members.

Morgan Boggs was the first full-time manager of the Country Club of Paducah; he also served as the golf pro. At that time, all income derived from the kitchen, bar, and golf course was given to Boggs, plus he lived in the house on the property.

The board minutes mentioned that members were allowed to bring food and drinks to the club and use the kitchen, a highly unusual practice. Naturally, Mr. Boggs protested about members bringing their own liquor; he eventually resigned.

W.R. Burnett filled in while the board searched for another manager. Bert Wilde came on board on April 8, 1950, and by May 30 he was gone. David Tosh was hired on June 10 and made it 11 months. Louis Czorney came next and was manager for a month, perhaps a record short stay.

Finally, the board hired Eddie Verplanke on July 5, 1951, which was the beginning of a more stable partnership that lasted until 1965. His wife, Anna Louise, was listed as the chef and assistant manager at the club from 1955-65.

The most memorable manager from the past was probably Bill Newcomb, according to some members and employees who shared their thoughts. He was a

Leonard said he was honored that the club accepted him, its first black manager, "with open hearts." He said being selected as one of the few black country club managers in the nation was an honor for him.

Gloria Livingston remembers Leonard well and said that he was a wonderful man. "His wife, Ruth, wouldn't move to Paducah, so Leonard's tenure at the club was short-lived," she added.

In 1984, Michael Henderson became the first manager at the newly opened clubhouse on Turnberry Drive.

"meeter and greeter" and enjoyed table hopping to hear all the accolades about the excellent food at the old club. Newcomb loved to play golf on his day off and may have loved playing cards even more, members say.

"Newcomb came from the best military restaurant in Europe (Germany) and he ran it. He gave us a 91 percent operating ratio," Bill Usher remembered. "We banked $200,000 in house operations during a two-year period. His food was great!"

"You never had a bad meal when Newcomb was manager," Bill Bone agreed.

Bone said that Newcomb talked him into playing golf one day when they were off duty. "It was about 35 degrees by the time we got to Mayfield. I think we played just a few holes and I told him I was freezing and not playing anymore. He would have played on. He loved to play!"

"Newcomb's wife made wonderful pies at home and brought them to the club," Ed Hough said. "He died in Hopkinsville a year after he left the club, I'm pretty sure." Members who remember him say Bill Newcomb knew food and beverage well and the club benefitted.

Harold Leonard was in the Air Force when Harry Livingston first met him. Years later, when Country Club of Paducah member, Neville Stone, called on Livingston to recruit a really good club manager for the club, Leonard was at the top of his list. He was a 20-year veteran of the Air Force in food service.

The first time Livingston tried to recruit Leonard, he turned it down, according to Harry's widow, Gloria. Harold was the dining room captain at the Philadelphia Country Club at that time. About a year later in 1978, the 48-year-old Leonard was hired for the Paducah position by house chairman Bill Paxton.

In a story that ran in the *Sun-Democrat* in September of 1978, a large headline streamed "Leonard gets his 'chance' at country club."

Joe Connor started as the manager in 1987 after working at Stacy's Restaurant, a popular place owned by Coy and Virginia Stacy. "Club Serve," an organization much like the Washington Tennis Service, sent Connor to Paducah upon request of the board. He was once a member of the Ohio State University golf team and a Toledo, Ohio, native. He stayed at the club until 1992.

Joe Connor

Jackie and Fred Nackley are the only husband-wife team since the fifties on the list of managers. Fred came to the club as a manager and Jackie replaced him. Jackie hired Debbie O'Malley in 1985.

The first General Manager (GM) was Charlie Lopez from 1998 to 1999.

Linda Carroll served as office manager for approximately 13 years and was the club manager from 2001-2004. Brian Hershey had a unique position in that he was the chef who also worked as the food and beverage manager.

Tim Straley was hired as General Manager/Chief Operating Officer in April of 2010. He is the first and only GM/COO the club has employed. With the assistance of the country's premier private

General Manager Tim Straley

club executive search firm, the board was unanimous in selecting Straley from a number of candidates.

According to President Mike Wyatt in the club newsletter, "The Board decided to adopt the GM/COO management model to insure the club's future viability."

Past President David Denton said, "Management of the club by board committees was cheap, but terribly ineffective. A professional manager with significant club experience and leadership was needed. In Tim Straley we found both."

Straley, a Penn State graduate, came to Paducah from Panther Creek Country Club in Springfield, Illinois, where he was the operations manager. He was trained in the Marriott Corporation restaurant and operations management. As the GM, Straley coordinates and manages all of the club's departments, including tennis and golf.

He and his wife, Becky, have a combined family of five daughters.

General Managers and Food and Beverage Managers and their approximate timelines

Ralph McRight, *part-time from 1942-49*
Morgan Boggs, *1949-50*
Bert Wilde, *April 8-May 30, 1950*
David Tosh, *June 10, 1950-May 4, 1951*
Louis Czorney, *1951*
Eddie Verplanke, *July 5, 1951, until 1965*
Bill Newcomb, *November 2, 1965-1978*
William McGlothlin, *1977*
David Cowles, *1977-78*
Harold Leonard, *1978-79*
Paul Stolle, *September 1979-July 1980*
Grace Murt, *1982, acting manager*
Randy Marcum, *1983-84*
Barbara Brownell, *acting manager until Henderson*
Michael Henderson, *1984-86*
Stephan Roth, *1986*
Don Schrack, *1986-87*
Joe Connor, *1987-88*
Joe Horvath, *interim*
Fred Nackley, *May 1988 and left later in 1988*
Jackie Nackley, *June 1988, asst. manager; manager starting in 1989*
Charlie Lopez, *1997-99, first General Manager*
Richard Centenni, *1999-2001*
Linda Carroll, *2001-04, club manager*
Jonathan Bennett, *2005-06*
Brian Hershey, *2006-09 chef, and food and beverage manager*
Shane Render, *2009-10, food and beverage director*
Tim Straley, *April 2010-present, General Manager*

Office Managers

One of the most important positions at the club is that of office manager.

Angie Skees, who is Tim Straley's office manager today, began her career at the club in 2001. She also serves as board secretary.

"Accepting the job as General Manger did not come without some initial concerns. Taking on the task of getting numerous department managers all working together and in one direction would have been much more challenging if Angie were not already present. She is an invaluable co-worker who is instrumental in keeping everything operating smoothly. Wearing the hats of accountant, controller, human resources, IT, communication manager, and others, she is always ready and willing to do whatever necessary to get the job done," Manager Straley emphasized.

Barbara Brownell was in charge of the office for several years at the old club. Linda Carroll was the office administrator from 1985 to 1997 and 2000 and 2001.

The Staff

The staff member who has been at the club the longest is Denise "Sissy" White, with 34 years under her belt as of April 2017. Sissy started unofficially at the old club helping out in the cloak room on the weekends when she was very young.

Sissy White

Her mother, Ruby Petty, was an institution at the club for decades. Ruby began working at the club in October of 1966 and retired in 2005. Her famous fried chicken came back on

Ramona (left) and Ruby (right) with another employee.

the menu recently because of its popularity in the days of "Family Night" at the club.

Sissy could tell many stories about her life at the club. In a discussion about the late Bill Usher, for example, she expressed her gratitude for the behind the scenes help Bill gave people. "He was always willing to help someone in need and never asked for anything in return," she said, recalling his support of her family's church as one example.

Debbie O'Malley is next with 22 years of employment as of 2017. She came to the club in April of 1995 by way of Stacy's Restaurant and still makes the best margaritas in Paducah. Members appreciate her service, dedication, and business-like approach.

James Mitchell, better known as "Mitch," was the club's bartender for decades. Mitch shared a story and a smile at every party he worked. He was well-known throughout the community.

Lisa Kupper and Debbie O'Malley (right) in the bistro.

Lucy and Bill Paxton with James Mitchell at Crissy Paxton's wedding reception at the club in December of 2006.

Edgar "Deacon" Stratton was a familiar face at the old club when he worked security. Deacon made history in 1961 as the City of Paducah's first black police officer. "We were great friends," Bill Usher said. He is remembered as a gentle and jovial man, always smiling. Bob Patterson, who was also a security officer of the club on Country Club Lane, became the City of Paducah's Police Chief.

Paul Patterson was another well-liked employee at the old club who members still mention today. He poured hundreds of drinks in the mirrored bar where some members gathered after work and during parties to share stories of the day. Nicknamed "Pick," he was also a server in the day of white coats and black bow ties.

Has an unkind word ever been spoken about Leroi King? He is the person whose name came up over and over in interviews conducted for this history. Tommy Whittemore, Jr., said everyone loved Leroi. He had a great wit and enjoyed his humorous exchanges with the members.

"Leroi King was a beloved member of the club staff who enjoyed teasing the members," Gloria Livingston said. "I'm moving to Kansas City!" Leroi would say when members asked what he was up to. The reference was to the popular song of that time and brought chuckles from those who knew Leroi. If a member inquired about another member or an incident, he would hold his familiar pipe and quietly sigh, "My memory fails me at the moment," Ed Hely said.

The names of the following staff members will surely jar the memories of long-time club members: "Means" who bartended and was a teacher at Lincoln High School, "Sledd," Laverne, Margaret Johnson, Hula Wilson, Merlene Kelly, Ramona, Jack Sims, Loretta and Shirley; and porter John Jordan who was on staff in 1942.

Alice Jones was hired on May 5, 1954, to be the club's one and only caterer. Lou Coots was

Paul Patterson (with Betty) wishes Dana Lee Reeves a happy second birthday in 1972. Her mother is Randa Fisher Dawson and her grandparents were Gene and Alice Fisher.

once an assistant manager in the seventies. Moving into more recent times, Mary Kay Sanders became the new dining room hostess and Mark Evans was named bar manager in the nineties. Chef John was famous for beer cheese soup and orange rolls, and Nick Cerbonne was a superb ice carver. Jack Sims was referred to as "maître' d extraordinaire."

Today members praise the food when Executive Chef Mike Harlow is in the kitchen. The Member Appreciation Night is one of the culinary highlights of the year.

Executive Chef Mike Harlow

Today's staff members who have spent five or more years at the club, in addition to Sissy and Debbie, are Suzie Thorn, Cindy Lewis, Rene Mastrorocco, and David Hurley. Heading maintenance is Philip Carter and housekeeping is Sandra Bridget. They all deserve special thanks.

The club also appreciates the kitchen employees who have more than five years of service—Leon Mason, Hank Lauderdale, and Nathan Dublin, the men behind the scenes whose culinary talents are enjoyed six days a week.

Carving station

From the bartender to the events manager, from the cooks to the landscaper, all personnel are on board to create a place for members to enjoy. Hats off to those who have come and gone, and to those still working at the club today...for 104 years of service!

Secretary-Treasurer of the Board

Although the secretary-treasurer of the board is not listed as an actual employee of the club, he or she has responsibilities that are paramount to the board's organization and functions.

No one proved that more than H.R. "Bunks" Dallam. Without knowing it, he wrote a 40-year history, taking the club through epic events such as the fire, the re-build, and the move, and he also recorded the mundane, quiet days at the first site. His minutes were meticulous, typed on a manual typewriter.

Bunks told stories of success and stress; he knew who was coming in and going out; who served well and who the "movers and shakers" were. He was named the designated agent of the club on May 8, 1941, and retired in 1980. When Bunks passed away in 1990, the newsletter said he was one of the most influential and dedicated members the country club has had in its history. "If we all could have only a little piece of his dedication in us," the tribute said.

With big shoes to fill, Marshall Nemer took the job when Bunks retired, and Ray Carlson after that. Nemer served from 1981-87, and Carlson from 1987-94. They, too, served the board well and deserve a special thanks.

In the following years, various board members handled the job. Board member David Massey was the secretary-treasurer in 2016 and 2017.

In the early 1950s, from left are John Welch, Victor Speck, Sr., George Prince, and "Bunks" Dallam.

The Presidents

History speaks well for the club's founding fathers and the leaders who came after them. The membership continues to reap the benefits of their labors.

When the Country Club of Paducah was incorporated in 1913, the first president was already in office. Charles K. Wheeler had the honor of being first. The second president was Muscoe Burnett, who served from 1914 to 1916, according to the club records.

Attorney Wheeler served in Congress for three terms between 1897 and 1903.

The next four distinguished members elected to govern from 1917 to 1921 were Elliott Mitchell, George Wallace, Louis Rieke, and P.N. Stewart. Each were elected for one-year terms. In those early days, the term "Governor" was used instead of "President." And govern they did. Recorded information indicates that those who held the title ran the club and everyone reported to them.

Burnett served again from 1921-24 for a total of seven years, the most years as president in the history of the club. W.F. Paxton, Jr., was president for five years from 1945 through 1947 and again in 1950 and 1951, and E. Palmer James served three years, 1943, 1944, and 1948.

The list of club presidents includes Louis Rieke as the first Rieke elected (1919). Then came William Rieke (1928-29), and J. Calhoun Rieke, Sr. (1930-31). James C. Rieke was the last member of the family who served. That was in 1956 and 1957. No other family was as well represented.

Two past presidents who served in the seventies passed away in 2016, Bill Usher and Lee Warren. They made their marks as club leaders for decades, serving in the top post during the seventies. Each of them was seen at the club they loved until their final days. Usher became a member in 1960 and Warren in 1964.

Charles K. Wheeler

Muscoe Burnett

Elliott Mitchell

Louis Rieke

P.N. Stewart

Warren P. Sights

James G. Wheeler

William Rieke

Paducah Country Club Presidents

1912-13	Charles K. Wheeler
1914-16	Muscoe Burnett
1917	Elliott Mitchell
1918	George Wallace
1919	Louis Rieke
1920	P.N. Stewart
1921-24	Muscoe Burnett
1925	Dr. Warren Sights
1926-27	James G. Wheeler
1928-29	William Rieke
1930-31	J. Calhoun Rieke, Sr.
1932	J.R. Smith
1933-34	George H. Goodman
1935-36	Stanley Petter
1937-38	Roy M. Shelbourne
1939	R.V. Green
1940	W.F. McMurry
1941-42	Jack Fisher
1943-44	E. Palmer James
1945-47	W.F. Paxton, Jr.
1948	E. Palmer James
1949	Pierce Lackey
1950-51	W.F. Paxton, Jr.
1952-53	Jack Piers
1954-55	Louis Kirchoff
1956-57	James C. Rieke
1958-59	H.L Sullivan
1960-61	W.M. Carson
1962-63	E.A. Cave, Jr.
1964	George Crounse
1965	Russell Lund
1966	Dalton Woodall
1967	Russell Shelton
1968	Gresham Hougland
1969	E.M. Jack Bailey
1970-71	Jack Wilson
1972-73	Ed Hough
1974	Lee Warren
1975	Lester Myrick
1976-77	Bill Usher
1978	Irv Bright, Jr.
1979	Dr. Henry Dallam, Jr.
1980-81	J. William Howerton
1982-83	Harry Livingston
1984-85	Doug Edwards
1986-87	John C. Trogolo
1988-89	Burton Washburn III
1990-91	H. Burton Banks, Jr.
1992-93	John D. Williams
1994-95	Rick Straub
1996-97	Edward Hely
1998-99	James Harris, Jr.
2000-01	Richard Walker
2002-03	Dr. Robert Garey
2004-05	Gorman Bradley, Jr.
2006	Wally Bateman
2007	Tim Farmer
2008	William O. Gamble
2009	Andrew Coiner
2010-11	Mike Wyatt
2012	W. David Denton
2013	Tom Greene
2014	Jamey Brown
2015	Kurt Averill
2016	Adam Chustz
2017	Jason Siener

President James G. Wheeler

William F. Paxton, Jr., (center) presenting awards in 1952.

Today's past presidents have contributed summaries of what they recall about their terms in office "in their own words," beginning with the Honorable Judge J. William Howerton.

J. William Howerton (1980-81)

My tenure as club president covered two years of rather troubled times. It occurred at the time when the club needed to close the old facilities on Country Club Lane, and get moved to the new location. Many members were very upset with the thought of moving, while others wanted to get on with the move and start using the new golf facilities. Serving as president, and especially at that time, was the last thing on my mind. However, a very persuasive Marshall Nemer and two other club officers came to my office and finally convinced me to accept the post.

We held a few full club meetings to let the members express their grievances and concerns, and to provide an opportunity to explain what really had to be done. At that point the move was inevitable. We modified the membership structure, and created several new categories with different rates and privileges, which helped satisfy some members, especially the older ones and diners only.

In the beginning, the golf facility and range were accessed from Olivet Church Road, but during the first year, we constructed the golf cart paths, and also put in a double-wide trailer, with a basement to have a pro shop for golf and tennis, which were reached from Holt Road. It was also a base from which we could have a few club parties or outings. The old club remained in operation during all this time. The new tennis facilities were started, and everything was beginning to take shape.

I was never elected to anything, during the first or second year, but the elected board members convinced me to continue for a second year. During this time plans and construction began on the new clubhouse. By the end of the second year we were almost ready to close out the old place and move to the new, but not quite. The final move occurred in the year following my "retirement."

All in all, we lost very few members, and in total the membership grew, at least a little.

If there is anything to be said for my "administration," it is: "The Club Survived."

Conrad Trogolo (1986-87)

I got on the board the first year at the new location. Doug Edwards was president. During my two years as president and 10 years serving on the board, times were different than they are today. We were lucky not to have the financial problems they have today. There were times that the regular membership was full.

I fully support today's board and give them credit for their leadership in these economic times.

Burton Washburn III (1988-89)

I served on the board one term before becoming president in 1988. When I was first elected to the board, I was appointed chairman of the tennis committee. I was fortunate enough to obtain the services of tennis pro, Brian Martin. Brian took the tennis league play to an entirely new level, and created enough enthusiasm to justify purchasing a bubble structure to cover two courts in the winter and allow year around play.

The next highlight was a thorough study of the original irrigation system for the golf course, and acquisition of a new system that provided total irrigation, including all portions of the fairways and rough.

Another highlight was that the dining service became self-supporting for several accounting periods without the necessity of being underwritten by member dues.

I recall about a year after my tenure ended, Burton Banks told me that the board had approved several new projects and exhausted the savings account accumulated during my term as president. Although Burton said this in a joking manner, I knew that the club members would be better served by the additional facilities rather than money in the savings account, which reinforced the value of new leadership.

John D. Williams (1992-1993)

I served as president for two years and offer a few comments. They were pretty normal times for our club with strong membership and financial condition. Many of you newer members would not know about how our food service worked. Most of the dining was done downstairs and most food was prepared upstairs and then transported downstairs via a "dumb waiter" system to be served. Obviously, this was not ideal but in most cases worked well. We added the Kentucky Room to the 19th Hole for expanded dining downstairs. This was a great and needed addition to our club.

Our initiation was $10,000, which we maintained for some time. This was adjusted in later years to hopefully interest new members. A lot of clubs had high initiation costs back then given the demand of people wanting to join. Just a different time in the club business compared to today.

Our golf program was great and why wouldn't it be in that we brought in Todd Trimble as our pro. He did a remarkable job in that position. We were very fortunate to have him.

One other comment about the past. I was on board in 1982 when Harry Livingston was president and during that time we had several meetings with the membership about leaving the old club and moving to our current location. There were many members against that move given the central location of the old facility. There was even some discussion of a split, but it was voted to make the move and most would agree it was the right decision. We moved to the new club and opened the new building in 1984. Doug Edwards was president and having been on that board also, the transition went very well.

I had the privilege to serve with seven past presidents from 1982-2005 and all did great things for the club. We have a great facility thanks to the dedication of all our members.

Rick Straub (1994-95)

I was on the board for three years in the early nineties and then president for two years. I was secretary for two of my years as a board member.

I consider two primary accomplishments to be the highlight of my tenure.

First, while president, we completely rewrote the club by-laws in a way that eliminated the male pronoun and paved the way for female members. Until the by-law change, that was impossible.

Second, despite the fact that the board was golfer dominated, I felt that our tennis membership was growing steadily and therefore we pushed through a several hundred-thousand-dollar project to create the first permanent indoor tennis facility. This replaced the "bubble" that had just about reached the end of its useful life. (In November of 1995, the board approved a plan to build an indoor tennis facility.)

Both Todd Trimble and Larry Hantle were hired while I was on the board and I think both of them have had a tremendous impact on our golf course and golf program.

Edward Hely (1996-97)

Because Ed Hely grew up two blocks from the original club site, he has a slightly different perspective of the club and its long history. He can tell stories about long-time employee Ruby White and how she "helped raise" the kids of members, and about Leroi King, who enjoyed teasing the children who were in and out of the club on a regular basis.

Hely also recalls Mr. (Jim) Davidson riding around the golf course turning off sprinklers every night. Hely's mother and father, Sue and Norman, were avid golfers.

Hely served on the board for six years and as president two. In his letter to the membership as he was finishing his term as president in 1997, he said highlights included the renovation projects on the golf course, pool, and driving range.

The proposed new tennis facility was one of his special interests and he worked hard on the project. It came to fruition in 1996 when Hal Sullivan was on the board, Hely said. (The grand opening of the tennis building was in January of 1997.)

Our new indoor facility and the hiring of a general manager, Charlie Lopez, were major things that occurred during my term. The club had not had a GM for many years until Lopez was hired. John Williams, Rick Straub, Connie Trogolo, and others served on the search committee.

The board was forming a long-range planning committee to study the physical facilities and services to meet the needs of the membership, Hely continued in the summary of his term. He urged members to serve.

James A. Harris, Jr. (1998-99)

During my board time in the mid-1990s, many people contributed to the effort to add indoor courts to our club. Hal Sullivan, in particular, should be recognized and remembered for his tireless efforts.

In a message to the Board of Directors and printed in the Club By-Laws handbook in June of 1998, Attorney Harris wrote the following: Since those early years, the club has had a set of corporate By-Laws, as well as Rules and Regulations for boards, committees, and members to follow.

These two documents represent the basic guidelines for governing boards while managing the affairs of the club. By all our membership following these basic guidelines, it will result in good order and consistency.

Over the years, our By-Laws and Rules have become more detailed to meet the changing times. Even so our By-Laws and rules have remained virtually unchanged since the 1980s. This booklet represents the first complete revision and re-printing since 1988.

Every effort was made to ensure these By-Laws represent a fair and equitable set of rules and standards for all our membership.

Richard Walker (2000-01)

Dick Walker was handed a difficult job when he was elected president because the club was in debt, improvements needed to be made, and additional funds needed to be raised, according to those who served on the board at that time.

Walker and the board moved to assess the members in order to go forward with plans for clubhouse improvements and to reduce the debt. We lost members over the assessment, but some of them came back later that year. Others left because of tough economic times in general, Walker recalled.

The action taken during Walker's term did pave the way for the next presidents, Bob Garey and Butch Bradley, to work on the clubhouse renovations.

Dr. Robert Garey (2002-03)

The main goal when I was president was to lower the debt. It was the only way we could make changes and improvements inside the clubhouse. The debt in December of 2001 was $930,901 and members were paying $202 per month for a full membership.

Dr. Jim Woods and I worked on this constantly. We wanted to run the club like a business. Every Friday morning for two years, the two of us met with Angie Skees at the club to sign checks and find ways to save the club money.

We changed insurance, re-did the debt interest, and eliminated many unnecessary expenditures.

I had been on the board from 1999 to 2002, and as a board member I was aware of the need to expand the club dining upstairs. We wanted to make it more casual and have less formal dining and a better view.

In 2001, the membership started declining, partly because of the downward turn of the economy and partly because of the assessment, although some members did return. I do thank past president Dick Walker for making the hard decisions that allowed us to have the facility we have today.

The scoreboard behind No. 18 green was built in 2008.

In 2002-2003, we had a difficult job to do, but by the end of my term in 2003, the debt was down to $399,940.

The board members and Jim and I knew that future board members would have a great start toward making the needed improvements to the upstairs dining areas, which began around 2005.

Also during my term, we celebrated what we thought was the 100-year anniversary of the club. In the early days, the club presidents acted as club managers, by the way. We had no major chef or general manager when I was president.

The lockers and restroom facilities downstairs were in bad shape and needed an overhaul. I asked 50 members to donate $500 each to pay for new lockers. The labor was done by the club's repairmen. The locker rooms and bathrooms were completely re-done.

Also during my term, Bill Usher was the greens chairman; the tennis "bubble" was in place, and Todd Trimble left to pursue another business. Dave Hutcheson still owned some small parcels of land on the course perimeter. I approached Dave Hutcheson and the land came back to the club. The club was re-carpeted and new dining chairs were purchased. The job back then was almost a full-time position. I spent lots of time putting out fires.

Gorman Bradley, Jr. (2004-05)

When I was elected as director in January, 2000, the board was considering a major clubhouse renovation. After the membership rejected the plan, the board voted to assess the membership to reduce the debt. As a result of the assessment we lost a significant number of long-time members. However, the loyal membership paid the assessment and the board pursued every possible avenue to reduce expenses and debt.

I was fortunate to follow four years of great leadership and major debt reduction. The board continued the debt reduction through mid-2005.

As a result of the debt reduction, and with the support of the voting membership, we were able to renovate the clubhouse and resurface the parking lot.

Regarding the highlights and important actions taken during my tenure, I would have to respond that I am most proud of the renovation and the overwhelming support of the membership.

Wally Bateman (2006)

The one item that sticks out the most is the board and membership approved our plan for remodeling and expanding the first floor dining experience to what it is today. The decision came out of a board strategic planning session and was our number one goal for 2006.

I am sure the members remember that the dining was very limited when in the basement, with no view and not many positive comments from members. The move to create the dining we have today was hoped to be an inspiration for an increase in new members and member satisfaction.

I know the planning and construction began under Bradley's term, but opened for business in April of 2006 during mine. Tim Farmer was the Building Committee Chairman and president-elect. He saw the project to its completion.

Also in 2006, the club became a smoke-free facility after the 2005 board approved the new policy.

Tim Farmer (2007)

I had the honor of serving the Country Club of Paducah as a member of the board of directors from 2001 to 2007, serving as chairman of the board in 2007.

Two thousand and six was my most memorable year. While serving as chairman of the Building Committee, the club completed a major construction project that included a new dining room, a complete kitchen redesign and the remodeling of the upstairs bar area and outdoor

patio. Most of my time was spent meeting with contractors and designers. I am proud of the fact that we finished these projects on time and within budget.

In order to take full advantage of our new facilities, we brought in an exceptional executive chef who was able to significantly improve the over-all quality of the food that would be prepared in the newly completed and redesigned kitchen.

Prior to 2006, dining at the club occurred downstairs in the old Kentucky Room. Although this venue offered a small, quaint atmosphere, it really could not have been considered "fine dining." With the completion of the new dining room, the country club began offering our members a dining experience that rivaled the best Paducah had to offer.

William O. Gamble (2008)

Club news during Gamble's presidency included hosting the Men's State Amateur and completing the scoreboard behind No. 18 green. Improvements were made inside the clubhouse, and repairs of the tennis facility after the hurricane force winds of September 14 were completed. Gamble served as chairman of the greens committee for several years.

Andrew Coiner (2009)

Mother Nature said, "Congratulations on being selected president by the Board of Directors of The Country Club of Paducah for 2009. Here's an ice storm of historic proportions." Snow and ice devastated Paducah in January 2009. Power lines went down. Kentucky Governor Steve Beshear called it the biggest natural disaster in modern Kentucky history. Trees fell on homes, businesses, automobiles, and the club.

On the morning after the devastation hit, I bundled up, got in the four-wheel drive and headed to the club to check on the damage. It didn't take much of a survey to see the trees lining the golf course were severely injured. Significant money would be needed to restore one of Kentucky's best courses.

I thought there has to be a silver lining to all this. I walked down the fairway on number one hoping the big tree by the pond fronting the green was down. It has ungraciously prevented a plethora of potential pars. But of all the trees to go down, it did not. It was there, stubborn and defiant. Silver lining delayed.

The Great Ice Storm was only one problem facing the club in 2009. The kitchen was in turmoil. Membership was stagnant. The club, like lots of private clubs around the country, was not in good financial shape.

Fortunately, like the tree down by the pond on number one, the Board of Directors was also stubborn and defiant. The club was not going down, or semi-private, without a fight. Things had to change. Numbers were crunched. The golf course was repaired and restored without a significant membership assessment. Our golfing members contributed manpower to assist in course cleanup and save money for the club.

The board did a little self-analysis. We expertly determined not a single one of us had ever managed a country club. If the club would survive it needed to be managed by a professional. We hired the best headhunter we could find. He found us Tim Straley. Tim, among other great things, brought in his own guy, Executive Chef Mike Harlow, to restore culinary competence to the kitchen.

Tim and subsequent boards of directors led by Mike Wyatt, David Denton, and Jamey Brown have increased membership and restored the facilities to an elite level. As of 2015, the club's financial outlook is bright. Membership satisfaction is evident by the number of people participating in club activities. Silver lining discovered.

The Country Club of Paducah is a tremendous asset to our area. It provides a place where families can create lifetime memories. It helps our area recruit new business and maintain existing ones. It was an honor and a privilege to serve as its president.

Mike Wyatt (2010-11)

I am honored to have served the Country Club of Paducah, as president in 2010 and 2011. Having already spent two years on the board, I was aware of many of the problems facing the club. The two foremost issues were the serious financial position the club was in and the dissatisfaction of the membership with food and service issues.

The club was in a negative cash flow position and the line of credit was close to its limit due to the ice storm of 2009 and continued monthly borrowings to meet our obligations. Because of our poor performance, banks had no interest in loaning us more money, which would have only been a Band-Aid. I had put Jamey Brown over the Membership Committee to reverse the trend in our declining membership. He did a phenomenal job growing our membership and revenue.

I appointed David Denton to secretary-treasurer, and we spent hours upon hours brainstorming what we could do to bring in more money to solidify our finances and make a plan for future catastrophes so the club would have a financial cushion in the event of another calamity by Mother Nature.

Establishing the Rainy Day Fund, reducing the mileage requirement for non-resident members and a plan aimed at bringing in more people into our underutilized clubhouse were some of the things we tried. Some of the programs were not well received by the membership, but did bring in over $250,000 to the club the first year. The other alternative was (and nobody likes the "A" word) assessment, which in turn would have cost us more members.

The entire board was supportive, but I mention Jamey and David because they were in positions to make a real impact on our finances.

In 2010, we hired Tim Straley to manage all aspects of the club. He was charged with adhering to the budget and improving food and service in the clubhouse. Tim brought Chef Mike on board and the food went from mediocre to outstanding. I feel that hiring a General Manager has been one of the best decisions the board made.

I would be remiss if I did not mention Larry Hantle who quietly, day after day, keeps our golf course in pristine condition and on budget. I was amazed at how clubs all around us were losing greens in the sweltering heat and ours had never been better. Our club is very fortunate to have key people like Larry, Tim and Mike; they can make the board look brilliant.

It was my personal goal to have the $250,000 line of credit paid down to $0 and to have the Rainy Day Fund fully funded before I left office. Thanks to the hard work of Tim, staff and board of directors, both of those were accomplished.

W. David Denton (2012)

Thinking about the Country Club of Paducah, I believe I have seen..."the best of times and the worst of times." (Charles Dickens)

My first term on the board was during the mid to late 1970s. The club was riddled with divisions and truly in a state of turmoil. One membership group advocated moving to today's location. Another hotly argued that it should stay put. Membership meetings were unruly and disruptive, often with everyone arguing and shouting at once. We did move. We have survived. I learned a lot about the resiliency of the club and its membership during that tour of duty.

After a long absence, I returned to the board in 2010 (President in 2012). The club membership, its finances, and its facilities were reeling from the effects of the historic ice storm of 2009. Dedicated directors worked diligently to get the club back on sound footing. Our indebtedness was reworked, dues were increased, a Rainy-Day Reserve was implemented, and new membership recruitment was given a high priority.

Most importantly, the club retained a national search firm resulting in our hiring Mr. Tim Straley as a full-time professional general manager. By the time I left the board, the downward trend had been completely reversed and the club continues on that positive course today. Again, I learned about resiliency.

The club's resiliency, witnessed over my 40 years, is, I believe, driven by the adaptability of its members. In the 1970s, we were a men's golf club. Today we offer a superb Robert Trent Jones golf course coupled with family oriented recreation, programs and dining experiences. We have changed with the times. We are still changing. It has been a true pleasure to watch the Country Club of Paducah evolve and grow.

Tom Greene (2013)

I was elected to the Country Club of Paducah Board of Directors in January of 2011 and served as president in 2013. The board of directors was made up with folks blessed with a strong business sense, enabling us to move the club forward and make a number of improvements. All of the improvements were done through cash payments generated from membership dues without adding new debt or drawing on the revolving credit instrument provided by our banking institution.

The club was also fortunate to have a talented and hard-working general manager in Tim Straley. In my years of being a member dating back to 1995, we have seen a general manager or two come and go. Sometimes we

Several past presidents of the club gathered at the end of 2016: Seated from left are J. William Howerton (1980-81), Conrad Trogolo (1986-87), John D. Williams (1992-93), Edward Hely (1996-97), James Harris, Jr. (1998-99). Standing from left are Dr. Robert Garey (2002-03), Gorman Bradley, Jr. (2004-05), Tim Farmer (2007), Andrew Coiner (2009), W. David Denton (2012), and Kurt Averill (2015).

would have a GM and at other times the board decided to run the club without a GM. When the board made the decision to bring on Tim, it may have been one of the best decisions I have seen since joining the club.

Several projects were either started or finished while I served as president. A few of those were construction projects. Among those, the design and completion of the main entrance and sidewalk after the previous canopy was destroyed when a too-tall truck tried to get through a too-small opening. The main dining room was renovated in order to bring more privacy to private parties.

Rock walls were constructed at the water hazards on holes one and two with the help of the Turnberry Foundation. The construction of the cart "barn" next to the pro shop was started in order to house the fleet of electric carts that replaced the aging gas carts. Finally, the placement of the Robert Trent Jones plaque outside the golf pro shop was completed.

Several first-time events for the membership were also started during 2013. These included the family campout on the range which was a huge success, the children's fishing tournaments, Ladies Night Out, and the reinstituting of the parent/child golf tournament.

It was an enjoyable, rewarding and educational experience serving the club. We are fortunate to have many talented members and staff.

Jamey Brown (2014)

To say that 2014 was a unique and challenging year, yet wonderfully rewarding, would be an understatement. We began the year with significant momentum and excitement from the prior four years that I had served on the board and were looking forward to taking advantage of that momentum in the upcoming year.

Little did we know that we were in for a historic winter that would have us facing one of, if not the most, difficult challenges we had ever faced from Mother Nature.

We began the year by instituting the first ever board retreat. I wanted an opportunity for the entire board to be able to meet for one whole day focused on each and every department of the club reviewing both challenges and opportunities that would help us to create committee agendas, which would prioritize the actions needed for the upcoming year.

Two years prior we had completed a survey of the membership and learned what they saw as our top attributes and also our top opportunities. From that we pulled away the words Tradition, Value, Family, and Excellence. Those four words became our governing mantra as we addressed all areas of the club and the decisions that we would face throughout the year.

By March of 2015, it was becoming more and more clear that we had a massive issue on our hands with the Bermuda fairways, just as most of the courses in our surrounding area. That said, our course was affected much more greatly than our most local peers. As time wore on we came to the realization that we had lost nearly 75-80 percent of our fairways. The following weeks were chalked full of meeting after meeting, with everyone from our insurance companies to agronomists working to figure out what our plan of attack needed to be.

Our decision was to either sod or sprig with Bermuda or to take this as an opportunity to move to a more superior surface in the form of Zoysia. The cost to sod was, of course, much more than the cost to sprig but the down time was going to be significantly less. The cost to go to Zoysia was going to be more than to use Bermuda, but it presented another advantage in that it was much hardier than Bermuda and would prevent something like this from happening again.

In the end, the total cost to sod with Zoysia was approximately $700,000. This was a financial hit the club could withstand but that would require a large draw on an unused line of credit that would hinder our opportunity to continue the process of rebuilding and refining all of the other very necessary areas of our club.

After countless hours of meeting one on one with members along with larger group meetings, we made the decision to move forward with sodding as much of the course with Zoysia as we could while sprigging the rest. The last wrinkle was how to pay for it. I had spent the last four years in charge of membership where we had

had wonderful success building all membership types, but most specifically the junior area, which was to be the foundation for our future regular membership.

I knew that if we assessed our membership to pay for this project we would lose approximately 20-30 percent of our members, which frankly would have threatened the closing of our doors. Therefore, it was not an option and I made it very clear that this would not be the route that we would go.

I then opened up to the membership the concept of our replacement choice and asked if they felt so inclined that they would give to our "Fairway Fund." As the weeks and months passed, I was blown away by the generosity of our membership. With their contributions and the insurance proceeds that we received, we were within a few thousand dollars of fully paying for the project while never putting at risk members in an uncomfortable spot.

In the end, I simply could not have been more proud of our board, our membership, and our management staff who all stepped up in their own way to take what could have been a devastating blow to our club and threatened its existence, and instead embraced the challenge and allowed us to come out on the other end in a better place than we began the year.

In addition to the fairway replacement, we used our down time to address over 100 projects that added to the refurbishing of our fine golf course. We also completed ten other projects touching all areas of the club, with total projects being completed reaching in excess of $800,000. We were able to do this and maintain a very solid financial position.

While the fairway issue might have been the challenge that defined the year, I am most proud that we were able to continue to focus on all areas of the club with the goal and accomplishment of addressing what our membership so clearly stated that they wanted, Tradition, Value, Family, and Excellence.

Kurt Averill (2015)

As the 2015 club president, six-year board member and member since 1990, I would like to say that the Country Club of Paducah is in great shape. With the most recent additions or enhancements to the club during the past couple of years such as Club Manager Tim Straley, Chef Mike Harlow, Tennis Pro Chris Dallas, stone retaining walls around the ponds, irrigation system, Zoysia fairways, cart shed, new fleet of electric carts, fitness center, club house entranceway and others, we are set for 2015 and many years to come to keep "Value, Excellence, Family and Tradition" as the foundation and future of the Country Club of Paducah.

We are and always will be the best full service country club within a 100-mile radius of Paducah, Kentucky. Why? Because of our members!

Our past is amazing and our future bright. I can't wait to see what the future holds for the Country Club of Paducah!

Adam Chustz (2016)

Serving on the board and as president of Country Club of Paducah has been a tremendous learning experience. Working with the GM and other board members, you realize what a capable, dedicated, and hard working group can accomplish.

We wanted to implement the "Wildly Important Goal" (WIG) focus this year and, as a board, decided that having positive cash flow at the club would be our primary goal, and all meetings and discussions were had with that one important thing in mind.

For the first time in no telling how many years, the club will actually generate a positive cash flow, putting us in position to do capital projects and continue to improve the Country Club of Paducah for our members going forward.

The time serving the club will always be an experience I look back on with fondness and appreciation to our staff, department heads, GM Tim Straley, and fellow board members.

Jason Siener
2017 President

Not only do all of the presidents of the Country Club of Paducah deserve recognition and gratitude, but also those members who have spent thankless hours serving as committee chairmen and board members.

About the Author

Vicki Russell Hunkler has a Master's Degree in Journalism and many years of experience both as a writer and photographer. She first joined the Country Club of Paducah in 1979 as a tennis player and later switched to golf.

Her interest in golf was second nature, having grown up in Mayfield with a father who caddied as a youngster and played the game for 40 years. Vicki attributes her creativity to her mother, Helen Frank, and her avid interest in sports to her father, Henry.

Vicki moved to Paducah in 1972 when she was hired as a reporter and photographer for the *Sun-Democrat* following graduation from Murray State University. She worked at the *Paducah Sun* most recently as a writer, photographer, and director of *Posh* Magazine.

A Florida resident from 1991 to 2008, Vicki was the Director of Marketing for a real estate development and BallenIsles Country Club in Palm Beach Gardens. She was named Marketing Director of the Year by the Gold Coast Builders Association and received the same award from the Florida Builders Association.

Compiling and writing this history of the Country Club of Paducah was the idea of Vicki's husband, Chris Hunkler, who retired from the PGA of America before they moved to Paducah and became active members of the club.

Index